I0008675

Talking
Outsourcing

Talking Outsourcing

Mark Kobayashi-Hillary

www.lulu.com

2009

Mark Kobayashi-Hillary

National Outsourcing Association

44 Wardour Street

London W1D 6QZ

United Kingdom

www.noa.co.uk

www.markhillary.com

www.talkingoutsourcing.com

Quoc-Huy Nguyen Dinh photographed the two author portraits featured in this book: www.qhphotography.com. The cover was conceived and designed by Sean Cook at Level 3 Creative: www.level3creative.com

First published in the United Kingdom by Lulu - www.lulu.com

ISBN 978-1-4092-8568-7

Copyright © Mark Kobayashi-Hillary 2009

The right of Mark Kobayashi-Hillary to be identified as the author of this work has been asserted by him in accordance with the Copyright, Designs and Patents Act 1988.

All rights reserved. No part of this publication may be reproduced, stored in or introduced into a retrieval system, or transmitted, in any form, or by any means (electronic, mechanical, photocopying, recording, or otherwise) without the prior written permission of the publisher. Any person who does any unauthorised act in relation to this publication may be liable to criminal prosecution and civil claim for damages.

Comments on *Talking Outsourcing*

"We are seeing that interest in outsourcing has never been stronger, and of course client requirements continue to evolve. Mark is clearly a leading commentator in this area; he provides perceptive industry leadership and facilitates thought provoking discussions. It is great to see this information and debate being brought together in this publication!"

Clive Harris

Distinguished Engineer, Chief Innovation Officer, IBM

www.ibm.com

"I always remember Mark bringing up trust as a key ingredient - usually never mentioned - for success in an outsource contract, and that sums up Mark, his work, and this book. An experienced assessor of all aspects of outsourcing though many years, whose views are well thought through, practical and most of all can be trusted for accuracy. This book represents an excellent collection of observations that combine to paint a very comprehensive overview."

Andy Mulholland

Global Chief Technology Officer, Capgemini

www.capgemini.com

"Mark's blog brings a fresh new angle to outsourcing news. This book-of-the-blog clearly highlights the key industry trends of the past few years. Read it, Buy it!"

Martyn Hart

Chairman, European Outsourcing Association

www.noa.co.uk

"Talking Outsourcing delivers the big picture without bias or facade – it is the go-to blog for telling it like it is with integrity. In a sea of global content, few stand out as influential or as passionate as Mark."

Doug Brown,

Author 'The Black Book of Outsourcing' (Wiley)

www.theblackbookofoutsourcing.com

"Mark brings a unique and valuable perspective to the table regarding the global outsourcing scene. His latest book "Talking Outsourcing" is a must read for all whose company and career are impacted by where things are and where they are going in the outsourcing market space."

Frank J. Casale, Founder, CEO

The Outsourcing Institute

www.outsourcing.com

"Keeping up with the frenetic pace of change in the world of outsourcing is almost impossible without a guidebook. And that is exactly what Mark has created. An essential guidebook to what's happening, why and where things may be headed next in our profession. It's a must read."

Michael F. Corbett

Chairman, International Association of Outsourcing Professionals

www.outsourcingprofessional.org

"Insightful, up-to-the-minute stuff. Mark's ability to get the messages out, using all the media available, is impressive. It's entertaining but also fundamentally highly useful indeed."

Professor Leslie Willcocks

London School of Economics, and co-author *The Practice of Outsourcing: From IT to BPO and Offshoring* (Palgrave, 2009)

www.lse.ac.uk

"Over the years, Mark has developed a unique expertise and insight into global outsourcing. His views are taken seriously by the industry in determining their strategy in this area. I commend Mark's excellent contribution to information and debate in his writings."

Dr Mohan Kaul
Director General, Commonwealth Business Council
www.cbcglobal.org

This book is dedicated to Angelica,
my beautiful one...

Contents

The Author

Mark Kobayashi-Hillary is a British sourcing, technology and globalisation expert and advisor based in London. He writes the *Talking Outsourcing* blog for Computing magazine and is a frequent media contributor on this subject.

He is the author of several other well-received books, including:

- Outsourcing to India: The Offshore Advantage (Springer 2004, 2nd edition 2005)
- Global Services: Moving to a Level Playing Field (British Computer Society 2007 co-author with Dr Richard Sykes)
- Building a Future with BRICs: The Next Decade for Offshoring (Springer 2007)
- VNU Outsourcing Yearbook (VNU 2007)
- Who Moved My Job? (Lulu 2008, Viva 2009)

Mark is a director of the UK National Outsourcing Association and a committee member of the British Computer Society (BCS) ELITE group. He was also a founder member of the BCS working party on offshoring. In 2008, he worked with the United Nations to design and implement the African Outsourcing Association (AOA) and he remains on the AOA board.

Mark is a visiting lecturer at London South Bank University and a business mentor for the Prince's Trust. He is an advisory board member of Saffron Chase Communications.

Mark is the founder and Chief Executive Officer of the international business exchange *peerpex.com*, a business network focused at linking smaller organisations from across the world.

www.markhillary.com

www.talkingoutsourcing.com

Mark Kobayashi-Hillary

London, June 2009

www.qhphotography.com

Acknowledgements

This is a book of a blog and so the vast majority of any thanks due have to go to the former editor of *Computing*, Bryan Glick, for calling me up and asking if I'd like to contribute to a new and improved web site he was planning.

That was back in 2006. I continue to contribute to the same blog and I believe that my personal experience of working within the outsourcing market nicely complements the news coverage of the magazine.

Mark Samuels, editor of CIO Connect, was also a key figure in the early days of the blog, back when he was the Computing features editor. These days Mark gets paid more to write less. If only we could all learn the Samuels secret.

My old friend Sean Cook from Level 3 Creative down in leafy Hampshire designed the book cover, and the cover used on my last book *Who Moved My Job?* He is a fantastic artist and designer and I thoroughly recommend his company.

I have spent a lot of time over the past year trying to see *Peerpex.com* become a reality and would like to add a note of thanks to Stephen Page and Jay Shah from Ortegra – I was probably working on this book when I should have been working on the site.

Vikas Pota asked me to join the advisory board of Saffron Chase this year and it has been a pleasure to work with him. The advisory work I do around sourcing has somehow veered towards the utilisation of my communication skills and Vikas has helped me to do this in a more professional way.

Finally, and most importantly, the period from 2006 to 2009 was quite traumatic for me personally so I'd like to thank Angelica Mari (herself an excellent tech writer) for helping me to eventually find my way through the woods.

Mark Kobayashi-Hillary
London, September 2009

Introduction

This book is a collection of all of the entries written for my Talking Outsourcing blog in *Computing* magazine from November 2006 through to July 2009 – almost three years of blogging.

Computing is published in the UK by Incisive Media and its focus is providing insight for IT leaders. If you are unaware of it then I suggest having a look at the website to learn more.

Despite the occasional commentary around the outsourcing news of the day, the blog entries are often about my personal experience or observation on the outsourcing marketplace – the idea is to shine a different light on the news agenda.

You might ask, where is the value in a collection of blog entries? They have already been published online - including the hyperlinks. I thought for a long time about listing the web sites referenced by each blog at the end of each printed entry, but I concluded that it was pointless. If you read something here and want to follow up with the online version, it is easy to find the content at the Computing web site.

It might also seem bizarre to move content from the modern world of the "blogosphere" to the ancient world of book publishing, but I believe that there is some method to taking hundreds of blogs and producing them within a book. It's true that the entries were originally written to be experienced within an online environment. However, after writing over 300 entries I have started looking back at my own blogs and I could see the value in collecting them together. They flowed as a business diary, rather than just a stream of news articles.

These blog posts reflect the nature of an extremely fast-moving business area over a period in which the economy turned from boom to bust. By bringing this material together into a book that can be easily browsed for relevant articles, I believe I will have managed to capture the essence of this business strategy during a turbulent period.

Look in your local bookstore, there are many books on the shelves that focus on outsourcing – I should know as I've been responsible for a few of them – but this book allows for an exploration of not just 'how to' outsource. This book is focused on how outsourcing is changing the very nature of business today, regardless of industry sector.

You might choose to sit and read this book straight through, but I suggest you dip in and out and explore how fast the themes and trends shaping global services can change in a short period of time. If you want to comment, you are welcome to come and join me on the Computing website!

www.computing.co.uk/about

Foreword

We live in very exciting and interesting times. This financial crisis has revealed some very seismic shifts globally. We have witnessed the rise of Indian offshoring in the last few years, and now we will see the rise of China. This dramatic change will once again change the nature of business globally.

We have failed to really recognise the change that is taking place at the grassroots level. There are major demographic changes happening; outsourcing and offshoring is just one part of the globalisation of the world. We should not run from it, nor should we just accept it, as is. It is taking a very strong hold on us. There is no point in moaning about it. There is no point in avoiding it. There is also no point in accepting it blindly. We need debate and discussion. We need to investigate what it means for us. What will it do to our businesses, our communities and, overall, our societies.

Mark Kobayashi-Hillary has been following this trend for many years. He is an author and writer who has plotted this change and made comments on its rise. He doesn't pull punches and he reports from the frontline. I have enjoyed his books and find this one to be read with interest... and humour. His collections of blogs and articles are an excellent way to feel the changing pulse of this world. I have followed his comments and thoughts for a while. He is both entertaining and has a sense of irony and intellect that is often missing in this discussion.

Mark has debated and discussed this area with the absolute conviction of one reporting at the frontline of this major change. He does not pull punches. I'd advise you to read this book. It is a way to get into the debate and see what has happened and what is happening to us. Enjoy a great read, like most of Mark's others books which I have personally enjoyed. Get into the debate and make sure you also get connected with one of the great documenters of this technological change.

Egidio Zarrella, Global Partner-in-charge, IT advisory

KPMG, www.kpmg.com

Talking Outsourcing

Mark Kobayashi-Hillary

November 2006

Monday, 06 November 2006

Posted at 10:56

India is catching up fast but still has work to do

I visited London Business School recently for the inaugural Aditya Birla lecture series, a new series of lectures on India that are now commencing on a regular basis at the school. The first speaker was suitably qualified to talk about the new knowledge economy; Azim Premji, is the chairman and managing director of Indian technology major, Wipro. Wipro, TCS, and Infosys are all now into the multi-billion dollar revenue league (and Wipro grew year-on-year by 41% last year!) so none of them are in the little league anymore, yet it's still hard for these companies to shift away from the 'cheap as chips' image of offshore technology outsourcing.

Premji did give a good talk and focused a great deal of effort on some of the key questions surrounding the offshore outsourcing model of business. I've seen him before in India where he appeared to be a bit more reserved and stately, here he was authoritative, humble, and funny too.

He only talked for about 20 minutes to a procession of Powerpoint slides - clearly put together by some eager Wipro managers who wanted to cram every possible statistic about India into a short presentation. To his credit, Premji was quite disparaging about the presentation and said that it's only people who 'work for McKinsey or MBAs who do good presentations...' to nervous laughter from those assembled, as a post-MBA job at McKinsey is like the Holy Grail to many of those in this school.

The best section was the open Q&A, which lasted for about 45 minutes, but zipped by extremely quickly as everyone had a question. Each time it felt as if Premji was coming to the end of an answer dozens of hands shot into the air, as if choreographed by ballet genius Matthew

Bourne, only to wither disappointed as he would continue to answer by saying '…and another thing…'

A friend of mine, Mahesh Ramachandran, managed to get his question in. Mahesh asked Premji about the fact that all the 'Western' service companies are all hiring in India – Accenture, IBM, EDS, etc, they are all hiring thousands of people and creating and Indian back-office just as all the major Indian players are hiring a stronger front-end in regions such as the UK and US.

Mahesh asked if Premji felt that there would eventually be some convergence in the IT services market. Premji replied with extreme confidence. He said: "Within three years from today you won't be able to tell the difference between an IBM, Accenture, or Wipro or Infosys…"

Given the Indian companies are hiring experienced consultants at an incredible rate here in London now he has a good point, but three years seems to be extremely bullish for complete integration. When one of the Indian majors starts paying a huge amount of money to a celebrity who 'embodies their values' in the way that Accenture does to Tiger Woods then I might believe it.

Wednesday, 08 November 2006

Posted at 11:10

Ban the buzzwords - please!

I'm always at industry conferences and events focused on outsourcing. Many are interesting and offer a good mix of new information along with the chance to meet interesting business contacts over a few glasses of the French stuff, but sometimes the presentations are interminably dull with speakers who can't speak. My worst experience was watching a fairly long PowerPoint-led presentation – by long I mean about 45 minutes – where the speaker did not face the audience at all, she faced the projected PowerPoint image on the wall and read it verbatim to the wall as we squirmed in our seats.

I'm not suggesting that technology speakers need the stage presence of Sir Ian McKellen or the raw talent of Amy Winehouse (how can her speaking and singing voice be so different?), but facing the audience helps. One of my pet hates though is the business buzzwords that go into many of these presentations as a sort of industry shorthand for normal concepts that we can no longer be bothered to talk about or define in any detail.

The outsourcing conference circuit is full of people talking about 'moving up the value chain', 'the war for talent', 'tackling the low-hanging-fruit'… It's a cornucopia of confusion and cliché. I was interested to see a new report about these business buzzwords from Investors in People, those people who give awards to companies for being good employers.

Investors in People surveyed about 3,000 employees and found that a third of them felt uncomfortable when management used these phrases; the needless verbosity creates a sense of inadequacy in the poor employee who is trying to figure out what the hell the boss is talking about. I'd actually suggest that while those employees unfamiliar with the terms are clearly going to have a problem, even those of us fluent in the dialect should not be letting it become a normal and accepted mode of communicating with each other. Can you imagine Lear talking to the Fool about his 'issues' or getting his daughters together for a 'brain-bang'?

In my experience though, these phrases are a language, a doctrine, a new world in which the 21st century business executive somehow needs to survive – even if we don't like it. In the 1950s and 1960s an extensive slang vocabulary known as Polari allowed gay people in Britain to talk together about more than just the weather, without feeling the long arm of the law. Polari also created a sub-culture where it would be social suicide to not understand the conversation, and so here we are in the modern business environment where it would be professional suicide to stick up your hand in a meeting to ask 'just exactly what do you mean by brain-dumping our plans to move up the value chain?'

Of course, complex subjects need complex terminology – try reading an academic paper and decoding it through the mist that descends from the ivory tower, but most of the business buzzwords describe very simple concepts. There is no need to mask these processes with little phrases that sounded great in your MBA lecture theatre. It would help if the business schools created a campaign for clear business

English, or at least taught the value of clear and direct communication. Now, if you start combining technology terminology and business buzzwords then the entire problem is multiplied many times over. Don't start me off...

Thursday, 16 November 2006

Posted at 15:38

How will globalisation affect UK skills?

I spend my days engaged in various aspects of offshore outsourcing, in whatever I am doing. In fact, I'm spending about half the week on paid assignments right now and the other half working on doctoral research at the London School of Economics (LSE) – trying to keep a foot in academia and the 'real world' of business at the same time.

As a result, I get even more invitations to related events, conferences, and parties than if I just focused on one or the other – though the PR parties are always fun! Last night, I went along to a slightly more cerebral event at the LSE where the state of the UK economy was being discussed.

It's a big topic and the director of the school kicked off the debate by asking if we had reached the 'end of history' for economics - Sir Howard Davies using a deliberately controversial turn of phrase and the evening itself was designed to plug his new book 'The Chancellor's Tales' – a walk down memory lane with former chancellors recounting the good and bad from their time in office. The speakers never failed to give a glowing reference to the book before launching into their own comments on UK plc today. I hope one of my own future book launches has such complimentary panellists.

Professor Charles Goodhart chaired the debate, himself a former member of the Bank of England (BoE) Monetary Policy Committee. William Keegan from the Observer, Shadow Chancellor George Osborne MP, chairman of Abbey plc Lord Burns, and director of the Institute of Fiscal Studies, Robert Chote all formed what was a very impressive group of capable people who managed to bounce economic issues around and make it clear and interesting – even for me, and I have never made any claim to be an economist.

What was funny about this debate though was that when panel members referred to the Thatcher years there was some authoritative feedback from the audience - with both Lord Geoffrey Howe and Lord Nigel Lawson sitting there and grasping the audience mic when they could!

They talked quite extensively on the image of Britain staring into an abyss, the fact that we have had years of 'Brownian' economic stability now and we don't really know how structures (such as the independent BoE) brought in by the present government might hold up if we move into recession again.

It's quite a concern and though I'm not making trying to make a partisan comment, it seemed to be George Osborne of the Tories who was most tuned into the need to plan for a complete social change in Britain over the decades ahead. Osborne was clearly well-briefed and talked of the need to consider difficult supply-side issues that will govern the future of the UK in a world where labour and services can be sourced from locations such as India and China. He was basically talking about how you get people to realise that the internet is a reality for connecting global business together – at some point the wave of opportunity for big companies will trickle down to SMEs and how will developed nations, such as the UK, deal with that?

Whichever political party takes the idea of future skills requirements the most seriously probably has a good chance of power, as this issue is connected to careers, social security benefits, immigration… it's a minefield of interconnected issues. Professor Goodhart brought the audience back down to earth when he reminded us that the talk was recorded and could be listened to as a podcast – in a non-plussed tone of voice that suggests he is more at home with micro-economics than micro-electronics.

Friday, 17 November 2006

Posted at 15:39

Image matters in outsourcing

The Canadian writer and publisher Tyler Brûlé isn't the kind of person one would normally associate with offshore outsourcing, yet as I work with more and more companies from a variety of continents I just cannot help feeling that some of them could sit and learn from his Fast Lane column in the weekend Financial Times.

Brûlé is a style guru, an icon of cool, an iconoclast, and arbiter of taste. He has a number of roles these days, including work on a new men's magazine titled Monocle, but he is probably best known for creating the style bible Wallpaper in the 1990s. In his FT column, he reports on what he has been up to in the week, favourite railway stations or airports, and what to pack in the ideal travel bag – and what brand that bag should be for maximum impact at check-in.

You might wonder why any of this matters in the technology industry? Well, although we persist in calling ourselves a technology industry because we use, define, implement, or design technology – the stuff we create is actually being used by other industries for other services. Think of the lawyers, architects, doctors, academics, shop designers, surveyors - they all use technology as an enabler for their own life.

Now think about companies that offer services using technology, especially those that we might often call outsourced services where you partner up with another company for delivery. It has become harder to find a good partner as the services have become ever more integrated into the supply chain. That's because the earlier ideas of procurement don't work in this new outsourced environment. You can't run a competitive tender based on price alone when the service that is being outsourced is a critical part of what your company does.

In this case, most modern outsourcing arrangements have to be constructed more like partnerships than supplier/buyer relationships. That sounds a bit like a cliché – aim for true partnership etc, etc - but the reality is that when suppliers are completely integrated into your product supply chain and you start trying to screw them to the floor on price or service then you are actually damaging your own service.

Last year, Professor Leslie Willcocks of the London School of Economics published some research funded by LogicaCMG analysing if it was possible to define a value for 'trust' between two partner companies involved in an outsourced deal. Willcocks found organisations that develop their firm's outsourcing relationships based upon mutual trust rather than relying on punitive service level agreements and penalties will benefit from a "trust dividend" worth as much as 40 per cent of the total value of a contract. At the time, Willcocks said that to ignore the value of properly managed relationships with an emphasis on trust is "tantamount to corporate negligence."

So where does our fashionista friend Tyler Brûlé fit into all this? Image. Gaining trust and respect is governed to a large extent by the way a company carries itself and presents an image to the market worthy of your attention. Look around at the various technology service companies, both the traditional players and the newer entrants, especially from India.

At a technical delivery level it has to be accepted that they are pretty much all the same. Everyone uses the Capability Maturity Model, or ISO, or BSI, or Six Sigma, or something else to put a framework on their services and ensure a reliable and consistent delivery. Everyone talks of global delivery, and innovation, and "leveraging synergies". Ho hum, if they are all as good as each other technically then why do so many companies – especially from India – attempt to keep on using these attributes as differentiators?

I know that butter purchased from Waitrose is just the same as butter purchased from Tesco, or Asda, or Sainsbury's, or Morrison's, yet I still go a little out of my way to shop in Waitrose, passing a Tesco on the way. It just feels nicer. Tyler understands that and it's about time the technology services groups did as well.

Monday, 27 November 2006

Posted at 14:15

Old Empire - New Economy?

I recently attended a very nice lunch at the Bombay Brasserie (great restaurant near Gloucester Road tube station) hosted by the Labour Friends of India. This is an association of Labour MPs and Peers who all have some association with India, either through a business interest or through representing their constituents.

There are many interest groups in the British parliament, with everyone being a friend of something, but this group is particularly strong and well connected. As I munched on my sag paneer and roti I found myself sitting next to the manager of ICICI bank in Knightsbridge. This is an Indian bank that started a few years back by opening a single London branch and which has now expanded to a small chain of branches in the UK. They handle a large percentage of the Indian money flowing into the UK and they are now looking at European expansion plans.

Opposite from me was an old acquaintance, Mohan Kaul, the Director General of the Commonwealth Business Council. Even the CBC has now decided that global sourcing is an issue they need to address and focus on, as he spoke about the need for more research into this area.

I usually focus on the technology industry and how it relates to the UK. The new book I have written with Dr Richard Sykes of hi-tech trade association Intellect is focused entirely on how our industry interfaces with the rest of the world, hence the title 'Global Services: Moving to a Level Playing Field'. But it cannot be avoided that when examining global services and the technology that makes this possible, India is storming ahead of its rivals. The UK should really exploit our long and historic association with India to ensure we can work together as partners in a knowledge economy environment.

Just look at some stats the Indian High Commissioner Kamalesh Sharma talked about over the Bombay brasserie lunch:

• 1.5 million people of Indian descent live in the UK

• Trade between the two countries was up 57% year on year from 2004 to 2005 – that's an incredible growth in trade and it is flowing in both directions

• We have more Indian companies listed on the LSE than Indian companies listed in the US – a very important point given the issues many companies have faced over the onerous Sarbanes Oxley legislation in the US

• 16,000 Indian students are here in the UK studying at university, with more wanting to come to the UK for an education

In 2007, India will celebrate the 60th anniversary of freedom from the British Empire. Though there was initial, and then sporadic, bloodshed as the Empire left the subcontinent to fend for itself, India is becoming a mighty superpower of the 21st century. Given our historic links and strong economic relations, shouldn't we be thinking about how to create a multinational joint venture focused on the knowledge society?

Tuesday, 28 November 2006

Posted at 14:19

Indian and Chinese sit on the same table

This week I enjoyed a very pleasant meal at the very hip and trendy Amaya Indian restaurant in Knightsbridge. My wife moans constantly about how I'm constantly out on 'business' in fantastic restaurants, yet when we go out it's more 'Star of India' than 'Tamarind', so I now owe her another expensive trip into the West End – these free PR-themed meals do have a cost if you are married.

This time, the meal was hosted by Satyam, the Indian technology services group who sit just outside the big 3 of TCS, Infosys, and Wipro, but well past the $1bn-a-year revenue milestone and are growing at a phenomenal rate.

The occasion was to talk about their increased expansion into China. Satyam has just opened a new 100-seat centre in Guangzhou with the intention of scaling up this new facility to host 1,000 employees by the end of 2008. This new office is in addition to existing facilities they have in Shanghai, Beijing and Dalian.

There are a couple of interesting points to note beyond the normal press release puff. Satyam claims that 97 per cent of their Chinese employees are local hires, meaning that this Indian company is growing into a serious employer of Chinese talent. The largest Indian technology group, Tata Consultancy Services (TCS), has a publicly stated aim to build up its own Chinese operations to about 50,000 staff. These are big operations and certainly larger than any of the indigenous companies in the same field.

What is also interesting is the general march of the Indians into China. India has the maturity and experience of remote technology delivery and China has bundles of raw talent. The Chinese technology services industry can benefit and create huge numbers of jobs through extending a warm welcome to the Indians and allowing them in to set up parallel India/China operations (the TCS future strategy predicts an equal number of staff in India and China), but will the welcome always be so strong and will the local companies always be so much smaller?

The Chinese military strategist Sun Tzu, who presided over battles approximately 400 years BC once said: 'If you know the enemy and know yourself, you need not fear the result of a hundred battles.' Once the Indian players have established a strong foothold in China and the industry benefits from the maturity of good techies with solid experience, from the foot-soldiers to the chief executives, then I'm sure a major Chinese brand name will also break through as a major supplier to the US and Europe. Until then, the safe money is on companies like Satyam to continue their extraordinary growth for the foreseeable future.

Tuesday, 28 November 2006

Posted at 14:24

Is business asking the right questions?

I'm writing from the annual conference of the Confederation of British Industry (CBI) in London. This annual shindig is where the captains of industry get together once a year to talk about the big issues of the day. Quite often this might be issues of tax, red tape, the minimum wage and various of pieces of legislation that the UK has adopted from diverse EU directives, but this year it's all about India, China, and the perils of globalisation.

The opening session of the day was titled 'China and India - facing up to the challenge' and immediately followed a keynote speech by Conservative Shadow Chancellor George Osborne. Osborne and his leader David Cameron have developed into the masters of spin in the same way Tony Blair did before his own rise to power in 1997. I was only just looking at the weekend newspapers featuring photos of Cameron helping destitute children in Darfur and as his Shadow Chancellor speaks in Islington, he is off to meet our troops in Iraq. They have a formidable PR machine driving the Tory image at present.

The CBI has become very concerned about the challenges presented by the powerhouse economies of China and India. They want to understand how do we compete in, and with, these exponentially growing economies. The conference blurb asked 'And what are the opportunities and challenges of working in partnership in third-country markets?' Is 'third-country' a new euphemism for 'third-world' that I just haven't run into yet? I thought 'developing world' was the standard, but when you find countries like India and China where immense wealth rubs along with grinding poverty 'developing' is somewhat of a misnomer. I heard a commentator on TV calling the developing world, the 'two-thirds' world. He might well be technically correct, but I don't think that one is going to catch on either, so for me I guess it will have to stay as 'developing' until someone comes up with a better definition for those countries that are newly-developed, but still poor in regions.

The main concern for the CBI has been to ask the question 'how does the UK shape up against India and China?' It's an important question and our news bulletins are becoming full of M&A activity that far exceeds the impact of a few call centre jobs lost here and there. The Indian Tata group makes the tea that's in your mug (Tetley), and could possibly be the owner of the old British Steel company – now known as Corus – if their takeover plans go through without any hitches. The hard-nosed face of Chinese industry was also exposed to the British consumer when MG Rover collapsed not so long ago and the state-run SAIC swooped in to scoop up the juicy bits of what was left over from the British marque.

Yet, the story is so much more complex than a raid on UK industry by those in the East seeking to grasp economic development as fast as possible, and at our expense. The Tata Group is also a major employer in the UK. In fact, most of the offshore suppliers in the technology industry (where I normally focus) have realised that they won't be invited to the table on large deals if they are not employing people locally; you just can't outsource everything offshore because it is cheaper. We are experiencing a fundamental shift in the way people are employed, creating what the sociologist Manuel Castells termed a 'network society'.

In my view, the concern about India and China should be seen more in the light of supply-side economics. I mean, we should not be too concerned about the now – because the truth is that UK companies are still world-beating, especially in services. We need to think more of the next generation and how our economy can compete in a global environment – where peer-to-peer systems will allow any company to located expertise in any location. Let's sort out the mess over A-levels and work out some better funding for kids at university, along with improving vocational education, because if we don't start training the people who will lead British industry in future then we all know where it will end up.

December 2006

Monday, 04 December 2006

Posted at 14:27

Bridging the gap between IT and academia

Riding two horses. That's what it feels like sometimes to sit astride the gulf that is the commercial world of information technology – in particular technology outsourcing – and the ivory tower of academia.

When I work within the 'real' world, I take great pleasure in being able to cite references to chunky texts on organisational theory or behavioural texts written by social psychologists that engaged in some form of experiment that is relevant to a problem I am bumping up against at work. When I have been engaged in change programmes, this theoretical knowledge has proven to be of great practical use. When I enter the hallowed halls of academia and talk to other people engaged in organisational research, they often express an admiration at the level of access I have to major corporations. Well, all that networking at trade shows paid off in the end by increasing the number of contacts on my mobile phone, but it can be hard to marry the two worlds.

I sometimes wonder why I keep on trying to ride both these horses and don't just focus on earning more money or teaching more students. Is it so impossible to have an interest in the behaviour of real companies and yet to also want to analyse how they function with the more detailed rigour demanded by academia?

What makes this task harder, and is the reason why you don't see very many people comfortable working in both disciplines, is that the expectations of business are very different to academia. The academic will generally try to drill down to a very specific problem, a tiny problem that can be manipulated without other variables changing – to try proving a hypothesis in a replicable way. This can sometimes take years to achieve, depending on the nature of the research, but it will almost always be so focused on a specific problem that it is of little use to the business leader.

The manager wants real answers to real questions. Why do my outsourced contracts fail? Why can't my suppliers in India make a promise and stick to it? Why does my supplier suffer such a high rate of attrition? Is it really easier to work with local companies or do my problems have more to do with corporate, rather than national, culture?

The academic world looks on in horror at the generalisations managers often use when making important decisions that involve immense amounts of money and resource; often decisions can be based on little more than stereotypes, personal experience, and a quick glance at Wikipedia.

Yet we won't see this situation changing soon. IT is a fast-moving business and sometimes it's better to take a decision and to repent later than to have asked for additional research before choosing what to do. The manager is responsible to business stakeholders and ultimately has to do something, the academic can sometimes prove only that a decision is hard to take; something most IT managers know only too well.

Tuesday, 05 December 2006

Posted at 15:53

Bringing globalisation home

How do you fight a general fear of globalisation? Indeed, is it even right to fight the fear – is there a genuine case for protectionism or is the flag-waving just a political game played by those who need to appeal to a populist agenda?

These questions are difficult to answer. Economists have argued the case for globalisation and offshoring extensively - the only successful economy is one that is open and engages with others. That means wealth and expertise will flow in both directions. Yet the popular view of the man on the street persists, all those pesky foreigners are coming over here to steal our jobs and big companies are just sending work offshore.

Last week, Deloitte published some new research that confirms the popular view and just demonstrates how far the man on the street really is from the business decision-maker. Some might choose to just ignore this as the fear of the uninformed – the tyranny of the majority -

yet these are the consumers who use and buy the products or services your company sells. The number of people prepared to switch bank account because of offshoring is limited to a few radicals at present, because the hassle is seen as too great, but what would happen if UK consumers could operate in harmony to boycott goods and services in much the same way as petrol stations have suffered consumer boycotts in the past?

It's worth reviewing some of the numbers from Deloitte. They asked 2,044 employed adults what they think about offshoring and found that in general the UK population feels increasingly threatened - with 82 per cent not wanting more jobs moving overseas. Some 65 per cent of those surveyed believe more investment is needed in skills and education for the UK to maintain its current competitive economic position. Just four per cent of those surveyed actively support the continuation of offshoring and almost 1 in 3 (32 per cent) believe UK companies should be forced to bring jobs back to the UK.

Here are a few other key and interesting statistics from the Deloitte research:

* 50 per cent of respondents believe that the UK status as a global power is declining while five per cent think it is increasing

* 69 per cent of respondents believe that gGovernment is responsible for global competition (down from 77 per cent)

* 38 per cent of respondents believe that business is responsible for global competition (down from 52 per cent)

* 66 per cent of those questioned said they would relocate internationally to be better off financially

* 64 per cent said they would move to improve their work/life balance

* 53 per cent would leave the UK for better education and skills training

It's interesting to note a couple of things about these answers. Two thirds of people in the UK said they would relocate to be better off financially. Yet, what do they think others who are relocating are doing –

or is it OK for Brits to relocate and not for others? Just four per cent of people with any level of support for offshoring really hammers home the point that the network society is a very misunderstood concept. Wealth creation, capital flows, second-round economic effects, none of these is appreciated as much as a company that hires locally and visibly creates local wealth.

It should be appreciated that many of the companies working within a global environment are creating wealth and jobs for the UK, but those same companies might want to consider how they can increase the local understanding of what they do for this country. Offshoring really does have an image problem. Japanese car manufacturers are seen as somehow 'better' than a financial services organisation based in the City because the impression of jobs created is still visible every time the factory whistle blows.

It might take the MySpace generation to really understand the opportunities presented by virtual networks of work, because in our present transition between those used to a career for life and those expecting to compete against others globally there remains a disconnect.

Tuesday, 12 December 2006

Posted at 11:52

Exploit the new internet business models

O ne of the key changes we are all facing with the IT industry is the concept of knowledge - or skills - being globally available in an accessible market, a level playing field. With the rise and rise of the internet over the past decade a platform has been created, a new public utility that can offer a delivery mechanism for the companies of today and those of tomorrow who are delivering things we have not yet even thought of.

When Thomas Friedman updated his multimillion-selling book 'The World is Flat', his focus was on this idea that many of us are not yet prepared for this change. We are hide-bound to the past and the idea that our competition is the other guy or company down the road. Friedman sees the change as a personalisation of competition using the analogy that in earlier times we saw nation states competing for dominance, followed by major corporations, and now individuals can peddle their skills via the internet to a global audience.

I can see what Friedman means. I have my own personal web site and I use it to promote my own writing and consulting. It's like a shop window where people can see what I do, and if they like it then they might consider hiring me. But things have moved well beyond personal web sites. There are people offering their services through peer-to-peer social networks and companies founding their own competitive offering on the peer-to-peer model, allowing the internet to be the driver of an entirely new form of business transaction that was not possible before this level of connectivity.

These new business models will either help companies to embrace the concept of global partnerships and outsourcing, or they will kill off those who fail to see that the client engagement model has changed. The business-to-business model (B2B) and business-to-consumer (B2C) organisations are blending and merging and utilising the concepts of the social network to gain online credibility.

Take a look at some examples. Zopa offers a deposit and loan service, much like a building society or bank, but different in the way that those prepared to place money on deposit are far more actively engaged in how that money is then carved up and loaned to those seeking to borrow. It would probably be possible to arrange a one-to-one loan service where someone is prepared to invest £5,000 and this goes to someone seeking a £5,000 loan, but by spreading each deposit across a number of borrowers the risk of default is reduced.

So what's the difference between this internet model and the old 'Building and Loan' operation we see every Christmas when watching repeats of 'It's a Wonderful Life'? Well, by connecting the buyer and seller directly and just acting as the utility that makes this possible then it should be possible to create a real win-win for both. Look at the difference between the rates that a bank will pay on money that is placed on deposit and the rates they charge a borrower. Now, if you can connect the saver and borrower directly and agree on a rate for deposits that is higher than a bank or building society would pay, but less that would normally be charged for a loan, then both parties win.

Foreign exchange specialists FXA World use this concept to their own advantage in the same way. Look at the huge difference in foreign exchange rates when you buy or sell any foreign currency, that's called the spread and for a good reason too because the banks make so much cash from this that they can afford to spread large end-of-year bonuses to their traders for continuing to rob the consumer. The Post Office is probably worse than the banks as those cute little ants talk about commission-free currency and then take more from the customer by charging an enormous spread (and they still try selling you a life insurance policy on top of the foreign exchange). FXA World connects buyers of currency to sellers and charges a minimal commission on the trade. So if you have pounds and want dollars then the system will find you someone with dollars who wants pounds and you can agree on a price that is between the buy and sell price a bank will offer – so again, both sides win thanks to the peer-to-peer possibilities offered by the internet.

I have to declare an interest, because I have owned shares in FXA World [2009 note: I no longer have any interest in this company] since just after the company was formed a couple of years ago, but regardless of any potential conflict of interest in bigging-up this organisation, the point is that companies like this – offering a way of connecting a buyer directly to a seller – are all taking the model perfected by eBay and applying it to new markets and services. There is no end to the number of examples where this model could totally change the entire marketplace.

Zopa (I don't have any connection to them at all, but I like their business model!) and FXA World are just acting as a new form of utility and it is becoming essential for every company to consider the implications of this possibility. Just imagine what might be possible if you could employ the best-of-breed service supplier for every service in your supply chain?

Tuesday, 19 December 2006

Posted at 12:04

A new form of competition

In my last blog entry, I was thinking about the changes in the way companies need to represent themselves, because of the internet and how it has created an entirely new world full of potential. There are so many new business ideas floating around now and the barrier to entry is extremely low. This really is an important consideration in the world of outsourced services, because outsourcing is all about slotting into the supply chain of the purchasing organisation and as service companies become more and more sophisticated in utilising the internet as a delivery platform, we will see a shift downwards from the FTSE 100 using strategic sourcing to much smaller outfits.

In fact, as I mentioned in the last blog, the ability to seek out individual free agents for specific ongoing or short-term projects where the internet has facilitated a global search for exactly the right person, has the potential to change the way any of us work. It could even change the nature of what we think of as a company today. We are already talking today about outsourcing as a change in the way that companies operate. The strategy of core competence described by Gary Hamel and CK Prahalad in the early 1990s (or even Charles Handy's Shamrock theory from the 1980s) really has come of age now, yet how much further can it go? The idea at present is that a company can maintain a small core of management and then employ experts via outsourcing to perform manufacture, marketing, public relations, advertising... the list goes on and this theory has become the orthodox view on strategy in our present age. Yet, does a company need to operate this way at all? Perhaps the notion of permanent employment by a single employer is about to go the way of the Dodo?

What if we had to justify our existence at work everyday because we are getting paid on a daily basis, with an almost-perfect market allowing the employer to seek out others to fill our role – so they always have the best team on the job at any particular moment? That's a scary thought and I would love to hear what Lucy Kellaway at the FT thinks about it. It's especially worrying for those who quite enjoy the snug security of a permanent role in a safe organisation. The final-salary pension (remember those?), the ability to take it easy now and then when a hangover prevents too much effort, the regularity of knowing that the bank account will be boosted on the 25th of the month, every month. That's the safe vision of permanent employment enjoyed by some, but the reality for most people is that even permanent jobs have been less than permanent for some time now.

The perfect market offering a way of tapping into an almost infinite pool of resource is also a nice idea in theory, purely from the perspective of economic efficiency, but given that humans are social animals and need some form of environment around us to function best, the idea that we will all be beating each other up on a daily basis for work seems unlikely – for now.

However, if we were going to look around for the best individual resource at present then where would you look? There is no really general employment "exchange" at present, other than some specific web sites such as Rentacoder or eLance. For the past few years I have put my eBay user rating on my CV – my 100 per cent record hopefully a demonstration of my personal behaviour over hundreds of transactions, yet that is not quite good enough to demonstrate my suitability for work in a particular role. Most employers make an assumption of honesty when they offer you a contract. The only places that might be considered appropriate (at present) for demonstrating the value of an individual to the world might be the social networking sites such as Myspace, Bebo, or even Flickr and YouTube – where credibility is earned through the content an individual creates.

If you want a really good example of this, and one that is presented as such in my new book, then take a look at YouTube and look out for the videos posted by a British girl who posts under the ID Cutiemish. Michelle Lam is 18, from Kent, and has been posting regular videos based mainly on her thoughts or ideas – with a few bits of song and dance thrown in (can you believe it, she really likes Elvis). It might not sound like much – and we are not even talking about the usual internet seediness here – but she has attracted millions of viewers.

It could be argued that Cutiemish edits her videos really well, or just has some original and fun thoughts (Angus the orange anyone?) and has a fan base all hanging on for the next instalment in her life. But it's unlikely that she could attract such a following – remember we are talking about millions here - without having some talent for performing and editing. If I worked in the BBC, or in A&R for a music company, then I'd be scouting what some of these YouTube kids are up to because some of them have real talent. Michelle is already going to appear in a Channel 4 movie scheduled for broadcast later this year, bringing the Old Testament book of Exodus into modern-day Margate – and conveniently titled 'Exodus'.

Although Cutiemish will probably end up in the performing arts, she is a clear example of my point that we will probably all need to become our own personal brand in a future where workers from across the world can compete with each other. So if you don't yet have the video-editing skills of Cutiemish then I guess you need to take a personal audit of where you really feel that you can compete – with anyone, anywhere - even if your skills are more suited to hardware performance than stage performance.

January 2007

Tuesday, 02 January 2007

Posted at 12:22

Innovation in outsourcing

I've been thinking quite a lot recently about innovation. Not innovation in the sense of fancy blue-sky thinking, but how the idea of taking new ideas and monetising them, or making them valuable commodities, can be applied to the outsourcing environment. After all, everyone in every service industry likes to talk a good innovation story. Every company wants to be seen as interesting, innovative, sexy, and exciting. Which company ever advertised their services as staid and boring? Though there is a lot to be said for positioning your company as a 'safe pair of hands' rather than something it is not, still everyone wants to be seen as innovative.

The US TV network NBC is making a series of five shows on corporate innovation and they are including outsourcing and offshoring as key areas in which companies are seeking to find new ideas. I know because they asked me to participate in the programme focused on outsourcing, which means filming at midnight in London this coming February in order to synchronise with the people at NBC in the US. The filming is scheduled to take place after a British Computer Society (BCS) evening event focused on outsourcing, so I'd better lay off the free BCS wine and canapés.

So if a major US network like NBC feels they can get five hours of TV from the innovation story then perhaps all of us should be thinking about how new ideas could stimulate our own company. After all, look at how fast the business landscape is changing right now because of the possibilities being created by the globalisation of services. I've been talking to a number of outsourcing supplier companies about this and I've tried to boil down the debate to five major questions:

• Why is innovation so important to you as a service company; try to explain your rationale for offering innovation as a value or attribute rather than any other (such as reliability).

• The concept of a global delivery model (GDM) has become increasingly important to all service companies; does your company see the GDM as a platform to offer innovative service delivery or is it just a response to market requirements?

• Offshore supplier companies – especially from India - used to promote robust quality control methods (the creation of the software 'factory') such as CMM, ISO, COPC, Six Sigma as the key to successful delivery across borders. How can these strict quality control procedures be adhered to at the same time as the creation of a more innovative delivery culture?

• Can innovation be commoditised and offered by your company as part of the overall package in service delivery?

• In your corporate worldview, where is the dividing line between innovation and invention?

Of course, this is not an exhaustive audit on where you are going with your thinking on innovation in outsourcing, but it offers a start on really thinking about whether you are going to take innovation seriously – or whether you treat the entire concept as nothing more than window-dressing your existing services.

Wednesday, 03 January 2007

Posted at 09:00

In memoriam - Sunil Mehta

I was scanning the news last weekend and I saw something in the Indian media where Kiran Karnik, the President of Nasscom – the Indian National Association of Software and Service Companies – was talking about "carrying on" and "managing". The article also mentioned a "Mr Mehta". Clearly something had happened to someone associated with Nasscom, but for some reason I never made the connection with

Sunil Mehta, the research head of Nasscom and one of Kiran's right-hand men at the association. I wasn't reading things very thoroughly, just scanning my various Google News Alerts.

I was chatting on the phone with Hilary Robertson, offshore development director at Xansa on Tuesday about the subject of the annual Nasscom conference in February. This is the biggest annual get-together for the technology industry in India, the one time when everyone (mostly) puts competition aside for a few days and meets in Mumbai to present a united face to the world and the Indian government – and enjoy a few Kingfishers together. She mentioned how it's such a shame that Sunil won't be there – suddenly I connected her mention of Sunil to the news story about Mr Mehta. I had never even thought that he would be talked of in the past tense – he was only 41, just a few years older than me.

Sunil had suffered a massive heart attack at the weekend and died immediately. Not only was he too young to go and leave his family and the Indian technology industry, but also he was a real pleasure to have worked with and I know I will miss him along with many others. As Hilary said, it's a real shame that the conference in February will be without him.

Last October, when Channel 4 aired the 'Dispatches' programme that aimed to expose data security issues involved in working with Indian companies, Sunil was instrumental in preparing the data to refute the allegations in the programme. In fact, all of us who worked to prepare for the broadcast of this documentary had assumed that there might be some allegations worth fighting, rather than the silly "I paid a shady crook in a back-street bar for some data" type of story. Sunil not only amassed a huge amount of valid material to defend the industry, he took on the job of updating the annual Nasscom report each year – the much-quoted annual snapshot of the Indian tech industry.

It was because of Sunil's research and roll-up-your-sleeves mentality that Nasscom, and India in general, managed to ride out the anti-offshoring union protests in the UK in 2003 and the presidential election battles of 2004 in the USA. A lot of people used to have the misconceived view that Indian technology was nothing more than cheap and cheerful, low-cost labour or software 'coolies'. Sunil and his work at Nasscom over the past few years has changed that perception – his research has demonstrated how India is already leading the world in the production of high-quality software and has already started moving into new areas of knowledge process outsourcing and complex R&D.

Whatever you think of globalisation, it can't be denied that India is now a major force in the global information technology industry. The fact that we have some quantitative publications that can prove the reality – rather than the el cheapo offshoring myth – is largely thanks to Sunil Mehta and his team. Thanks Sunil.

Monday, 15 January 2007

Posted at 13:51

Drop the jargon - in outsourcing as well as IT

The BBC dubbed one fateful week in early January 'Geek Week'. The reason? The huge Consumer Electronics (CES) show in Las Vegas, plus MacWorld in San Francisco were both taking place in the same week – the two largest shows in the world for electronic gadgets and everything Apple. The ideal opportunity for technology reporters to worship at the altar of new kit – and to ogle at all the young girls employed to display that kit (or question why sexy gadgets need sexy girls to make it more interesting).

Apple famously launched their new iPhone at MacWorld to the gasps of the assembled crowd (I wouldn't mind one myself when they are launched in the UK) and BBC technology correspondent Rory Cellen-Jones described his incredulous amazement at the CES crowd, who would call out in joy and wildly cheer speakers describing a new software feature or bug-fix.

He was talking on the BBC Radio Five Live radio show 'Wake up to Money', which is usually a non-tech zone, and often focused on the financial results of brewing companies. Rory wrote something similar on his blog and commented on how annoying it is that people involved in technology cannot communicate what they are using or selling without resorting to a wave of acronyms and numbers.

The comments to the blog showed that most techies reading the BBC blogs felt quite patronised by this. Most were happy to fly the flag of geekiness with pride and considered that the ability to understand arcane tech-speak was the result of hard work. One comment on the blog even told Rory that if he wasn't describing something very technical or that the reader could not understand – and therefore had to work to understand – then he wasn't doing his job as a technology writer. Rory has some stern critics in the blogosphere.

The outsourcing community is as guilty as those in consumer electronics. The suppliers, the advisors, the users, all have their own language and one glance at any article or book about outsourcing can leave the uninitiated reader dazed as terms such as captive, offshoring, GDM, KPO, BPO, LPO, APO, RPO, SLA, or KPI, all blend into confusion.

I have to admit that I'm with Rory on preferring a good understanding of what is going on without the jargon. Outsourcing is just a description of partnership, two companies working together, something that has taken place for hundreds of years, yet we now have this confusing management-speak that obfuscates what is really going on. If we want the benefits of outsourcing to be better understood by those in the public who are not a part of the technology industry then we really need to do a better job of making our case in a clear and consistent way. There is power in simplicity!

Thursday, 18 January 2007

Posted at 13:58

Marketing fails to cross international divide

One of the downsides of having quite a well-known email address is the amount of spam that I get; a positive deluge of the stuff. Of course, the filter snares most of it, but something from an Indian technology vendor got through the net yesterday and it made me smile because it is the very opposite of where everyone in the outsourcing industry is headed. It's just one of those sorry tales of someone buying a spam database and blasting millions of poor suckers in the hope that one might just be about to buy a technology service and the incoming spam will influence their purchasing decision.

To start with, the mail in question was not addressed to me, it was a generic spam mail opening only with a cheery "hello!" It went on to say: "I represent an IT Company, XXXXX Pvt Ltd. We serve in all the different industry domains including Finance, Healthcare, Tourism, Education, Automobiles and infact all others that are greatly leveraging INFORMATION TECHNOLOGY to support the actual business Processes. We are INDIA based offshore IT solution provider for clients in US, UK and around the globe."

To start with, considering this is a marketing mailshot the grammar is pretty hopeless. The capitalisation is interesting to say the least – do they need to shout INDIA from the rooftops? We all know India – in general -has a great reputation for technology outsourcing, but I doubt that a dodgy little email like this is going to help the company in question. One of their fatal mistakes is to say we can do anything – just give us a contract, please, we can do that, the pleading being reminiscent of Yosser Hughes for those who remember the gritty 1980s drama 'Boys from the Blackstuff'.

So the message is unsolicited, the English is dreadful, and the company has no focus. What else could be wrong in such a short message? Well how about the classic techie problem of bombarding three-letter acronyms at decision-makers and hoping they don't understand? Or maybe they think it is impressive?

This paragraph is worthy of James Joyce for its ability to bamboozle the reader: "We are using .NET Technologies using C# .NET, VB.NET languages. Also, we are doing web development using ASP.NET and .PHP and Manual testing as well as Automated testing. We welcome software work including development, Web Development, Quality Control, QA Automation OR we can provide offshore consultant for direct staffing who will work from our offshore center.

Here are some key facts about the company with Technical expertise. We provide offshore software development services to clients globally through our vast experience in PHP, ASP, ASP.Net, C#.NET, VB.NET, Java, J2EE Programming.

- ASP .NET 1.1 and 2.0
- .NET Framework 1.1, 2.0, 3.0 based Development.

- C#.NET And VB.NET
- Visual Studio .NET 2003 and 2005
- J2EE, Java Technology
- Oracle JDeveloper, Eclipse
- XML/XSL Technologies with .NET
- MS SQL Server 2000 and 2005
- Oracle
- PHP
- MySQL/PostgressSQL
- LoadRunner, WinRunner, QTP"

That's quite a mouthful. It's a shame that while the big guys have realised this is not the way to promote an international service, an entire tranche of small and medium companies continue to market themselves in the worst possible way. This is a problem because the small and medium sized business sector in the UK needs help finding reliable partners to work with for technology services, and they usually don't want to work with the big companies for fear of being the smallest and least important customer. Who else can they turn to if the smaller Indian companies are so bad?

Monday, 22 January 2007

Posted at 14:18

Is terrorism a threat for outsourced IT?

I read in one of the Indian newspapers that their security services were on the verge of closing down a terror operation focused on the international outsourcing industry. It claimed that the Indians suspected a new threat where well-trained Pakistanis would obtain jobs in Indian companies where the service provided formed a critical part of the supply chain for a Western company, allowing them to strike at the very heart of Western civilisation by bring various companies to their knees in some form of co-ordinated effort.

It all sounds far-fetched and positively paranoid – rather *Casino Royale*. This reporting also perpetuates the animosity that still simmers between India and Pakistan. For all the diplomacy and recent thawing in relations there is still a great mistrust between these two nations. I recall being at the Indian Independence Day party of one of the larger technology firms in Bangalore a couple of years ago. I was there to interview the chief executive, who was held up, so I joined the staff in their Friday afternoon celebrations.

One group were conducting various 'what-if' scenarios – asking each other what they would do in certain outlandish situations. They question to one young software developer was: "What would you do if you personally could control the Indian nuclear arsenal?" His immediate reply was: "Destroy the whole of Pakistan!" Cheers went all round. I was shocked. These kids were young, in good jobs, and had the benefit of a college education yet they still continued to hate their smaller neighbour - for no apparent reason I could see.

I don't want to get into the rights and wrongs of the India and Pakistan conflict – there are plenty of other bloggers doing that job, but I did want to comment on the idea that supply chain terrorism might be a genuine threat and not just because of this particular geography. There are conflicts in many other regions beyond just this one alone.

Think about the changes in technology over recent times. Technology used to be physical; there was a tactile quality to it. You could go to an equipment room within your office and touch the servers, even if backups were located offsite. In addition, the architecture was all locked together and tightly coupled – systems that integrated together did so in a very pre-determined way.

Now we have far looser architectures, such as services-oriented architecture (SOA), that focus far less on the physical kit and far more on defining the service you need from technology. You no longer care where the kit is located, so long as the service is delivered when you push a button. Changes to the services are far more likely to be outsourced to someone outside the company, and possible even outside the country.

Imagine the chaos if the website of every retail bank in the UK was brought down simultaneously, or the customer helpline of every major insurer was cut off. There are many new routes to terrorist disruption that may not result in lost life, but can cause financial loss and disruption and in all our plans for a new era of outsourcing we need to bear some of these real issues in mind.

Thursday, 25 January 2007

Posted at 14:26

IT debates must look to the future

I attended a dinner at the Royal Society recently, hosted by the British Computer Society (BCS) and focused on the question: "What are the right things to do to sustain UK competitiveness in 2025?" It was an invitation-only event designed to collect together a broad group of thinkers and decision-makers from the IT industry in the UK. BCS President Nigel Shadbolt gave a talk about the direction of the BCS and how these events are useful in gathering opinion – essentially it was like a focus group, giving some direction and policy input to the BCS.

It was an event controlled by the famous 'Chatham House' rules, so direct reporting where any comments are attributed to people is not allowed, but I want to make a few comments on the discussion.

I personally was a bit disappointed that one of the key themes that underpinned the debate was a concentrated attack on Nicholas Carr's book "Does IT Matter?: Information Technology and the Corrosion of Competitive Advantage" – a book that was published almost three years ago and has been debated ad nauseum ever since. The debate focused on how important IT has become for any business and therefore the utility model Carr has defined could not possibly be correct.

I've just written a new book for the BCS with Dr Richard Sykes of Intellect and in there we have analysed the Carr hypothesis. Although we have also been critical of some aspects of the Carr book, we also accepted that he has some excellent points. Utility computing is becoming a far more attractive proposition. Software-as-a-service is becoming a reality that is changing the local requirements for IT architecture and support. All of this impacts on any potential outsourcing decision. The way IT services are consumed is changing and this affects the way any IT service group needs to operate and market itself.

My fear is that we might debate the IT industry in terms that are outmoded. I have a lot of time for the BCS and I respect what they are doing to promote the Skills Framework – helping to guide people through a career in IT, but the bottom line is that those of us in IT have to accept that the industry is changing and that means the idea of a career in IT also has to change. It's no good harrumphing about the fact that 'in my day we were considered engineers' – let's just consider how information technology as an industry can progress and give people valuable work for many years to come.

Sunday, 28 January 2007

Posted at 14:32

Let's discuss the future of IT services - not just offshoring

I recently chaired a debate at the illustrious London School of Economics (LSE) titled "Hi-Tech India, Challengers at the Gate? Will India build on its lead in technology or lose out to China and the new players in global services?" This was just one in a series of lectures and events focused on India, as a part of the annual LSE 'India week'.

The LSE asked me to get some people for the debate, once I had agreed to chair it, so I did have to work a little to bring the whole event together. I was pleased to have three real leaders from the world of India and high-tech up on the stage with me though. Arun Aggarwal (Tata Consultancy Services, European head of consulting), Srikanth Iyengar (Infosys, European head of strategic sourcing), and Rajiv Dey (NIIT SmartServe, senior vice president) all joined me to debate the issue of where India is now and where it might go in future.

Srikanth went first and he painted a positive picture for India, though acknowledging some of the local issues regarding infrastructure – a fair and balanced picture. Rajiv had done a lot of homework and he reeled off one statistic after another – a real mountain of data that he felt proved the Indian advantage – especially in terms of demographics. It was such a glowing tribute that I quipped 'if India really is that great then I don't know why David Beckham has gone to play football in the US...'

Arun departed a little from the stated objective of examining the potential for India to maintain a lead in this industry, based on what others are doing. He felt that there is no point in watching what China, Vietnam or other regions are doing; the question is more importantly what will the IT services industry look like in a decade, because it won't be the same as today, and that uncertainty is the real challenge – not competing nations.

I was really keen to go down this track - I wanted to question Arun a bit more and to see what the others felt. In my mind I was thinking about the future for outsourced systems integrators in a world where software-as-a-service has really taken off and most tools are browser-based. Who would need to pay for big package rollouts then? Or who will be paying for customised software if the open source movement matures into an environment where business customisations can be undertaken? There are so many changes taking place because of technology virtualisation that it would be hard to predict where the classic IT service company is going to sit in future and this is important not only for outsourcing, but for the way the entire industry operates.

In the event, I wanted to let the audience get in as many questions as possible – and they were keen to ask! There was a good debate and we talked a lot about the branding of nations, how trust can be developed, and why there is no Indian version of Google or Yahoo, but ultimately I think the points Arun raised could form an entire day of debate – that could be captured and reported on the internet. I missed my immediate chance to follow up, but I hope to do so at some point this year!

Monday, 29 January 2007

Posted at 14:41

How leadership attitudes differ

I was talking to a friend of mine – Nick Hadjinikos, who heads up Kallinos Communications – last week, about the different approach to management taken by Indian and Western IT leaders. It was interesting because as we compared some of the differences we had encountered when talking to the 'Western IT outsourcing companies' compared to those from India, there were a few key themes – regardless of the specific company.

One of the most obvious is the difference in attitude of the leader and what this means for a company that is trying to market itself through the media. Think of famous US technology chief executives - Bill Gates, Steve Jobs, Larry Ellison, Sam Palmisano - they are all larger than life and prepared to speak to the media (or Second Life gamers) about their company – and more. There is a real sense of the CEO as a 'hero' – leading the company to its future destiny. The bookshelves are filled with management books from ex-CEOs telling us all how to run companies – probably the most famous is Jack Welch, formerly of General Electric – who is treated as a demi-God on the campus of most business schools.

Now look at the Asian outsourcing companies, the big technology players from India are the best example. The leaders are far more humble and less brash. This is at a personal level probably a good thing, yet it doesn't help a great deal when trying to sell a story to the world. When Steve Jobs makes a statement about Apple, the media and the world listen. When the leader of an Indian technology services group makes a statement, there is usually nothing more than a wave of indifference.

Yet, it's not because they have not got something important to say – we all know how important the Indian tech companies are becoming. But even the über-geek himself, Bill Gates, has managed to master the art of behaving like the übermensch. Infosys is probably the major example of a company that bucks the trend, managing to be both Indian in its heritage, but also presenting a face of global leadership, thanks largely to Narayana Murthy and Nandan Nilekani, but also a corporate strategy of making sure they get noticed in the places that count – such as the World Economic Forum in Davos.

I'm going to comment a bit more on this in another blog because there are some specific ideas around Web 2.0 that I'd like to mention, but I think it would be useful to paste in a chunk of text on this topic from my earlier book 'Outsourcing to India: The Offshore Advantage', as I observed this and wrote about it quite a while back, but there does not seem to have been much progress:

"A parallel can be drawn with the theory of the philosopher king in Plato's Republic. A major difference is that Plato was hypothesising on a desirable form of leadership in a time of ignorance, where knowledgeable leaders would be groomed to their future position from an early age. Plato desired this form of leadership whereas in India something similar exists today in the modern world. Thomas More developed the Platonic argument further in his Utopia; however authors such as George Orwell and Aldous Huxley managed to twist these ideal mores into frightening visions of benevolent dictatorship.

"In Western society, the individual player is often rewarded for an ability to work without 'disturbing' the manager. Indian subordinates often require more guidance than a Western manager will be comfortable with, as he may expect them to 'get on with it' rather than frequently asking for advice, but this state of dependency on the manager is a very normal situation. Sharma explains: 'Dependence-proneness is a tendency of the subordinates to seek support, advice and help from superiors even in situations which do not warrant such dependence. Dependence-prone persons tend to avoid responsibility and do not show initiative. But in a nurturing climate of warmth and emotional support, dependence-prone persons are likely to perform better than others.

"The emphasis on that last statement was added by Sharma. In a Western context, this means that there will be many situations where a person can be a valuable member of the team, but they need to be taken 'under your wing' in order to perform. Just think of all those Hollywood movies with a rookie cop or cub reporter and you should have a good appreciation of how to help these people grow in stature. Just don't use

'Dirty Harry' as a management role model; the rookie was always shot before the end of the movie."

Tuesday, 30 January 2007

Posted at 09:00

The brave new world of Web 2.0

When I see things like Matt Harding's video of him dancing around the world it makes me think 'Wow. How on earth did he think of doing that and how could something similar be applied to the companies I work with to help them reach out to new customers?' After all, he has over five million hits on YouTube alone for the video; now add in Google videos, Yahoo, MySpace... that's a lot of eyeballs.

However, my experience in general of companies adopting Web 2.0 has not been positive. Most are caught up in a world in which they have control over what is released about them and their services. Like a despotic government controlling what the press can say, modern service companies that present themselves as the ideal partner, exciting, innovative and flexible – all recoil in horror when presented with some ideas for reaching customers that go beyond the norm.

So everyone is working on creating corporate blogs? Well, my experience is that the first thing people are concerned about is the uncontrollable nature of the blog environment. What if the reader comments say something negative about us? What if the competition starts making a point of commenting? What if the chief executive can't spell – shouldn't we run everything through three levels of editing first to check grammar and adherence to the corporate line first?

And what about other interactive environments such as Flickr, MySpace, or YouTube? I recently arranged for punk legends Buzzcocks to play a 1977-2007 celebration gig at the University of London. They agreed to give a talk in the theatre pre-gig on the relevance of punk and youth culture in 2007. Now, as Buzzcocks were probably the first band to create their own label – and therefore the creators of the indie movement – I thought the connection with bands of today using MySpace to usurp the record labels was so strong that a corporate sponsor wanting to reach a youth audience would be easy to find. However, it proved harder than I thought – all the companies I have good connections to thought I was nuts to suggest that they should sponsor a rock concert. So although I had the band on board with the idea, I couldn't go ahead with it. No points for forward thinking and the potential advantage of being seen in front of 1,200 of the best and brightest young people in London then.

One of my own companies is using YouTube in an interesting way, but then that is because I gave them the idea and I don't immediately benefit from giving away my ideas to them, apart from them hopefully doing better as a result!

I have discussed the idea of using YouTube with a number of the outsourcing service providers. I thought that it would be a great way to present a young and funky (hey, this is Web 2.0!) and global image – just what many of them are striving for. The problem I kept hitting was a fear of people uploading spoof videos that might reflect negatively on the brand. Oh well, whatever happened to the old adman's saying (apologies to Oscar Wilde) that "all publicity is good publicity?" Is the fear of talking about outsourcing still so powerful that companies would rather lurk in the shadows than enter a brave new world?

Wednesday, 31 January 2007

Posted at 17:36

There is one thing the Indians should outsource...

Next week is the equivalent of Oscar week for the Indian hi-tech industry. It's the annual conference of Nasscom in Mumbai – the National Association of Software and Service Companies – which is basically the voice of hi-tech in India as 95 per cent of the industry belongs to Nasscom. So I am off there on Monday and even planning to speak about knowledge process outsourcing (KPO) at the conference, though I still don't know on which day or at what time, but the timezone is IST - Indian Stretchable Time - and as I am attending the entire conference I am happy to get roped in and to help out where I can anyway.

One of the less pleasant things about travelling to India is that you need a visa – it's not like flying into most countries with a European passport and just getting waved through. In India, you need a visa in advance of travel or else they won't even let you board the plane at Heathrow. So I went this morning to the Indian High Commission at Aldwych to get a new visa, as my earlier one ran out just after Christmas.

I know that a lot of people I work with and who also have friends at the High Commission might just give a call in advance to their staffer friends, call in for cup of tea and allow some flunky to deal with the paperwork, but that sort of cosy corruption never really sits well with me – so I go and line up like everyone else. In my opinion, the Indian High Commission had really improved their visa service over the past few years, getting the process down to something that took not much more than an hour, which has not been too much of a hardship for me in the past.

Today though, it was dreadful. I wanted to try getting it done quickly, so I got there almost one hour before the doors opened. The queue of like-minded souls snaked around India Place and down Aldwych. It was pretty cold this morning and I had cycled about eight miles to get to the High Commission, so I was pretty miserable and freezing; my feet no longer existed. When I finally got to the front of the line and collected my chit, telling me my place in the processing queue, I found I was after 326 other people. I got there at 7.30am and finally got the passport back in my hands with a new visa at noon.

It doesn't have to be like this. It's about time that India outsourced the whole visa application process to a company that can offer a turnaround of no more than one hour. I heard a rumour that the High Commission was considering a private sector operator for this, but nothing seems to have been confirmed – and certainly nothing is happening at the coalface, things just get worse! Perhaps if enough of us - who regularly travel to India – kick up a fuss then something might happen? Spending half a day just to get a stamp in the passport is just not acceptable and doesn't help the process of working with India at all.

February 2007

Monday, 12 February 2007

Posted at 12:06

Cut the jargon

I spent three days at the annual Nasscom conference in India last week. Three days is a really long time for me to consider spending at a conference – I'm as busy as everyone else and blocking out that much time for networking is rare for me, but Nasscom in February has become the de facto meeting place for everyone involved in global IT and outsourcing.

Almost as soon as I walked into the conference though, I was disturbed by one of the sponsor booths. I've always championed the cause of simplicity in IT. I mean, I know that IT is a complex subject – I studied computer science and software engineering when I was a teenager, but then I later got myself an MBA – so I hope I have some appreciation of what is going on under the hood (all that Babbage and Boole wasn't wasted), but also why it matters to a company or industry.

I walked up to the stand in question – the Polaris software company. Now, I know Polaris is a serious technology player. They were spun out of Citigroup and so they know financial services tech as well as, or better than, most. But my eyes were drawn to the information they had plastered all over their stand proclaiming them to be the first company to be offering a banking solution based on SOA (services-oriented architecture). Hmmm.

I asked the nice young man on the stand (who was very pleasant and helpful and even laughed at my jokes) if they normally talk to their banking clients about SOA, rather than the solutions that the technology offers. He claimed that banking clients are really excited about this development, although on probing further he did say that every client has a different idea of what a service oriented architecture really is, and with so much legacy kit in place, any SOA implementation can only be bolted onto the environment, not designed from the ground-up.

Every time I asked him about how wise it is to use jargon, acronyms, and technical terms in marketing literature my words seemed to fall on deaf ears. I've a lot of respect for Polaris as a company, but I can't understand this approach at all. Cut out the jargon guys and talk in terms of solutions to the problems bankers have, rather than selling technical architecture. I mean do you buy a PC just because it has Windows installed on it?

Tuesday, 13 February 2007

Posted at 12:16

The political risks of offshore outsourcing?

On 5 February I chaired a session at a conference organised by the Royal Institute of International Affairs – better known as Chatham House – on the political risk involved in offshore outsourcing, with a focus on outsourcing to India as the company chosen to talk on the topic was from India.

Rajiv Dey, a senior vice president of NIIT SmartServe, made a presentation to the Chatham House audience after which they probed and questioned him in detail. The NIIT group is well known to anyone with any experience of India as it has become a leader in technical education, with thousands of colleges and schools now running its courses. In fact, I met its chairman Rajendra Pawar for a breakfast in London quite recently and he told me about an entire university he is building in India – from the ground up. SmartServe is NIIT's business process outsourcing (BPO) division, the area that focuses on back-office services.

Now, I had originally thought that I would just introduce Rajiv, let him talk and take some questions, and I would just need to chair proceedings and keep things moving along by making sure I had some questions in case the audience dried up. But I then found out that I was expected to draw up a summary of the session to present immediately as a 15-minute presentation, based on what just happened, and to speak alongside Clive Cookson – the erudite science and technology editor of the Financial Times. So I ended up furiously taking notes on what Rajiv was saying, and then found that when I was supposed to summarise, I had five pages of notes to browse.

To summarise some of the key points Rajiv brought up:

• Some of the economics measures talked of are a bit crude, such as the terms laid out in the much-talked-of BRICs (Brazil, Russia, India, China) analysis – all these countries will develop, but they will do so in different ways.

• India is the largest democracy in the world, but the poor and disenfranchised are not yet feeling the effects of the IT boom.

• Consumer views are still quite negative towards outsourcing and so there remains a political risk of protectionism from major economies.

• The technology industry has grown and developed this far despite, rather than thanks to, the government.

• Companies now believe that the business sophistication is available for really complex services from India – not just grunt work. Cisco has even made Bangalore a joint-head office.

• There are some political conflicts or disputes at present in the sub-continent region, especially in Bangladesh and Sri Lanka, but these have not affected confidence in India.

Rajiv did make some good points and he looked beyond the typical business perspective to give a wider perspective on the effects of working with another country and the risks this can bring.

Wednesday, 14 February 2007

Posted at 09:00

Summarising Nasscom 2007

I spent some time last week at the annual Nasscom conference in Mumbai. Nasscom is the trade association that represents the Indian hi-tech industry and it effectively represents the entire industry in India as 95 per cent of companies in this sector are members. The annual conference really sets the agenda for offshore outsourcing around the world.

This year there was not a single issue that dominated the event, as there has often been in the past. I felt this myself and heard it from a few others. This could be viewed as a good thing – maybe a sign of maturity – as the unifying force for the industry has often been negative, fighting back from poor impressions overseas or data protection disasters. Now they are well accepted as leaders in India they have less and less to fight against.

There were a couple of thousand delegates and so I spoke to a lot of people over the three days, but I have captured a few thoughts here in my blog to give you an idea of what people were saying about the industry at Nasscom 2007.

Alistair Cox, chief executive of Xansa told me: "There hasn't been a single burning issue this year, but there have been a number of simmering issues as you might expect. One of these is can the Indian growth rate continue at the heady heights that everyone has enjoyed over the last two, three or four years – firms growing at 40 per cent or 50 per cent a year? How long will it continue and is the bubble about to burst? But frankly, people have been talking about this for more than the last year anyway!"

Anant Gupta, chief operating officer of HCL infrastructure services division, focused on the idea that collaboration and genuine partnerships (not the ones we always see in the sales literature) will become ever more important. He said: "One of the biggest themes this year is alternative sourcing and alternative ways of sourcing IT services. I think that services such as remote infrastructure management, will be focused more on a collaborative model."

The old problem of attrition and human resources management reared its head again, but this time in partnership with the fear that India is eventually going to run out of skilled people to keep fuelling the industry. V. Sreenivasan, vice president of strategic relations and consulting for ITC Infotech said: "The key issue is to understand the sustainability of the outsourcing operation – we need to sustain the present growth over the next five to seven years. The challenges are around talent management, attrition management and repeatability and how the Indian and global players are going to identify their respective places."

Ashank Desai, chairman of Mastek took a long-term view on the war for talent and identified that the entire education sector needs to change. He said to me: "We need to move on from liberalising the technology sector to consider how to liberalise the education sector. In fact, when I spoke with the Indian Prime Minister Dr Manmohan Singh earlier today, I raised this issue with him directly. We really must impart a good education to all Indians. There are some excellent universities, but we need to consider the full scope of education right down to the primary level."

Of course, there is always a company looking for a new way of doing things and Francisco D'Souza, president and chief executive of Cognizant Technologies, highlighted this when he said to me: "The central theme coming out of Nasscom this year is how do we drive innovation. How do we continue to innovate in our business models and continue to drive growth rates and increase the levels of customer satisfaction that we have become known for?"

Although there really was no driving single concern, Xansa's Alistair Cox was right - there are some simmering and important issues across the industry. I do feel that the Indian technology industry has matured a great deal since the heady days of the millennium and is going to develop itself further into a leadership position. Mastek's Ashank Desai talked to me about this in his car as we travelled to the closing gala dinner together. Ashank has a strong belief that the Indian industry can help the IT industry globally by breaking free of any low-cost stigma and starting to behave like leaders – to demonstrate best practice to the world. And I think he is probably right.

Tuesday, 27 February 2007

Posted at 11:52

Listen to the new generation

I recently participated in an event hosted by the British Computer Society Young Professional's Group (BCS YPG). The focus was on government technology and I was talking about the use of outsourcing by the UK government alongside Kate Silver from the Cabinet Office.

The event was interesting to me for a couple of reasons. I was keen to see the type of folks involved with the YPG in the first instance. Even though I'm sadly now over 35 and therefore not officially eligible to participate in their events, I thought it would still be interesting to meet them and to hear their views. And as it turned out, I was right.

This was a mixed crowd of 20- and 30-somethings, some entrepreneurial, some corporate, and I'm pleased to say some women as well. What I did not find was the stereotypical young geeks - everyone could talk about more than just C++ or widgits. I have been a member of the BCS since the 1980s and I flirted with the YPG on a number of occasions, but whenever I got close enough to consider increased participation – to the extent that I might feel I belong to their flock – it started feeling a bit like the young Tories. The BCS has really changed in a positive way if the crowd at the meeting last night is anything to go by. It was more like a First Tuesday event.

The questions from the floor on outsourcing were a lot more mature than those posed at many other events I have spoken at or chaired. The focus of the questions was far more on building a skills framework for a 21st century career than building a wall around the UK borders to prevent any interaction. It was a refreshing change to talk to an audience that has already accepted some of the unchangeable realities of the internet, cheap communications, and low-cost travel. These guys have accepted that globalisation in the IT industry is taking place and they already have a focus on managing their career a decade from now.

Instead of paying mega-bucks to visionaries and gurus such as Malcolm Gladwell, some of the companies asking questions about where technology is taking us might want to consider asking groups such as the YPG. Just think about it, young adults graduating today cannot even remember a world before mobile phones and the internet. That earlier time is ancient history and they can only appreciate it in the same way as I might appreciate the music of the Beatles – great tunes, but all recorded before my own birth. The young have a different relationship with technology just because they are young – those of us with a few more years work experience should learn the value of that experience.

Wednesday, 28 February 2007

Posted at 11:58

The easyLife

Sir Stelios Haji-Iannou – founder of low-cost airline easyJet - was talking about innovation at the London School of Economics (LSE) the other day. It's a subject that everyone is talking about in the outsourcing community at present. Everyone is wondering where the next major areas of growth will come from. Will it be a new ability to tap into the small and medium-sized enterprise (SME) sector, or a wave of disruptive innovation that will entirely change the marketplace?

Stelios was on top form. One of his opening lines was "I bet you are all wondering how I could start an airline at the age of 28 and achieve such success – well, I have a rich dad..."

He went completely off-piste and did not focus on a structured talk in the way that one normally expects in a university lecture theatre, especially where the talk was billed with a specific theme. Instead he cracked a few jokes and then took questions from the audience for the entirety of his allotted time, so he allowed the audience to decide exactly what he should talk about.

The general theme was innovation, but he did not really talk about it in any way that might be of use to anyone interested in outsourcing; the real focus of the talk was climate change and entrepreneurialism. However, a couple of points are worth mentioning because they cross over to some of the work I am often asked to get involved in with outsourcing suppliers.

The first is knowledge of your own market and the value of the service you are providing. There are untold numbers of IT specialists now climbing onto the gravy train of consulting, with the intention of 'moving up the value chain' and being paid to advise companies much earlier in the purchasing cycle – advising before the client has even decided to outsource. Stelios gave the example of using his own brand to found a new university – easyUniversity. Imagine the concept, the value-for-money easy brand offering a 20 per cent discount on LSE prices. Unfortunately, the association with cheapness does not work very well with education and it doesn't really with consulting either.

The idea that the brand can be flexible within limits is something else that Stelios shared. He gave the example of his easyCruise service, a cruise ship that spends winter in the Caribbean and summer in the Mediterranean, operating rather like an upmarket bus – going from one resort to the next. When he launched the ship, it was bright orange inside and out. I even read one newspaper travel writer who complained that he needed to wear sunglasses when going to bed because the gaudy bedroom decoration meant it was impossible to sleep at night.

Stelios admitted that this was a mistake. Bright and in-your-face works on planes because no customer has to spend more than a couple of hours in that environment, but that same livery applied to a ship - where someone might be living for a week - causes a greater emotional problem.

This does directly correlate to many of the offshore suppliers coming and working in the UK market. Web sites, white papers, and marketing collateral all remain directed at consumers in the home market, with an assumption that it will be OK because it is all written in English. Attitudes to marketing, advertising, and public relations - they can all be so different and yet they should really be aligned to the market in which you are trying to market a service, not where the head office is located. Reading some of the white papers produced by Indian suppliers is like trying to spend a night in an orange bedroom courtesy of easyCruise – painful and likely to result in lost sleep.

One final comment on brands. One audience member at the LSE lecture asked Stelios if there was any truth in a three-way merger between easyJet, Virgin, and Air Asia – which Stelios denied, saying there had been some talks and ideas bounced around, but no serious discussion and talks had ceased a long time back. The questioner then shot back the comment that it's a shame no merger is planned as the joint venture could be called Easy Asian Virgin... The entire LSE audience laughed - along with Sir Stelios.

March 2007

Monday, 05 March 2007

Posted at 13:21

Where are these IT sweatshops?

There has been a lot of talk recently about IT sweatshops, not over in India or China, but right here in the UK. The allegations being that offshore outsourcing companies are now abusing work permit regulations on intra-company transfers to bring cheaper people over here, before sending them home again.

Last week, the Home Office revealed that 33,756 permits were issued to overseas IT workers in the last year, which is about a third more then the year before. Most of these work permits – 79 per cent to be precise – went to Indian IT workers. These figures were released under the Freedom of Information Act to the Association of Technology Staffing Companies (Atsco).

There are a couple of things to remember here. First, some of the 'talking heads' have expressed opinions on sweatshops and staff who cannot speak English – essentially making accusations of abuse or trafficking. Just look at the exact words of Ann Swain, Atsco's chief executive: "They are working in sweatshop factories, not learning English, some are in hostels and most are not learning the culture. We have had calls from people saying they are earning less than half what they could on the open market."

Let's deal with the issues in turn then. First, how about the IT sweatshops? Atsco, please tell me where are they? Tata is in Grosvenor Place. Infosys is in Canary Wharf. NIIT is in leafy High Wycombe. HCL is in Bishopsgate. Wipro is in the spanking new Paddington Basin complex. I could go on. If Indian techies are not working in these pleasant surroundings then they will be on client sites and given that the client companies of these IT suppliers are world-leading organisations I can only assume that they have pretty nice offices too. We are not talking about pre-war Cable Street here.

Second, on the question of the movement of labour itself – I'd immediately state my own view that just because legislation on work visas exists, it does not mean that it is automatically correct or the best way of doing things. In fact, it is impossible to roll back the clock to a time before the internet or cheap telecoms made it possible to deal with Bangalore instead of Basingstoke.

If an Indian company takes on a technology contract then it seems perfectly fair for them to bring in some staff from overseas to work on the knowledge transfer. They don't need to suddenly get UK salaries because they are being based in the UK for a period of time. They have their expenses covered and they receive their salary back home, which is a lot more than most people outside the IT services industry.

I'm involved in some recruitment in Mumbai right now and staff in their 20s are getting something like eight times the salary of a high school teacher. That's another issue entirely regarding the change in societal values and the power of the market, but the point is that these guys are not being exploited by getting peanuts in their pay packet back in India. On a purchasing-power basis most of them are probably richer in India than on the British salary for a similar job.

The one area where Atsco and the unions may have a fair point is if those transfers of staff from India to the UK are on a long-term basis and the transfer does not involve a switch to a UK employment contract. Clearly if people are transferred over for project work and they end up on expenses in the UK for a year or more then there is an issue – they should either be getting a local employment contract or someone local should be hired.

What's funny about all of this is that when I worked as an IT manager for the French bank SG, when I expatriated people out to India, they would continue to get their European salary PLUS an additional monthly bonus to compensate for the inconvenience of having to move to a developing country. If my wife had not insisted on staying in London I would have considered a deal like that myself. If the Atsco people are correct in what they say then expatriation in the other direction should result in a hefty pay cut.

But, here is some more food for thought. International service companies such as IBM, HP, and Accenture are amongst the largest private-sector employers in India – and they are all hiring at a prodigious rate. Indian players such as Infosys, Tata Consultancy Services, Wipro, Satyam, HCL, NIIT Technologies et al, are all trying to build their own 'global delivery models' – meaning they need local people on the ground where their customers are located. So they are hiring extensively in the UK. TCS now has around 5,000 people in the UK working for them – at local salaries. There is a merry-go-round taking place where the international brands are hiring in India and the Indians are hiring in the UK, in addition to the temporary transfers of labour taking place, to allow flexibility on individual projects.

The real issue here is not that Indian companies are abusing the work visa system or even 'exploiting' their workers, it is that government regulation fails to understand the consequences of a network society. Both labour and tasks can relocate in our present environment through migration or outsourcing. And they will relocate for reasons of cost and quality – or specialisation. Government policy needs to connect these two topics together with a third issue – what kind of education do British kids need if they are going to need to compete with the best the world has to offer? Because that's the environment we are entering.

Education, Migration, Outsourcing – the EMO trinity. EMO should be the real focus of the unions and organisations such as Atsco – and I don't mean the angst-ridden EMO music scene documented on a weekly basis by the NME.

Wednesday, 07 March 2007

Posted at 13:30

Building BRICs

I had a quick chat the other day with Dr Ganesh Natarajan who is the deputy chairman and managing director of Zensar Technologies. Ganesh is also on the executive council of Nasscom, so he is one of the key players steering the Indian IT industry at present.

I asked him for his views on the key trends in technology outsourcing at present. He said: "The key trends are the integrated IT and BPO offerings that are enabling services firms to provide true end-to-end transformation solutions to their clients. Another trend is the move towards rapid productivity improvements by replacing high-cost manpower with lower experienced folk and automation."

I personally would question the first comment. Not that I think Ganesh is entirely wrong – it's true that BPO companies need to use better and improved technology in order to improve the services they offer – but I think there is also a distinct difference developing between those who are offering IT or BPO services. Ganesh added: "The days of pure play IT or BPO providers is over and as the need for process understanding and innovation increases all successful players will follow this path." Let's see how the market plays out over the next year or so.

Ganesh is also a strong believer in the BRICs theory (first published by investment bank Goldman Sachs in 2003) that Brazil, Russia, India, and China will be the economic leaders of the 21st century. He explained: "I completely agree with the BRICs hypothesis - three out of these four (the jury is still out between Brazil and Russia) will surely dominate the world."

I think he is right on this count. India and China are set to dominate this century in a way that historians will compare to the dominance of the British Empire in the 19th century and US influence in the 20th Outsourcing is one of the options available in the strategy toolkit for these regions and they have certainly seized on it in a way that is allowing us to witness one of the most exciting periods of economic development – ever.

Thursday, 08 March 2007

Posted at 13:36

Call centre outsourcing is growing up

The 'Quit India' movement was a wave of civil disobedience that was itself a response to Mahatma Gandhi's call for Indian independence from the UK. As we are now fast approaching the 60th anniversary of

Indian independence, some might argue that we are now seeing a new form of 'Quit India' – only this time it is the call centres serving customers in the UK.

Last week, Lloyds TSB decided to move all their customer-facing call centre work being performed in India back home to the UK. They will continue work on some back-office processing work, but customer calls will no longer be answered in India.

This is just one more major UK company that has reviewed its offshore outsourcing policy. Recently, the insurance giant Norwich Union said they would not move any new work to India, and companies such as PowerGen and eSure have also turned their back on the Indian call centre.

I have been talking about this and predicting it at various industry conferences for some time now. Think about the reasons why Lloyds TSB might want to shift their customer phone calls back to the UK. There is the issue of corporate image to start with. It's now really easy to switch bank in the UK, so retail banks can't rely on the old sense of inertia – the horror of switching dozens of direct debits and standing orders – all the problems that used to keep people with a bank for life. Nowadays, rivals such as NatWest are actively promoting the fact that their phone calls are answered only in the UK – and even going further by localising customer service back to the local branch.

The comparison of being able to call your local branch to only being able to reach a call centre, especially one in another country, is quite a stark difference. It positions the point of customer contact as a potential profit centre for the bank and not the cost centre it has been considered to be – the call centre has become a key differentiator.

The other reason why companies such as Lloyds TSB might want to see a change is for quality of service. It's hard to knock the Indian business process outsourcing companies, because they have actually written the book on quality in this space. Companies such as FirstSource (formerly ICICI oneSource) that have major operations in both the UK and India are exporting the quality controls of their call centres in India to the UK, not the other way.

However, the issue is that timeless problem of culture. In the early days of Indian call centres we used to hear western names and semi-scripted enquiries about the football last night. Things are a lot better than that now, but the business of banking has changed. Operating a current account is an expensive business and consumers in the UK are vehemently clinging onto to the idea that banking should be free.

Retail banks need to cross-sell products such as mortgages, personal loans, credit cards, insurance, and foreign exchange, anything that is in addition to the basic banking service. The best sales teams are going to have a cultural identification with the customer, because that cultural connection lets them identify when they need to be formal, when they can be casual, when they can joke about Red Nose Day, when they ask about insurance needs. The best cross-selling can't be scripted and the best sales teams just can't learn how to do it by reading a Dale Carnegie book.

So I do predict that we will see some more major companies following the example of Lloyds TSB. However, this is not the end of the road for outsourcing in India. In fact, this is the beginning of a new maturity in outsourcing. A lot of call centre business has been won in the past five years because of the reduced costs in India, but the role of the call centre itself is changing. Services are more complex and require more cross selling - the call centre has gradually become the only point of interaction between many companies and their end customers. It's therefore absolutely critical that companies consider the best location for their voice-based customer interaction – for complex services that is most likely to be somewhere local to the customer.

Many forms of remote call centre can, and do, work well. Technical support can be performed from anywhere provided the agent has the required skills. I recently called Apple for help with my own Mac and was directed to an Indian agent who had a very pronounced accent, but knew his stuff – and that was all I was concerned about – he fixed my Mac and I thanked him profusely.

As Lloyds TSB has noted, they don't intend to stop doing back office processing and other work that does not require direct interaction with their customers in India. So the anti-outsourcing lobby will crow that a major British bank is pulling out of India and hiring in the UK and the pro-outsourcing lobby will point out that the back office work remains in India. Both sides of the debate will argue that they are right, but what we are really seeing is the idea of globally sourced services - and voice-based services in particular - growing up.

Monday, 19 March 2007

Posted at 10:43

Outsourcing and SMEs

I had a conversation the other day with Marc Vollenweider, chief executive of Evalueserve. Evalueserve is well known for their research into the phenomenon known as KPO – Knowledge Process Outsourcing. In fact, I have often asserted to anyone who will listen that I believe the Evalueserve India head – Ashish Gupta – created the term KPO. At least, I cannot find any earlier use of the term before Ashish started talking about it, so I guess that's decided.

Marc is Swiss, but he lives in Austria. I have often talked to Marc in person and on the phone in various countries, but I don't think I've ever managed to call him and find him at home in Austria before – so that's a first. Maybe his wife told him to stop living on airline food - for a couple of weeks at least!

Marc explained a couple of interesting things during our chat. We talked a lot about KPO in general and the market growth at present and then looked a little more at the sustainability of the sector. To begin with, look at what Marc said about KPO today in India: "We believe there are now about 75,000 KPO professionals in India – that depends on your definition of KPO – but if you look at people with two degrees then in this type of high-end task I really think it is around 75,000 people, right now generating around $3bn in revenue for the companies they work for."

Marc also explained that he felt the build vs buy model – should you have your own 'captive' operation in India or outsource to a suppler – was a very different question in KPO: "At the moment, about two-thirds of KPO professionals still work in captives, however this is going to change significantly in the future. The remaining third work with vendors and about 70 per cent of those work for large and medium companies and the rest are focused within the small to medium-sized enterprise (SME) segment – that's interesting because it shows that KPO is far more able to serve SMEs than IT or BPO type outsourcing has been."

This is a really interesting observation. SME outsourcing is often talked of as the next wave, the place where everyone should be focused, yet the realities of outsourcing – the controls and contracts and agreements and monitoring – don't lend it to work well in the small company environment. However, where a company needs just a few people offering a very high-end bespoke service, Marc is arguing that there are KPO vendors now developing expertise in managing that kind of SME requirement.

Evalueserve predict that KPO will grow to employ around 200,000 people in India alone by 2011 – generating $9.9bn in revenue in that market. From today to those numbers is significant. It's even more significant when you consider that KPO did not exist at all until 1999 or 2000, when major captives such as GE and McKinsey started asking their offshore operations to perform complex work they would normally have always done locally. They were forced to do it for themselves, but soon the vendor base grew and over the last couple of years the stable of KPO vendors has been maturing.

I asked Marc about the issues of recruitment in India. Everyone asks about staff attrition in outsourcing suppliers, but recently Nasscom published some worrying research that indicated India may struggle to keep supplying graduates to the industry if things keep growing at the present rate. He expressed some concerns for those involved in BPO, but suggested that KPO is an entirely different beast.

He said: "I do believe that people and recruitment is crucial for KPO, but KPO players won't be exposed too much to any crunch. KPO companies are far more attractive to work for. We are seeing a lot of people coming to us from the high end of BPO, IT, or consulting - all trying to join us. I think this is partly because of the exposure the KPO segment gets in the press and from groups such as Nasscom. We recently won the Nasscom award for most innovative business model in India and got an award from the Prime Minister – we had 600 job applications arrive the next morning."

Marc has some interesting views on the salary increases in India. Many commentators have pointed to the double-digit percentage pay increases in India leading to an erosion of the cost advantage. Marc believes that this is true in the more commoditised services, such as BPO, but he feels the pay gap is actually getting wider in KPO. He explained: "Look at absolute cost increases in the West and with India – the gap is widening, not closing. Last year in the UK, an employee in a similar role with two degrees might have expected something like a six per cent raise on $80 an hour – now compare that to a 15 per cent increase on $20 in India. These are average numbers, but in general you can see that in KPO it is more likely that there is not an erosion of cost advantage – the gap is actually getting wider."

These are some quite important comments. If the cost advantage is increasing for higher value services in offshore locations and these services can be more focused and controlled for SMEs then there is a vast market in the UK just waiting to be tapped.

Tuesday, 20 March 2007

Posted at 10:48

Indian IPO shows market is still booming

When I was in India last month, one of the things that caught my eye were the posters for the Initial Public Offering (IPO) of a company called Mindtree Consulting. It's very interesting to see these IPO offer posters strewn across the city in the same way as we might expect to see car advertisements – IPOs are a little different in London and certainly don't involve posters on street corners, the Financial Services Authority (FSA) would have something to say about that. Yet, there they were all across Mumbai – huge posters urging investors to put their money into the initial offering of shares in Mindtree.

I had a meeting with Krishnakumar Natarajan, the chief executive of Mindtree, on the day the IPO commenced, but we were actually talking about another important subject. He was wearing his Nasscom hat and I was wearing my National Outsourcing Association hat, so we were focused on trying to explore new ways for Indian and

British SMEs to work together. He was clearly excited though; his mobile phone was going into meltdown and had to be ignored for a while so we could get through our small business agenda.

What is interesting about the Mindtree IPO is the level of confidence shown by investors in both the Indian stock market (in general) and an advisory firm known for its expertise in working on outsourcing deals. To be strictly correct, Mindtree is not just a consulting firm – despite the name. They do have their own service offering for IT and back-office services, but it's interesting that they are perceived as an advisory firm first and supplier second – where a lot of the Indian suppliers would like to be. The IPO raised £28m to help Mindtree expand, but it was massively oversubscribed – by 102 times to be precise. By the end of the first day on the market in Mumbai, the shares were up in value by 47 per cent compared to the issue price.

Clearly this would have been a great short-term investment for anyone wanting to ride the wave of enthusiasm for anyone associated with outsourcing, yet the influx of capital is designed to make Mindtree a major global player in IT services. It is investing some of the proceeds in new facilities in India, so it can hire more people within India – allowing the firm to serve more international business – and with a strong brand already developed, it would be no surprise if it did quite well.

If a company in India releases £28m of stock to the market and investors come to the table with nearly £3bn, cash in hand and ready to invest, then it would appear that the Indian outsourcing story has yet to reach any kind of peak. It's still on the up. In fact, the Mumbai stock exchange might be worth exploring for your own investments with this level of market confidence, but I'm not a financial advisor so don't turn to me for stock picks – ask all those who made 47 per cent in a day on Mindtree.

Wednesday, 21 March 2007

Posted at 11:14

Educating for the networked economy

Heather Hamilton is a human resource executive at Microsoft. In her blog recently she was talking about how Bill Gates was called to testify in front of Congress as a part of the US research into connections between the work visa system and education policy.

It's striking that the US has made this connection and got so far as to calling in the big guns from industry, because the UK seems woefully far behind. Yes, we have started reorganising the work visa system, but where is the intelligent redesign of the education system that takes into account the network society - the movement of skilled people, and the movement of jobs through outsourcing? In fact, our own visa changes are starting to get bogged down by protesters complaining that "too many Indians" are coming to work in the UK IT industry. The changes may not even settle in before they are changed again.

This is a fairly large quote, but I think it is worth echoing some of what Bill Gates said to the US government:

"Our current expectations for what our students should learn in school were set 50 years ago to meet the needs of an economy based on manufacturing and agriculture. We now have an economy based on knowledge and technology. Despite the best efforts of many committed educators and administrators, our high schools have simply failed to adapt to this change. As any parent knows, however, our children have not - they are fully immersed in digital culture.

As a result, while most students enter high school wanting to succeed, too many end up bored, unchallenged and disengaged from the high school curriculum - "digital natives" caught up in an industrial-age learning model. Many high school students today either drop out or simply try to get by. For those who graduate, many lack the skills they need to attend college or to find a job that can support a family. Until we transform the American high school for the 21st century, we will continue limiting the lives of millions of Americans each year."

Bill makes an important point, a really important point. Kids graduating from university today have not known a life without technology. If you are just about finishing university today then you probably don't remember a time before mobile phones and the internet. So there is an entire generation coming through that is familiar with technology and its application in their everyday life, yet our technology training has not moved so fast.

If you enter university and start to study for a technology-themed course believing you have an interest in technology because of your experiences of personal computing use (blogging, social networking, using the web and so on) and then find yourself engaged in three years of analysing Boolean logic, Babbage and Smalltalk, then its no wonder kids become disengaged.

The National Outsourcing Association has been working with a number of universities in the UK to try introducing the concept of outsourcing and partnership into a number of courses. The idea being that this knowledge is going to be useful in the real world, so anyone who can combine a strong appreciation of how outsourcing works along with a willingness to learn about the practical aspects has to be a better potential employee than one who can demonstrate only theoretical knowledge.

The British Computer Society (BCS) has in effect gone even further and has almost reinvented itself over the past few years to become an organisation completely focused on maximising the career of its members. The BCS these days is entirely geared up around services such as CareerBuilder and networking events – they have caught on to the fact that technical jobs have social requirements, like any other job.

Where Bill Gates has really hit the nail on the head is in his views that we should be connecting the idea of the digital society – or network society as sociologist Manuel Castells calls it – to policy formation. If a technology company needs access to experts most easily located in India then does it make more sense to offshore the work itself to India or to bring the Indian experts into the UK, so long as they then pay local taxes? And over the long term how do we ensure that our education system can ensure that the young people we are educating are getting the right blend of skills needed to find employment in a future 'networked' environment? If the universities are teaching highly commoditised skills that can easily be sourced from overseas then companies will source from overseas.

The UK government needs to connect these issues together now. Work visas and migration of skilled labour into the UK cannot be separated from work being offshored and this cannot be separated from higher education. The network society demands that we formulate government policy with a global vision, not just with an eye on populist measures that win elections.

Thursday, 22 March 2007

Posted at 11:20

Getting the business right

So what can we observe of the decision by Prudential to undergo a major review of their business that could potentially involve the loss of 2,000 jobs in the UK and 1,000 in India?

One thing is clear; it's not a simple slash 'n' burn offshoring story and the review involves potential job cuts in India as well as the UK – certainly not the typical 'jobs to India' scenario. Despite all the speculation, there is no real decision at present; all that has been made public is that something will happen during the fourth quarter of 2007.

However, a couple of things are clear. Prudential has a substantial investment in its Mumbai delivery centre. I visited the Pru's Mumbai centre in 2004 and found a very impressive facility – brand new towers emerging from a relatively undeveloped part of town offering a complete lifestyle and work environment for those lucky enough to work there. With great facilities and people, there is no reason to not undertake more of the back-office functions there and the jobs-at-risk being discussed are centred on roles such as back-office and customer services.

Castigating the Pru over offshoring doesn't help matters. Remember, it hasn't announced anything concrete yet anyway, but even if it goes ahead with a major offshoring programme driven by cost reduction later in 2007, it is a reflection of the business environment the firm operates within.

The business of insurance is changing. It's becoming more automated. Internet price comparison systems are destroying the old ideals of brand loyalty, the old practice of the 'man from the Pru' knocking on your door to collect a premium is as archaic as believing your kids can walk to school without being attacked by nasty folk lurking around every street corner. Well, maybe they can – it depends which newspaper you read. Even those who are not quite tech-savvy enough to be comparing prices online are using the services of discount insurers such as – calm down dear – eSure, who will match or discount what you are currently paying. The whole business has changed, yet the companies that have been in the market a long time have a legacy of closed book life policies they need to honour in the coming years.

Clearly, automation and technological advance is really the great destroyer of employment as we know it, because it changes the environment in which every organisation operates. But change has always existed and industries have always advanced and new jobs have always been created. In the era of thinkers such as Alvin Toffler, the future was imagined as an era where automation would create more leisure time – the reality is that we are all busier than ever and worried about what will be automated next, because the next step of progress might just make our own role redundant.

In the debate over the ethics of offshoring it's worth remembering that sometimes it might be a necessary step to help a company within an industry that is changing so rapidly that they either change or die. Prudential has to think about what the insurer of the future will look like and how it will source the required expertise to make that happen. Whether the resource is in India or Britain is not really all that important; it's the business itself they need to get right.

Friday, 23 March 2007

Posted at 11:26

A personal invitation

I wouldn't want to abuse my position writing this blog for Computing by plugging anything or anyone I have some interest in, but I hope you will excuse me mentioning my new book – because there is a book launch party coming soon and you, dear reader, are invited.

The book is being published by the British Computer Society (BCS) next month and is titled 'Global Services Moving to a Level Playing Field'. I have co-authored it with a friend of mine, Dr Richard Sykes. Richard is well known in the outsourcing community as he chairs the outsourcing and offshoring group at Intellect and he used to be chairman at outsourcing advisory firm Morgan Chambers.

Richard and I wrote this book as a reality check on outsourcing and an exploration of some of the wider issues surrounding the globalisation of services through the use of technology. We really took Thomas Friedman's award-winning book 'The World is Flat' as a catalyst – go and look back at what Friedman said about globalisation, because almost everything he wrote about is supported by IT. The BCS book breaks down our argument across eight key themes:

1. The Millennium; the dawn of the new trust in offshore outsourcing, when everyone was forced to try the offshore model because they just had a fixed deadline and no choice.

2. Business Processes Develop into Knowledge Processes; fixed and determined processes mutating to complete trust in a partner to make decisions on your behalf.

3. The Maturing Vendor Community; deep relationships being forged through risk-sharing and gain-sharing, working in a way that creates an interest for both supplier and client.

4. The Development of Technology; the virtualisation of the technology itself through changing architectures and software as a service.

5. The Real Matrix; the growth of the internet as a commoditised consumer delivery platform and the transition to being a robust business tool – growth of Web 2.0, Youtube, Flickr, Myspace, Bebo, and consumer interaction with the web.

6. The Globalisation of Services; man vs machine, automation, and the export of services – especially what is the UK exporting to the world?

7. Skills Needed for a Future Economy; what kind of education is needed for a digital society and how do we prepare for that future?

8. The New Globalisation; how are service companies reacting and offering services from multiple locations?

I hope that gives you a picture of what it's all about. It's not a defence of offshoring or a halcyon picture of outsourcing, it's a broad look at how outsourcing fits into the changing way companies do business today and how IT underpins that change.

The book is already available on Amazon with a five per cent discount, but BCS members can order it direct for £20 instead of the normal retail price of £25 – so there is a good reason to join the BCS, if you are not already a member!

I mentioned at the beginning that there is a launch event, and as you are reading this blog I guess you might be interested. It's on 30 April at the London School of Economics (LSE) and will feature me and Richard talking about the book – as you might expect. LSE director Sir Howard Davies and the TCS UK country manager A.S. Lakshmi will also join to talk about the issues raised in the book. Following the talks there will be copious amounts of wine and networking – do come along and say hello if you can make it.

Send your details to bcs@markhillary.com to reserve a place at the launch.

Monday, 26 March 2007

Posted at 10:15

Speaking the language

I've written recently about some of the cultural issues surrounding offshore voice-based customer services. Recently, Lloyds TSB canned its offshore customer services, though it retained other back-office processes. It's an issue that is very now.

This led to me think in a bit more detail about some of the issues faced by the contact centres. I've been to India often enough to know that the people in the contact centres there are well educated and respond well to training. Is it really just a question of customer attitudes to offshoring, or is there something about servicing customers from another region and culture that is just too difficult to get right?

So, I asked Tim Bond, chief executive of Launch Offshore, a few questions. I've been watching Tim's company grow for a few years now with some interest. He has carved out an interesting niche in providing jobs in offshore service companies to Europeans – sending the European workers over to the jobs in India! Tim's company has placed about 70 UK contact centre staff into Indian contact centres. He is working on about 50 positions at present and he has placed around 80 people into Central and Eastern Europe (CEE). He also sees this escalating quickly – he believes the rate he is placing people into positions will double during 2007 as demand from the offshore centres is very strong.

Of course, the first thing I asked him was the package these Brits and Europeans get if they take on a job in an Indian contact centre – and why they are going. Tim explained: "In India these new staff help by providing cultural inputs which help Indian contact-centre agents understand the idiosyncrasies of British English (which differs greatly from Indian English) ultimately allowing them to build a rapport with British customers on the telephone. They get their flights and accommodation paid, travel/health insurance, and an attractive local salary with performance bonuses."

So, they are essentially working alongside the Indian teams at similar rates of pay, but with travel and accommodation paid for. I did something similar myself when I finished college and took off to the US for three months on a Camp America programme. It's an interesting idea and one that has been used to a certain extent in the past by companies such as eBookers, but not in such a professional manner – with a company that can handle the process for both the agents seeking an offshore job and the contact centre looking for some non-local staff.

I asked Tim about some of the challenges faced by offshore contact centres that handle voice-based processes. He explained: "The problem with offshoring voice-based contact-centre operations to India is that English is the Indian call centre agents second language and it is old fashioned – using grammar, words and phrases which were inherited from the British in the early 20th century. As well as this, the agents in India come from a very different social and cultural background and are taught at school and managed in the office differently to UK people, resulting in a telephone manner that can appear strange to the UK ear, at least until they have a number of months practice and experience."

Tim went on to emphasise: "When UK customers are frustrated because of the poor service received by a utility, such as wrong billing information, or an engineer has not turned up, the customer rings a call centre in an emotional - and perhaps irrational - state of mind. If the Indian agent misunderstands the subtle nuances in the tone or manner, the customer will become even more frustrated, resulting in further brand damage to the company - this is the crux of the problem."

Tim is having some success in Europe as well. Of course, with so many languages used within the European Union nations alone, this is not just a problem that exists between call centres in India and the UK. His company has found that contact centres set up in the CEE region particularly struggle to service customers in the Netherlands and Nordic region. He said: "The reality is that whilst local people [in the location of the contact centre] speak English, German, French or Dutch fluently, it is their second language and the customers they speak to may not receive the level of comprehension required to complete tasks quickly and efficiently."

Although it's true that a lot of large companies may be reviewing their strategy of offshoring customer services at present, it's a fact that the industry is still growing at a healthy rate. That should indicate good times ahead for Tim's company – he is even putting together training and accreditation programmes now for individual agents. If Tim had been doing this back when I was listening to Depeche Mode on a cassette Walkman then I might have been making tracks for India instead of Uncle Sam. The food is a lot better – that's a good enough reason to start with.

Wednesday, 28 March 2007

Posted at 11:03

Offshore providers need to take you home

I went out for a grand lunch yesterday at the town hall in Kensington arranged by the High Commission of Bangladesh, with the acting High

Commissioner as host. The occasion was the 36th anniversary of independence and it was a good opportunity to interact with London-based Bangladeshi executives along with all the UK folks who interact with South Asia. I did see Anwar Hasan, the UK head of India's Tata group, in the crowd and I met my co-author, Dr Richard Sykes, as I was munching through some dhal.

I came away feeling a bit disappointed though – and not only because there was no vegetarian food (even the rice had meat, and I had promised my wife a nice lunch!) Sometimes I get a bit frustrated talking to trade representatives of countries about the way they conduct their promotional campaigns. Bangladesh is not the only place that is guilty of this, but all too often, when a region wants some promotion they rent a venue in London, pay for their business leaders to come over and then expect hordes of British managers to show up, all eager to sign business deals.

It really doesn't work like that. Even the likes of IBM and Accenture have to work hard to get people out of their office, let alone outsourcing companies that are unknown to most British managers. Everyone is busy and anyone with any authority to spend on behalf of their company already has a myriad of free conference opportunities. If the guys with a well-known and trusted brand have to work hard at getting people out to their events then what chance do the unknowns have?

Fortunately, I ran into Forkan Bin Quasem at the lunch. I know Forkan as we have spoken on many occasions in the past as he represents Basis, the trade association that represents the Bangladeshi software and technology-enabled industry. Basis is the Bangladeshi equivalent of Intellect here in the UK, or Nasscom in India, and they have been doing quite a good job (on a tiny budget) of promoting technology in Bangladesh over the past few years.

Forkan told me that he has found the US more receptive to the Bangladesh business story than the UK over recent months; in fact he has been spending a lot of time in the US while his wife stays in London. Clever woman. She knows that Knightsbridge is the shopping capital of the world.

Forkan did ask me for a frank opinion on some of the promotional tactics used by Bangladesh, and I gave him one, the main point I am now repeating on this blog. If regions want to promote their outsourcing story then they actually need to get influencers over there to take a look. Anyone can throw a party in London and hope that the right people come, but it does not really help anyone – those trying to promote the destination or those seeking information. It doesn't educate the decision-makers and it rarely results in any business being transacted.

It would make more sense for a country such as Bangladesh to get all the prominent writers and commentators on outsourcing out there to meet the people on their home turf, and then to report back on what it is really like. This would help to establish the brand of the region and stimulate interest and trust, especially through documenting some examples of what is really going on. I'm not angling for a free trip to Dhaka by writing this - fact-finding missions usually cost me money because of the opportunity cost in not doing paid work during the travel period. It's important to think logically and for the long-term when analysing what it is about a region that people buy into when outsourcing. Is it political stability, a pool of experienced companies and educated people, distance from home, cultural compatibility, or something else?

It's certainly a blend of all these factors, and an X-factor that could be broadly described as trust. Trust is not created overnight, but it can be stimulated through seeing some examples of the region working for others. The India outsourcing story took off mainly because executives thought 'if it works for GE then it can work for me...' Investing in contracts with partners in distant regions is certainly not the result of a free glass of wine in London.

April 2007

Thursday, 12 April 2007

Posted at 11:00

Celebrating 20 years of outsourcing

I am on the board of the National Outsourcing Association (NOA) in the UK. I'm the director with the offshoring portfolio, hence my constant interest in things offshore, especially India where I have worked extensively. The NOA is a trade association with several hundred corporate members who comprise users of sourcing, advisers, and suppliers. It is a not-for-profit body and exists to promote best practice, provide independent research into outsourcing, and provide opportunities for networking for people who work in member companies.

Something that might be of interest to readers who feel that the furore over offshoring and outsourcing is a recent phenomenon is the fact that the NOA celebrates its 20th birthday on May 17 this year. Twenty years ago I was a sixth-former eagerly anticipating the release of the last ever album by The Smiths, but those board members who are older and more wrinkled (sorry, experienced) than me, were forming the trade body that is now the modern NOA.

The NOA has hired the walkways at Tower Bridge in central London for a party on May 17 to celebrate the anniversary. If you don't know the walkways then imagine having a few drinks suspended 45m above the river Thames – it's a really nice location and the NOA team has all sorts of entertainment planned as well. Everyone there will have an interest in outsourcing so it will be a great occasion for informal networking, but this is essentially a party – you are getting a 'no PowerPoint' guarantee. Take a look at the NOA web site if you are interested in learning more and joining us on the evening to raise a glass to the next 20 years of the association.

Thursday, 12 April 2007

Posted at 11:34

Why it's good to be a programmer in India

I had lunch recently with Peter Bendor-Samuel who is usually based in Texas, but was over in London for work. Peter is well known as the founder of the Everest Group, a long established US consulting and research group that's starting to be a lot more active in Europe these days.

Peter is extremely tall and very knowledgeable. He has a sort of rapid-fire delivery of information that demonstrates quite a formidable mind – he obviously thinks about his subject, a lot. It also makes quite a refreshing change from some of the analysts in the market. It's clear when you talk to Peter that he has lived through some outsourcing triumphs and disasters – he talks with real examples and cases, not from the 10,000m up big picture of the corporate world preferred by some. I like his approach, but you need to be sharp to stay on top of what he is talking about.

One example of his no-nonsense approach is the debate over which country or region is the most attractive for offshoring. Everest has tossed all the conventional wisdom out of the window and started focusing on city-by-city comparisons. They have researched about a hundred cities now, examining key variables such as population demographics, local universities, and traditional industries, to map out how attractive investment in that particular city really is. It's a logical approach. We all know that Bath isn't much like Glasgow – why would we judge Chennai in the same way as we do Delhi?

I thought I would take the advantage of our lunch to ask him about one of the classic issues everyone is talking about at present, labour arbitrage and the skills shortage predicted for India. At the recent Nasscom conference in India I listened to speaker after speaker worrying about how the industry will not be able to continue growing at the present stratospheric rates when the source of skilled young graduates starts drying up.

Peter said to me: "The fundamental problem with labour arbitrage and the inflation factors in India and Eastern Europe – but especially India – is not the size of the underlying population. The population is plenty big and there are plenty of educated people. The problem is the rate of growth. The ability of the economy to mint new graduates and the get them into the equation is a function of the rate of growth, not of the fundamental economy."

He then gave one of his typical examples that sheds a bit of light on how attractive it really is to train to be a computer programmer in India: "There's more than a billion people in India. To give you some perspective, a programmer in the UK gets paid about 1.7 times average pay, so it's a relatively attractive thing to be a programmer in the UK. In India a programmer gets 14.8 times the average, so it's really attractive to be a programmer in India! And it's just getting more attractive."

His point is that the industry remains extremely attractive for people to move into and so they should naturally move towards a technology career without too much coaxing. He argued: "Labour will move into these attractive areas, but if you are growing at 30-plus per cent then you just can't absorb it all that quickly so as the growth slows – and it will slow as prices rise – then eventually you will see prices drop again, so this isn't going to be a problem when you look at it over a number of years."

Peter's very direct and interesting example put paid to a lot of the fears I had heard recently. It's clear that you cannot just keep extrapolating wage inflation forever based on the inflated numbers we see at present, because in the short term there are a lot of large companies scaling up quickly. Let's start looking over a longer period of time and thinking about how attractive it really is to be a programmer in India.

Friday, 13 April 2007

Posted at 09:57

Indian IT beats the doubters - again

This morning I caught a taxi at 4.45am to go to the studios of BBC World, so I could talk about the annual results of Indian hi-tech giant Infosys on the World Business Report programme. The market view up to yesterday was that rising salaries, the rising strength of the rupee, and a shortage of labour would start causing a serious issue for Infosys – and as the other major Indian IT companies won't report results until next week, the Infosys results are seen as an indicator for the entire industry. This was the line that the BBC had planned to report on, that the industry might need to take a breather and regroup before growing further, yet we got the results about five minutes before the show went live on air at 5.30am and had to completely change the interview questions and approach.

Infosys managed to beat all analyst expectations to declare a 67 per cent increase in profit over the last quarter. The word in the City was that they would possibly manage 50-53 per cent, so this is an impressive rise in fortunes. Business is booming for the second-largest software exporter in India and these numbers prove that there is still a lot of strength left in the Indian outsourcing story.

It's not such a surprise in my opinion. If you just look at some of the posts I have made to this blog recently you can see that I'm not so concerned about perceived labour shortages in India. What is really interesting now though is that the Indian companies are managing to ride out the negative perceptions and are winning larger and larger contracts, really moving into the territory of the big boys.

When you look at the technology export sector in India as a whole, it's no surprise that Infosys is still growing strongly. Software services exports have been around $33bn in the past year and are predicted to rise to twice that figure by 2010 – growth is generally still strong. If Nasscom (the technology trade association in India) can focus on ensuring the infrastructure is strong enough to keep on providing enough new people to the industry then there is no sign of the Indian tech companies slowing down. Just imagine what they could do if they could market themselves more effectively; the incumbent global service companies have a lot to fear.

Friday, 13 April 2007

Posted at 11:46

Who is really more secure?

I was speaking recently at an event in London hosted by The Indus Entrepreneurs (TiE), which is a network of over 10,000 professionals in nine countries all focused on various entrepreneurial activities, and usually with some link back to India. TiE is a global not-for-profit network of entrepreneurs and professionals dedicated to the advancement of entrepreneurship. TiE's mission is to foster entrepreneurship globally through mentoring, networking, and education and they host a lot of events such as this, combining information and networking.

The talk I took part in was focused on the new frontiers and challenges to India within outsourcing. The debate was chaired by Arun Aggarwal, who is the European head of consulting at Tata Consultancy Services. Others on the panel included Rishi Khosla, the founder of Copal Partners and Peter Brudenall, a partner at law firm Simmons & Simmons.

I ran into Peter recently at a drinks reception in Mumbai, but we've interacted quite a bit in the past as he is the UK chairman of the International Association of Outsourcing Professionals and he edited a book, that I contributed to, titled 'Technology and Offshore Outsourcing Strategies'.

Of course the debate touched on a number of topics, particularly on where the next threat to India may emerge, but one of the most interesting sections was when Peter gave quite a spirited defence to India and the issues suffered around data protection in the past couple of years. He didn't claim any in-depth expertise of Indian law, but he probably still understood the nature of the laws there better than anyone else in the room and he made a strong case for Indian service firms being as secure, if not more so, than their local counterparts.

I chipped in with some of my own experiences as well at this point. I know that it's hard to get into any of the more secure Indian back-office operations with any form of storage device - phones, iPods, USB keys – they are all removed at the entrance lobby. There is a greater culture of security in most of the Indian service firms that we would find unusual here in the UK – would you tolerate being frisked every time you had popped out for a sandwich? I know that my friend Kevin wouldn't mind a daily frisking from a burly security guard, but that's beside the point.

The general debate over security and the comparison of security reality and perception was recently brought home right here with the news that retailer TK Maxx had suffered at the hands of hackers for 18 months, compromising secure credit card information detailing some 45.7 million cards owned by UK and US consumers. And the scale of the problem is so vast that they can't even predict if any of those with compromised details will have suffered a loss – it's up to the consumer to check back on their card statements.

This does contrast with most of the issues in India, which have often been sting operations mounted by journalists determined to prove that Indian contact centres are not secure. The fact is we live in a society that is far more dominated by information than ever before. We give our banking details to strangers every time we buy dinner or a round in the pub using a card. It's a bit harsh to single out one specific geographical domain as 'less secure', especially when the experience of most people in the industry is that this perception of insecurity has actually led the Indians to take security a lot more seriously than we do back at home.

Tuesday, 17 April 2007

Posted at 12:40

A sense of deja vu

This week kicked off with an early start at the Gartner Outsourcing Summit. Gartner is one of the biggest and most well-respected global consulting and research companies and its summits attract a huge amount of attention. The London summit is possibly the single largest conference of the year focused on outsourcing. I counted at least 600 seats in the main auditorium, though someone I was chatting to over coffee told me that there were around 800 delegates at the conference hotel – all focused on learning new information about outsourcing.

Yet, for all its prestige as one of the largest events of its kind I felt a sense of unrest amongst many of the delegates. The huge line of people waiting to collect their ID badge might have sowed the initial sense of unease. If I had paid €2,695 to get in then I might have been a bit miffed to find a queue longer than most women have to endure when visiting the bathroom at a West End theatre.

The first couple of conference sessions were no more than extended adverts for Gartner and its services. Come and use our new research portal. Come and use our consulting services – we have all the answers you are looking for. When Gartner analyst Linda Cohen took to the stage for a keynote on the topic of multisourcing, the delegates around me were distinctly restless and already making attempts to use their mobile devices, but we were trapped in a 'no signal' Faraday cage. The sweat began to pour down the brow of assorted Crackberry lovers reduced to working in offline mode until the opportunity to walk to a window, where reception was just about possible.

Something I was interested in when I saw the theme of the conference was that it was entirely themed around multisourcing – again. I was wondering if anyone was going to ask why last year's conference was all about multisourcing, and here we are again with the same theme. Was it just me having a Bill Murray 'Groundhog Day' moment or was there much that had been left unsaid in the conference last year?

Linda Cohen started to explain the reasoning behind this. Last year was all about introducing the concept of multisourcing and this year was about drilling into detail and talking about real cases and examples of how it works. The fact that academics such as Professor Leslie Willcocks at the London School of Economics have been writing about this subject for at least a decade appears to be largely forgotten, or ignored. And Leslie's books are probably a lot cheaper than the research published by analyst firms.

The presentation on multisourcing was too long – a keynote presentation shouldn't be scheduled at more than one hour (and it ran late too). The audience might tolerate speeches of this length from characters such as Bill Clinton reminiscing about his time in office, but to keep the attention of hundreds of business executives through a series of slides showing graph this and graph that is a tough job for anyone. I'm not saying that Cohen does not know her stuff - she wrote the Harvard book titled 'Multisourcing' - but given that this year was supposed to be about drilling into some detail, I can't recall a single concrete example from the presentation that I can now talk to other people about as a case study supporting multisourcing as a strategy.

I found a few examples as I wandered the crowd, but the general response from most delegates was that they felt the topic was being spun slightly too much – they all had years of experience of working in various consortia and arrangements where they might need to partner with a competitor to deliver a programme.

My general impression after talking to dozens of delegates though is that the Gartner conference used to be the place that you had to be. Companies fell over themselves to sponsor booths in the refreshment area just so they could be seen to be there as part of the thought-leadership pack. But it feels to me more as if the industry itself should be wielding its power over the analyst community. Why should some of the companies I saw yesterday – Capgemini, Cognizant, TCS, Infosys, Zensar, HP, IBM, to name a few – pay handsomely just to be seen near to the coffee table when the entire event promotes the research and consulting services of Gartner anyway?

In fact, the only company I noticed doing anything a little more innovative was Cognizant. They decorated some quad bikes in Cognizant livery and had them charging around the road by the hotel and the lifts and Oyster card readers at Lancaster Gate station were covered in adverts for the company. Anyone who went to the conference on the Underground can't have failed to notice this before they even got to the Cognizant booth. I like that little touch of originality. Perhaps next year they might get a plane to loop over Hyde Park skywriting the corporate URL?

I have a few friends in Gartner so it's not easy to write and publish this blog, but then if I only ever blogged good news stories about my mates in the industry it would not exactly be compelling reading. Let's hope they can take it as constructive advice and do more of the type of presentations that Capgemini managed – on stage verbal blogging live with Capgemini execs Andy Mulholland and Steve Jones. Unprepared and off the cuff live blogging, but speaking rather than typing. Now, that's a lot better than death by PowerPoint.

Wednesday, 18 April 2007

Posted at 08:00

Outsourced - the movie

As I was browsing YouTube a few months ago I noticed a movie trailer that looked interesting. The movie was titled 'Outsourced' and from what I could see in the trailer it was the story of a US office worker sent over to India to set up a call centre. Some of the scenes in the trailer are certainly worth a smile; the cow in the office, the locals stealing electricity by re-wiring the mains, the call centre agents learning how to speak with a Chi-caaaa-go accent.

I got in touch with the production company and asked them when this was going to be distributed in the UK. They told me that it has been screened in the US already (and has picked up a few awards too), but has not had any European distribution - and they are still looking for a distributor. The director even got in touch with me and we kicked around the idea of a pre-Cannes private screening for London outsourcing professionals at Bafta in Piccadilly.

The timing proved a bit too tight to make that happen, but the production team are off to Cannes in a few weeks on a mission to find a European distributor. Assuming they get UK distribution for the film then the National Outsourcing Association has already agreed to help them host the London premiere. It will be a lot of fun to be hosting a movie premiere and quite different from most industry events focused on outsourcing. I might even need to buy myself a bow tie.

Thursday, 26 April 2007

Posted at 10:32

China - myth and reality

I attended a National Outsourcing Association event focused on China this week The subtitle for the event was 'Myth and Reality', perhaps underlining the duality that exists in the market today regarding China. Yes, we all know the potential is there and China has dominated global manufacturing since I was in shorts, but in the area of IT and IT-enabled services there has been far more myth-making than reality to date.

Paul Morrison chaired this conference. Paul is a consultant for Alsbridge when he is not on NOA duty. There were several contributors, but these are some of the stand out comments that made me tap a few notes into the computer:

Nigel Stamp, a partner at law firm Morrison & Foerster said: "We all know about the labour costs, the larger labour pool – which is in a country with a population of about 1.2bn people. What is not immediately apparent is that education is very good – something like 99 per cent literacy for those under 25 years. Infrastructure is also very good, good bandwidth with 137 million internet users and over 70 per cent of those on broadband."

Stamp made some interesting points and he capped it by adding: "Five years ago people would be impressed if you had a China strategy; now investors should be asking questions if you don't have one.

Gordon Milner, another Morrison & Foerster partner, joined Nigel and made some comments on confidentiality and intellectual property rights (IPR), topics that always rear their head when talking about China: "Remember that confidentiality is not very well respected. Employees share ideas and information and this is a cultural aspect – it is quite dangerous to rely on non-disclosure agreements (NDAs) alone when talking to companies, especially in arrangements such as when working with sub-contractors. IPR is not business as usual in China. There are lots of regulations and sometimes too many, it can be hard to understand without local advice."

Milner pointed out that most companies outsourcing to China are doing so through their own captive operation: "Most players are engaging with China using captives, but pilots are really popular at present – companies are looking to try out the model in a less pressured environment," he said.

At the end of the debate Paul Morrison did comment that many of the issues being debated are the same ones we talk about when examining any geography – there is nothing special to fear in China. However, back on the IPR issue once more, Russell Brown from accounting firm LehmanBrown mentioned that a few months after Ikea launched its first store in China, every local store was selling similar furniture at lower prices. Forget about the prices, if they could copy Ikea design and get rid of the queues then I'm there.

Friday, 27 April 2007

Posted at 10:36

Do you 'get' Web 2.0?

When I blog personally or for Computing I usually like to name names. I hate reading those corporate PR puffs that read 'we helped company X save $99m...' just as much as anyone else and so I like to mention who I am talking about. But I'm in a sticky situation here because the topic I want to mention affects so many companies in the IT services sector.

The topic is new media, or Web 2.0, or whatever the media is calling user-generated content and increased consumer interactivity this week. I have been talking to quite a large number of companies that might usually be considered outsourcing suppliers, offering B2B services without a care for the nasty world of online opinions and teenage interactivity. The topics have ranged from how to make the company more attractive to young techies, how to generate more media coverage from doing something sexy and exciting, or how to do something genuinely innovative, right through to how on earth to take some of the consumer internet tools and find a use for them in the corporate world of IT services.

Yet there is something wrong, because although most of the IT service companies want to embrace this new world, they almost all find it hard to move away from the old notion of the IT department defining how everything is used and locking down the kit to the point at which it's impossible to actually do anything new or innovative.

I published a podcast of one major IT services group. The employees could only listen at home because iTunes is banned for 'security' reasons. I have been trying to record an interview with a senior executive of a global IT services group and the marketing head asked me to send transcripts of published podcasts. 'But they are podcasts, not text...' seemed like an obvious question for me to ask, but they already knew that, it's just no one in the marketing team knew how to listen to one.

So even though I know where the bodies are buried, I'm only going to share that information with my dog. I do appreciate that blogs and podcasts are quite a new experience for those who think that the 'Paul O'Grady show' is cutting-edge television, but these are all major, major IT companies. These are the guys you hire when you want advice on how to set up your own new media strategy, how to improve your own web presence, how to set up a blog. I have certainly found out who really is embracing innovation and changing IT standards and who dreams of a return to the good old days.

All this terminology such as change, leverage, synergy, innovation – these terms are completely abused by corporate marketing teams who talk like the fictional FT columnist Martin Lukes, and yet possess none of the skills to deliver on what they promise. Where is the Creovation™ in that?

Friday, 27 April 2007

Posted at 13:00

Indian IT is creating jobs in the UK

Tata Consultancy Services (TCS) is the biggest of the Indian technology service companies, recently posting annual revenues for the past year of well in excess of $4bn. Although much of the Indian IT services market has focused on the outsourcing of applications development and maintenance work. TCS is now trying to focus on a new area, innovation.

This week TCS launched a new innovation lab right here in the UK, at Peterborough. I was at the launch event along with about 80 other industry analysts and potential customers all eager to learn more about why this large Indian player is conducting technology research over here. Aren't the hi-tech jobs all supposed to be moving India, not the other way?

Charles Hendry, the Tory MP for Harrow and Shadow Minister for Energy, Science and Technology, also picked up on this point when he made a speech welcoming investment into the UK from TCS. Hendry talked at length about education and he lamented the recent university admissions figures showing fewer and fewer young British people studying core science topics at university. He was also concerned about the potential for the Department of Trade and Industry to be broken up if Gordon Brown enters 10 Downing Street in the near future. On a lighter note, when he talked about Thomas Friedman's well-known book 'The World is Flat'. Hendry quipped that he learned more from the first chapter than in all his years in parliament.

This is certainly an interesting move by TCS. They have appointed Mike Scott as their innovations head in London and asked him to build this lab, which is focusing on a number of key research areas such as voice over IP, search technologies, and communications. The aim is to offer access to the expertise of an IT company within a lab environment for companies from other domains wanting to trial or 'hothouse' new technologies. TCS has a number of key partners such as IBM and Microsoft supporting this lab, so it's certainly not a lone-wolf effort to get some good marketing copy.

The politicians are interested because it means an Indian company is hiring people over here. Even the Mayor of Peterborough showed up to formally launch the new lab. TCS is interested because they now have 19 different labs globally doing this after the Peterborough launch and they see it as a key differentiator in the crowded IT services market. A lot of potential clients turned up at the launch, including almost every large company you can think of – so the customers also seem to be interested. Lets see if it works out as TCS hopes and the Indians manage to successfully sell innovation as well as just regular IT services.

Monday, 30 April 2007

Posted at 09:54

Favourite Worst Nightmare

I was up early this morning. It's not every day I get to publish a new book and today is not only the day of the book launch – tonight at the London School of Economics – but also the day I should get to see a copy of the book for the first time.

The book is titled 'Global Services: Moving to a Level Playing Field' and I have co-written it with Dr Richard Sykes from the hi-tech trade association Intellect. The British Computer Society (BCS) is publishing the book and it's exciting because I think this is possibly the first book from the BCS that looks more at the business potential for IT, rather than being a more technical how-to guide. I'm really pleased that Sir Howard Davies, the director of the LSE, is going to open the launch proceedings tonight – he also penned the foreword.

The printer promised the BCS that the books would be in London by last week and yet I still haven't seen a copy, neither has the BCS. That might explain why I was awake at 3am this morning thinking about a book launch without a book. Obviously it would still be a nice get-together and party where we could all talk about the book and what it contains, but it's not quite the same as being able to grasp a physical copy in your hands and to declare that the knowledge in these pages might be quite useful. And if you don't have copies then you can't sell them either!

Throwing a book launch party is quite a feat of logistics and this has been planned for several months so I really hope the printer comes good on their promise this morning. Richard and I started emailing our friends in the industry a couple of months ago, asking them to join us to celebrate the new book. Today, we have about 330 people confirmed and looking to join us for a drink. I'm sure not everyone will make it as plans change and people sometimes end up too busy to come out on a Monday night, but most of those who expressed an interest will turn up.

Although Tata Consultancy Services (TCS) has sponsored the launch party (the firm had to take my word that there was something positive about it in the book as they have not seen it either!), so TCS is meeting the expenses required for the bar, food, the close-up magician, and the live music, I have still had to cope with the logistics of organising the reception myself. It's a lot of work and involves arranging projectors, tables, chairs, security, microphones, the theatre booking, reception hall booking, and speaker bookings! Now I can see how event companies justify their fees – it's a big job and you can be sure that the next time I arrange a big book launch, I'll be outsourcing some of this work.

May 2007

Tuesday, 15 May 2007
Posted at 10:!4
A Handy guide to outsourcing

I picked up a book by Charles Handy the other day – The Elephant and the Flea. It was published about six years ago and I have read it before, probably not long after it came out, but for some reason I started flicking through it again rather than tidying up my bookshelf, as I had intended.

I have a great deal of time for Charles Handy. In my view he is the finest living writer focused on management and organisations. My admiration is borne from his accessible writing style and his ability to tell the truth about his own failings, without needing to shout from the rooftops about his incredible ability to observe what most see as 'normal' in a different way. Most management books proclaim the way things are in a 'guru' type manner, Handy observes and guides the reader to his way of thinking without needing to yell.

Here is a short extract from The Elephant and the Flea, where Handy recalls the 1980s, when he started describing the way company structures would change to accommodate outsourcing:

"I was promoting something rather different, what I called the Shamrock organisation – an organisation with three integrated leaves made up of the central core, the contractual fringe and the ancillary workforce, a concept that I argued was the way to incorporate a necessary flexibility within a corporate whole. A shamrock, I pointed out, was three leaves that still remained one leaf, which was why St Patrick used it to describe the Christian doctrine of the Trinity – three Gods in one God. I worried that in their haste to dismember the organisation and save money, managers were throwing away the sense of belonging that the old companies fostered, and that they would come to regret it. That worry still niggles today."

His fear was, and remains, that companies would see outsourcing more as a slash and burn cost-saving strategy, rather than a tool that can allow companies to structure themselves more efficiently. And I guess it could be argued that both scenarios have come to pass since he originally wrote about his Shamrock theory in The Age of Unreason.

Yes, a lot of companies have rubbed their hands together as layer upon layer of workers could be dispensed in favour of flexible outsourced resource. But, there was a huge consumer backlash against rampant outsourcing after Naomi Klein published her seminal book No Logo in 2000. This documented the 'brand bullies' as she called them, sitting in offices and designing products that were manufactured in union-free sweatshops thousands of miles away.

In services, things have been rather different. The dynamics of the industries involved are very different to, say, stitching together a pair of football boots. Skilled computer programmers are sought after and well looked after by the companies they join. Even the much-maligned call centre agent who can do their job well is a valuable commodity and won't suffer abuse at the hands of a nasty corporate bully.

But consumers of end products have still reacted against the offshore outsourcing of services they could previously see were locally delivered, because of fears over employment. Coping with structural unemployment is a real issue for developed societies – the UK has about 600,000 vacant jobs being advertised at present and a growing domestic contact centre industry, yet the fear is still there that one day everything will vanish to India.

Contact centre growth everywhere is more to do with the demands of an ever-accelerating 24x7x365 global society than just cost reduction by companies alone. Consumers today demand more of the companies they interact with. I bought a new car insurance policy online at the weekend. Can you remember when you had to go to a high street broker to do that? I tried ordering some books on Sunday and found it irritating that the call centre was closed, with a message advising me to call back on Monday. What if I am busy on Monday?

As Charles Handy predicted, outsourcing has enabled a new world of flexibility in services. It has also created genuine opportunities to save money. But the companies that are doing it well are finding that they can look after their staff, look after their clients, save money, and create flexibility too. It's no longer a one-trick pony promising little more than untold savings at the expense of service quality – at least not for the companies that are doing it well.

Tuesday, 15 May 2007

Posted at 15:18

Driving for outsourcing success

The Financial Times recently featured a full-page advert for the outsourcing services of Accenture.

What is interesting about the advert is there was very little copy. About 90 per cent of the page is just an image; in this case it shows a golf driving range with someone who is clearly able to hit a ball 400 yards in practice. Accenture is continuing on its golf theme, with Tiger Woods being the global standard-bearer, and the metaphor works a lot better than a page filled with facts. But the marketing people who believe that everyone in the senior echelons of corporate life enjoys golf always baffle me. How about some cricket-themed adverts with corporate stamina implied by how far an England batsman can ride his pedalo without drowning?

In four short sentences Accenture basically says the days of outsourcing to slash costs is gone. The company claims that by working with it you can 'outperform projections'. That's a bold claim, but the sentiment is in the right place. It's a lot like the psychology of the golfer who can hit the ball 400 yards, just because they believe they can do it. If a company enters an outsourcing contract to save money, but dresses it up for the media as a 'strategic move' then it will be all over the media within a couple of years as another outsourcing disaster. If they go in with a view that they can fundamentally improve their business by working with experts, then maybe they really can outperform their own projections.

Wednesday, 16 May 2007

Posted at 09:00

Never mind the Bengaluru

'Out to lunch,' sang the Sex Pistols' Johnny Rotten three decades ago on Pretty Vacant. Mr Rotten might have been observing the present behaviour of the government of Karnataka in southern India, the state where Bangalore is located and therefore is spiritual home to the Indian high-tech industry.

Changing the name of Bangalore was clearly not enough for these meddling politicians. For those of you who may not have noticed – most of the world in fact – Bangalore has officially been Bengaluru since November last year. After years of India building trust in the Bangalore brand, some local officials decided to flush away all that hard work in the stroke of a ministerial pen.

Now, the political classes are flexing their muscles over a generally ignored law that makes it illegal for women to work after 8pm. Of course, the business process outsourcing companies depend on teams working into the night – to serve customers in Europe and the US. And one of the greatest things this industry has achieved in India has been a blindness to gender, a move to meritocracy. Basically if you can do the job in this industry then we don't care if you are a guy or gal – that's been the mantra of the IT companies and it is blowing a wind of change through Indian society in general.

There has been genuine concern for the security of women taking taxis home after late shifts, though the cars are generally provided by their employer – these are not cabs hailed in the street – so there is the possibility for employers to start raising the level of background checks they do on drivers. But security concerns exist late at night in any major city. I wouldn't walk around certain parts of London on my own late in the evening – unless I'd had too many drinks to think of my own safety.

The politicians in Karnataka are trying to start enforcing the existing law preventing women working in the evening, offering 'advice' about how they should be with their family. These political leaders need to consider a couple of things. First, it's none of their business making a moral judgement on whether someone wants to work in the evening or not. Second, are they really going all out to ruin everything the private sector has worked for so many years to achieve in Bangalore? I can just imagine the state legislators up in Gurgaon – close to Delhi – rubbing their hands together in anticipation of the exodus from the south. And it will happen if those in power keep on behaving like this. Their time should be spent abolishing these archaic gender-specific laws, not reviving them.

Monday, 21 May 2007

Posted at 09:00

The art of living - and working

I entered the Palace of Westminster last week and mentioned to the security guard checking my bag that I was meeting Stephen Pound, MP for Ealing North in west London. The guard said there had been a lot of people coming in to see Stephen: "What's going on this morning?" he asked.

I told him I was going to participate in a lecture by Sri Sri Ravi Shankar. "Oh great, have we got a sitar concert in here today then?" answered the guard with a genuine sense of excitement.

When I met Steve in the committee room - we were both due to be speaking before Sri Sri gave a talk on business ethics - he got a text from an Evening Standard journalist asking about the famous sitar player – could Steve get them an interview?

Sri Sri Ravi Shankar must get this confusion over his name all the time, especially from people who are not immediately familiar with his work and think he is the famous sitar player, nowadays also known as the father of singer Norah Jones. Sri Sri actually heads the Art of Living Foundation, one of the largest NGOs in the world – his work is supported by the United Nations and he has been on the Nobel laureate shortlist three times now. He is on a UK tour spreading his message of healing and stress reduction.

Tonight he is talking to an audience at Wembley Arena. That's a pretty big audience for a speaking gig, and it's sold out.

The Art of Living foundation programmes have already been utilised in companies in the UK including GE and Shell. I was exploring some of the ideas around business ethics and the difficulties of creating an ethical working environment across borders. They had asked me to talk about some of my own experiences and I talked about the difficulties of working with the modern corporate environment, particularly when structures such as outsourcing can complicate our old certainties of whom we work for and what is expected of us as employees.

Sri Sri speaks very well, and he had answers without notes for every possible question thrown at him by the audience, but I had a nagging doubt. It's not even nice to admit this because when you meet someone who is so clearly spiritual and has the respect of millions, it feels hard to sometimes doubt the message. Sri Sri has helped over 20 million people with his training and guidance, so who am I to say that businesses often behave differently to individuals?

The problem is that every company does not take Corporate Social Responsibility (CSR) wholeheartedly, certainly not all the ones I have run into. It's often considered to be a branch of marketing – a way of giving something back, but in a way that also looks good. Yes, there are sporadic attempts to help the local community, but rarely does a company go all out to help the local community, the various nations it works in, and the workers themselves. It happens, but not that often.

What is interesting, and what supports the efforts of people such as Sri Sri is that a lot of people are not satisfied with where they are in the corporate world. Globalisation is changing how our companies work and we just feel less secure these days. Even trying to imagine what your company might be doing in a year can be depressing.

I saw some recent research by human resources firm Towers Perrin that quantifies some of this uncertainty. This was a study of 86,209 people in 16 countries, and it showed that just 12 per cent of staff in the UK are highly engaged in their job. The least engaged people are mid-level managers and supervisors. Crucially, for the advocates of a genuine approach to CSR and staff engagement, the study showed a causal connection between company profitability and levels of staff engagement.

Just think about that for a moment. Only 12 per cent of UK employees are excited and engaged about what they do for their company. And - not surprisingly - the research shows that if individual staff are engaged, interested, and happy, then company profits rise.

So although the message of Sri Sri Ravi Shankar is a spiritual one about an improvement in the emotional lives of individuals, there is also a real business case that should encourage companies to be involved with the work of such a guru. It helps the bottom line.

Companies are hard to change. They often care more about that bottom line in the short term than the effects they have on the world around them in the long term. Large corporations are rife with personal rivalry and politics and to approach every problem at work with a smile and belief that love will find a way appears naïve to most hard-nosed executives. Yet if researchers are proving a genuine connection between caring for staff and other business stakeholders and an increase in profits, then it is certainly worth supporting more of these initiatives. My best wishes go out to Sri Sri for the Wembley gig tonight.

Friday, 18 May 2007

Posted at 15:29

It was 20 years ago...

Last night there was a rather special birthday party in the walkways above Tower Bridge; at least it was for those of us involved in outsourcing. It was on 17 May 20 years ago that the National Outsourcing Association was created by Martyn Hart and a small band of others, particularly from telecoms giant BT – who were just finding out about the possibilities outsourcing could offer their business.

I'm sure nobody at BT could have imagined the present world of wholesale line rental – BT Group companies having to compete on a level playing field with competitors for access to the phone and broadband infrastructure. And thinking ahead was really the theme of the event.

Of course a party is a party and NOA board members could be seen quaffing champagne along with sourcing suppliers and users, but the party also raised a considerable amount for the charity Champions and Challengers. Atos Origin sponsored the event and so they managed to get an Olympic spin on events (they handle all the technology infrastructure at each games for the IOC) through their choice of charity.

Martyn Hart is now the NOA chairman. He led us through a series of reminiscences about the old days in the 1980s. Venerable businesses such as British Airways were only just being privatised, so the metrics-driven world of outsourcing was hardly on most business agendas at the time.

Roger Cox from Atos Origin did a good job of dodging a tough question, the obvious request for 'what will happen in the next 20 years?' A couple of his points resonated with me though, such as the atomisation of businesses, increasing specialisation, increased automation and industrialisation of the technology industry. In fact, as Roger suggested, I really don't think we will recognise what we think of as a 'technology industry' 20 years from now.

I bumped into Elizabeth Sparrow at the party, another British Computer Society author, with her book on Global Sourcing published in 2004. We have interacted on the BCS working party on offshoring and I was pleased to hear that she is taking a more senior and formal role at the BCS now, taking up a trustee position – the equivalent of board director in a normal private company (legally the BCS is a charity). Congratulations, and good luck for the new role Elizabeth. The BCS is now leading a charge to work out what a 21st century career really is and the effect of outsourcing on people working in the technology industry has been one of the major changes that we all need to cope with.

The NOA birthday party worked well as a summary of the past 20 years and the organisation still has much to do, it just gets busier. The NOA is focused on education at the corporate and university level, along with new independent research and study tours. It's an organisation that is focused on genuine best practice; a safe environment for buyers and sellers to discuss what works best for the industry, so here's to the next 20 years...

Wednesday, 23 May 2007

Posted at 13:16

Outsourcing gets personal

Person-to-person offshoring (PPO) - this could really be the next hot thing in offshore outsourcing.

Why is it so important? Well think about how the outsourcing trend has developed. Large companies paying experts to help where they either don't have the expertise in-house, or find that it is cheaper to pay someone else. The snag is that all those company-to-company relationships need contracts and time to oversee and manage. It's no surprise that the much-discussed new wave of small to medium-sized enterprise (SME) outsourcing has never really grown.

But as a potential market, just consider the number of small companies that are out there. There were an estimated 4.3 million private-sector businesses in the UK at the start of 2004. This compares with an estimated four million comparable enterprises in the UK at the start of 2003. Almost all of these organisations (99.3 per cent) were small (less than 49 employees). Only 26,000 (0.6 per cent) were medium-sized (50 to 249 employees) and 6,000 (0.1 per cent) were large (250 or more employees).

So all the outsourcing action has generally been restricted to those 6,000 companies at the top. There has not been much action at all from the really small micro-companies and one-man bands. However, even small companies need some IT maintenance, a web site, some bespoke systems, and databases. The very small companies are actually more likely to want to explore the outsourcing option than the mid-sized, because they have a greater need. Owner-run companies don't have any spare resource and the owner generally wants to run the business, not design a web site. And that approach is not because of any IT strategy plan, it's through necessity.

The India-based research firm Evalueserve has just published some analysis of the possibilities for very small-scale outsourcing in the US. In particular the research focused only on the possibilities for person to person offshoring, because small companies generally want to work with small companies – a small company would not commission an IT giant to build its web site. At present there is no UK data, but I hope they run the same study here soon, because it would be really useful to see how the 99 per cent of UK companies that fall under the label 'small' might be able to use outsourcing.

The Evalueserve research and analysis shows that between April 2006 and March 2007, the revenue from this person-to-person offshoring sector was more than $250m and is likely to grow to over $2bn by 2015, representing a cumulative annual growth rate of approximately 26 per cent. Furthermore, because this set of consumers (the small business owners especially) has diverse requirements, the breadth of offshoring services offered is also likely to be fairly large. Expect every service under the sun to be on offer. Many of these offshoring trends are in the beginning of their life cycles and others only have a few early adopters so it is not clear that all of these services will, in fact, enjoy mass adoption in the long run.

The Evalueserve report concludes that: "The value proposition of receiving such services at a significantly lower cost and 'just in time' is clearly irresistible, and therefore the overall sector shows the promise of rapid growth."

I'm watching PPO closely now and I've seen real examples of how this might work in the past few months. I think PPO is going to usurp the dreams of SME outsourcing.

Tuesday, 29 May 2007

Posted at 14:41

Who is really affected by globalisation?

Last December the European Union approved a "shock absorber" fund and pumped €500m into it, hoping that this would allay European fears of globalisation – and in particular the French fear of delocalisation - or what we generally know as offshoring.

The European Union created this globalisation safety fund because it wanted to – paradoxically - demonstrate that the union supports free trade and open borders, but at the same time has a level of compassion for any workers who might be displaced by offshoring. The cash is sitting there in the bank and is ready to compensate anyone who loses their job because of a change in world trade patterns.

This is particularly difficult game to play. Anyone who has followed the election campaign of newly-elected French president Nicolas Sarkozy can see that politicians are masters of double-speak. Then again, forget about France and just listen to our own leaders. One moment the audience hears that the government will crack down on shirkers who don't contribute to state coffers, the next the elected representative is outlining the cash available to help those affected by globalisation.

Yet, how does anyone define who is and is not affected by globalisation? In half a year, only France has applied for any money from the fund and that was to support the retraining of workers affected when a car component factory went bust. Does this mean that in the past half-year only one country in the union has been affected by globalisation, and even there in France, only one factory has been affected? Who says that it was globalisation that caused the company to go bust in the first place?

There are a lot more people displaced by companies going bust or moving location than displaced by offshoring. I recall speaking in New York about three years ago and I had checked some statistics at the time that showed companies moving from one state to another caused about 10 times the job losses of international sourcing. But who starts painting placards to protest against companies who move their operations from New York to California?

It's a fact that we need to consider the training needs of a workforce that has to now compete on a global scale, but the creation of a compensation pot in Brussels is not really the best way forward. Regions such as France that are extremely concerned about global competition might want to examine the red tape restricting their own businesses from competing. The compensation pot is really putting the cart before the horse if they don't analyse their own business infrastructure. London is now the seventh largest French city thanks to the large number of French entrepreneurs and workers finding the UK a far better place to do business – and to compete with the world.

Wednesday, 30 May 2007

Posted at 09:00

Are Indian rivals to blame for LogicaCMG's problems?

So it's all change at the IT services group LogicaCMG. Martin Read, chief executive and leader of the company for the past 14 years has decided to step down, though he remains in post until a successor is found.

There are a couple of interesting observations one can make from this turn of events. Read himself attributed his decision to go to a single project overrun that cost the firm about £10m, plus generally depressed trading. The formal line from the company pointed to unsettling speculation in the market following its recent announcement that half-year revenues would be lower than last year. When the profit warning was made last week, nine per cent of the share price value vanished immediately. Both could be right, but there is always a bit of short-term market uncertainty when a listed company announces a profit warning.

Some commentators are suggesting that LogicaCMG can't handle the competition from the Indian IT companies all ramping up their service offering in Europe. The Financial Times even went so far as to name Wipro, TCS, and Infosys as the key rivals making life hard for LogicaCMG these days. LogicaCMG is engaged in its own programme of hiring in India, creating its own blend of offshore as well as onshore local expertise, so the firm has already embraced the concept of a global delivery model for IT services.

But there must surely be more to it than just this though. So LogicaCMG has announced a downturn in profits and a hit on a particular project. That sounds pretty much like life as normal in IT services. Most of the time projects work out well, but now and again there are overruns and the service provider has to take it on the chin. LogicaCMG is still a name and brand that has exceptional value in the IT services marketplace. If the Indian players are really troubling the company then it can't be down to reputation or branding as the bright yellow logo of LogicaCMG in the Hampstead Road is generally trusted a lot more than the offshore operators, no matter that they are ramping up UK operations.

I don't have any inside knowledge, so I can only speculate as to what is going on, but it wouldn't be a surprise if some of those companies being named as international competition (Indian or not) are running a sliderule over some European IT service groups, as a way of consolidating their entry into Europe and leveraging off an established brand. With the LogicaCMG share price taking a tumble and the management situation uncertain, it would not be a surprise if the next chapter in the story were a bid for the group from an erstwhile rival.

Wednesday, 30 May 2007

Posted at 20:00

Is bigger, better?

IBM is the big IT service player that everyone wants to beat. The up-and-coming players all chart their ambitions along the lines of 'being the next IBM', yet IBM is not sitting around on its laurels. Though it does have plaudits to flaunt – the International Association of Outsourcing Professionals (IAOP) recently voted IBM the number one outsourcing company in the world, with the IAOP top 100 being published in Fortune magazine.

To give an idea of the scale of investment in seeking the next big thing, IBM spends over $5bn a year on research – a lot of that in the UK at the Hursley research centre. That's about a billion dollars more than the entire annual revenue of the largest of the Indian outsourcing companies, Tata Consultancy Services - not exactly small change.

So to find out a bit more about what they are up to, I had a chat with Bruce Ross, who is the general manager of IBM Global Technology Services. I put a few questions to Bruce about the IBM view on outsourcing.

First I wanted to know more about global delivery, or the global delivery model (GDM) as most service companies have started calling it. Bruce explained some of his thoughts on this:

"Global delivery has been a hallmark of IBM capability for many years now," he said. "About three years ago we went from a geographic model to a true GDM. We look at hardware, such as servers in Bangalore, the same way as a server in Moscow, and India is now the second biggest IBM geography by headcount. India is not the only place we are delivering globally - we have invested in Brazil, South Africa, China, and in Eastern Europe as we look to find the best mixture of skills and economics; the best skills at the best price for our clients. We believe that the GDM is essential for success."

Bruce mentioned some of the efforts by the Indian tech companies in this regard: "The Indian firms have made significant investments in this area, but we really truly believe that the differentiator for IBM is that we have a well-integrated and mature portfolio of services. We are not just the service provider, but the innovator of new technology that is used to run mission-critical systems."

It's true that the delivery of many services from remote locations is a given, consumers are getting used to it and it's normal in many sectors now, but companies are talking more and more about creating innovation through outsourcing. Conventional wisdom says that you outsource to a partner only those processes that are fairly standard and can be documented in a contract, with agreed service levels. Innovation is all about experimentation and exploring new ideas, that may or may not yield a benefit – how can companies contract for innovation through an outsourcing partner?

When I asked Bruce about innovation, he said: "There is a push in the marketplace for capabilities that the service partner can bring to the environment to make the client better – I call this a 'merger of capability'. So in other words if I have a capability at IBM and it's something the client is looking for, then the merger of that capability with the client service is what is going to drive the innovation agenda."

Bruce went on to mention some of the interactions he has been having within virtual worlds, such as Second Life: "Innovation is something we look to bring to all of our sourcing partnerships. For example, Web 2.0 is a really exciting area. It's going to create a whole new mechanism for how businesses interact with one another and with their clients. And that frankly creates a whole new set of clients in the marketplace that are yet to be served. Over 100 million people today are interacting with virtual marketplaces such as Second Life. You have probably heard about mash-ups – using publicly available data to create new applications. Those can be internal or publicly available and it really speeds up the time to market for new services and ideas. We are already leveraging on some of those principles within our client relationships."

They are the biggest, which doesn't always mean they are the best, but it's hard to avoid mentioning the old adage 'you never get fired for buying IBM'. In our less certain world it might be updated to 'you probably won't get fired for outsourcing to IBM.'

Thursday, 31 May 2007

Posted at 09:00

The outsourcing target frenzy

In The Observer newspaper last Sunday, management editor Simon Caulkin wrote about the dangers of managing by numbers. He wrote particularly about the recent case where the BBC Panorama programme exposed some allegedly dubious practices at several leading supermarkets, where food that passed the sell-by date was reprocessed for resale. In my opinion I am surprised that anyone is shocked by this news – I remember stacking shelves at a supermarket in the 1980s and it was going on back then, so the BBC has taken its time getting this scoop.

The problem of phoney figures and massaged targets all relates to fear: the fear of not achieving head office targets and the consequences of not doing so. Caulkin wrote that in his view "targets are a substitute for the thought needed to organise work to satisfy real demand".

He is right. As I read his article I immediately thought of the target-hungry outsourcing environment, which is awash with measurements and performance indicators. It's understandable because when you pay a company to deliver a service, you want some kind of metrics to show if they are doing a good or bad job.

Most management don't question that they never used to measure the efficiency of their internal team performing the same task.

In fact, the very first task that has to be undertaken by outsourcing suppliers - where a retained task is being outsourced - is an audit, because it's usually the case that nobody has any idea how much the service costs right now, so there is no way of working out a price until the whole process is audited. Half the time people don't believe their own internal costs as well, because the well-hidden annual cross-charge looks a lot cheaper than the transparent monthly bill from a supplier.

I can immediately think of three major areas where we see too much measurement in outsourcing:

1. Service Level Agreements (SLAs) and Key Performance Indicators (KPIs). Less really is more, but people don't seem to believe it. Ask yourself a question, how many of the dials on your car dashboard do you actively monitor while driving down the A40? Now look at all those charts and dashboards designed to monitor your outsourcing relationship.

2. Flexibility in contractual arrangements and service level agreements. When the IT support was just down the hall you really could shout and tell them that this is a serious problem and they need to help out – now. When a level of service is contracted it remains hard to create any sense of crisis, the 'backs to wall' mentality can't be written into a contract so the only way to get a service you can depend on 100 per cent is through good relationships.

3. Too many measurements have just become hygiene factors in the sales process, and that leads to suppliers adding more and more measurements to show that they have more than their competition. Of course there is a value in measuring software quality, but when every supplier is rated at the same level then all that documentation just creates a level playing field and everyone looks for more and more certification. Just look at the long list of certificates most suppliers demonstrate with pride, then they don't even offer you a cup of tea when you arrive at their office – what matters most?

It's not just schools, hospitals, and supermarkets that have gone target-crazy. Within the field of outsourcing we are probably guilty of forcing many other industries into their target-frenzy – it's time for a bit of pragmatism and good old-fashioned customer service.

June 2007

Tuesday, 05 June 2007

Posted at 14:47

Enter the NOA awards

The National Outsourcing Association (NOA) has announced that entries can now be sent in for the annual NOA awards. The NOA awards are now in their fourth year and provide a platform to reward excellence and best practice across the entire outsourcing industry. They are certainly the biggest awards around that specifically reward people specifically involved in outsourcing.

Of course, I'm a judge so I'll be looking out for some interesting and innovative entries into the competition. I remember last year there were a lot of interesting entries and me, along with a group of other NOA directors, spent a long day in NOA towers at Wardour Street judging who would win.

The competition is free to enter and there are 15 different categories, all related to outsourcing. Entry closes on 27 July so there is plenty of time to fill in the application form.

A word of advice from someone who has judged this before though - take a few moments to actually answer the questions on the application form. Last year there were a number of entrants with interesting projects, but entered into a completely inappropriate category or sent in with some sales literature rather than a completed entry form. It's not really that hard to complete a form by answering the questions is it? It's a shame to see these entries getting filed in the waste paper basket rather than being considered for the accolades they sometimes deserve.

Tuesday, 05 June 2007

Posted at 14:55

Tackling inequality and the effects of globalisation

The first place I ever visited in India was Mumbai. I took a flight there from Singapore and one of the strongest memories I have is of looking down from the aircraft – in the final approach to the runway – and seeing an unimaginably large slum. It was a collection of corrugated iron huts and shacks the likes of which I had never seen before. As I made the mistake of booking a hotel in south Mumbai – which is a long way from the airport – I had the dubious pleasure of my first Indian cab ride also including a tour through the shacks.

One of the questions often asked, when people look at the developing wealth in India from the globalisation of services and boom in offshore outsourcing, is how come so many people are still living in slums? India has a population of more than one billion, yet the IT and high-tech services industry only employs about a million people – that's similar to the number of people working in IT-related services in the UK, a country of 60 million people. High-tech service jobs are certainly not going to offer a ladder of opportunity to everyone.

India remains an enigma to most visitors. The business leader Mukesh Ambani, chairman of Reliance Industries, is planning a 60-storey palace in Mumbai as a new house for his family – at a cost of around £500m. Yet in the same city, millions don't even have access to fresh water or sanitation. It's no wonder that European business leaders who head over to Mumbai to check out their suppliers can be taken aback as they scan the horizon from their business class seat.

Academics use the Gini coefficient to quantify the level of inequality in a society – the effect of the rich getting richer and the poor getting poorer. What's really interesting is that income inequality, measured using the Gini coefficient, is greater in countries such as the UK or US, than it is in India. At face value it seems this must be wrong because at least the poor in our country have a social security safety net and legal protection, such as a minimum wage.

Dharavi, the huge slum by Mumbai airport, is now being redeveloped in a controversial new plan led by the state government of Maharashtra, where Mumbai is located. some 57,000 slum structures will be demolished and 30 million square feet of land will be developed for the existing slum dwellers. Of course, other development will take place. Twenty million square feet will be parcelled up for luxury homes and commercial use, leading to accusations from some critics that the government is scrubbing up the commercial heart of India at the cost of the poor and defenceless who can't do a thing about the development.

This blog is about outsourcing and not necessarily about the social impacts of globalisation, but any of us involved in the changing global nature of services cannot be blind to the effect that remote sourcing can have on employment in the developed world, and the creation of opportunities in the developing world. When we sit in London and examine analyst charts comparing the best global locations for offshoring, it's worth thinking about some of the impacts – positive as well as negative – and engaging with local communities in far-flung regions beyond just staking out a claim to be 'generating employment'.

Wednesday, 06 June 2007

Posted at 07:00

A model for outsourcing and skills

I had lunch with Tony Virdi from Atos Origin this week. I know Tony as he is a fellow director of the National Outsourcing Association and so we see each other at the monthly NOA board meetings, but we had decided it was time to catch up over a slightly longer meeting where we could exchange a few ideas.

I knew that Tony had wanted to get some of my views on the industrialisation of the IT industry. This is a familiar refrain to those of us who have been involved in software development in the past. The 'software factory' was often mooted in the past as the next logical progression as software development languages moved ever closer to natural language, yet it is a concept that is now only just approaching reality.

Tony described some ideas to me. He asked me to imagine all the usual logical steps in an IT process lifecycle from left to right as columns; analysis, design, specification, coding, testing, cutover, support and so on. He felt that we are starting to approach a level of maturity where the input and output from each column is beginning to be clear. Overlaid onto these columns though would be the various subdivisions of the IT sector, such as software development or application maintenance, creating a grid of IT 'components'. The entire grid would represent the industry as a whole.

What someone expects from a business analyst can then be more clearly defined and should function very much as a black-box component – something familiar to software developers. And the same expectations can be made for testing; it should be possible to create a test factory that can test any software, provided the standard inputs are all satisfied.

Some of these concepts, such as the industrialisation of the IT industry, have been discussed at length before – probably even before I was born – but the difference now is our experience of outsourcing. Companies that have experimented with outsourcing have found that the process-driven nature of the sourcing process does introduce efficiency. Even those companies who experiment with outsourcing and then decide to bring processes back in-house continue with some form of measurable internal market – they don't discard outsourcing in favour of the chaos they used to have. It creates defined inputs and outputs, just as Tony describes in his industry grid model.

So I think Tony is onto something with his component model. What is even more interesting though, is how Tony described the potential issues related to skills in countries such as the UK. If you create a component-based model of the entire industry in this way then you can observe where different geographies can add value. It should be possible to view the industry model with different areas shaded out, meaning they are of less value in this geography. Though the selection of component specialists is going to be based more on company rather than country, it is likely that some regions will specialise in particular components – and UK higher education institutions need to be aware of this. If they are not then we could find the doomsday scenario of highly-trained people leaving university with the wrong skills at the wrong time in the wrong location.

Wednesday, 06 June 2007

Posted at 09:00

How to stay secure when going offshore

C ommentators in Computing have been writing a lot about the security threats facing us all in the IT industry these days and offshore outsourcing opens companies up to cross-border risks far beyond the usual organisational threat. With global supply chains comes greatly increased risk to the company.

Recently, I've been fielding more calls than usual from commentators in the industry trying to gather information on the security threats involved in offshoring. Newspapers have been calling, company leaders have been calling, and even the UK government has called me on this topic. And yet, I'm wondering to myself, what has changed recently? It's always worth recalling a few basic points about offshoring risk though and keeping those thoughts fresh.

The main security threat everyone is afraid of in the offshore environment is a breach of personal data – employees or customer data being 'lost' or sold on the information black market. This is typically the fear of those with customer contact centres, and therefore employing a large number of people with access to the customer data of your own organisation. There have been a number of newspaper sting operations and even a Channel 4 documentary about this over the past couple of years. We all know the story – low-paid offshore call centre worker ready to sell personal financial data on UK consumers for a few meagre dollars. Only the money is not so meagre these days, so we might expect the risk to be increasing, as criminals are getting savvier about how outsourced operations function.

I think there are three quite separate areas you need to audit and examine if you have an existing commitment with an offshore supplier that involves the processing of sensitive data, or if you are considering which supplier to use:

Legal: In the legislative environment you have chosen, what kind of deterrent is there from the law to help prevent information theft? If there are measures in law to protect you then what actual case precedents exist – it may be that the law exists, but the process of going to court takes many years or is just too painful for other reasons so try to determine how well the law really protects you.

Process frameworks: You want the supplier to guarantee it will use process frameworks such as BS7799 to ensure that the business processes are secure, according to internationally agreed guidelines.

Additional measures: On a company-by-company basis you will observe that some suppliers go much further and are more secure than the process frameworks require. Make sure you determine how secure you need to be and work with a supplier who understands that data will not be secure, just because they passed a security audit.

Thursday, 07 June 2007

Posted at 18:11

Is the London 2012 logo an example of viral outsourcing?

C an you outsource to the public and get people to work for you for nothing? It's one of the possibilities created by the interactive nature of Web 2.0, but why on earth would anyone do something for nothing? Kudos and respect are the most obvious motives; in much the same way as expensive software developers give their time and expertise for free to work within the open source community.

But I don't think that software is the only type of service that can be outsourced to experts for free. Take a look at the furore kicking off at present over the logo for the 2012 London Olympic games. The branding company Wolff Olins has recently created a logo for the games that appears to be universally hated.

When it was unveiled on Monday this week, the detractors started an immediate hatchet job on the logo. Doctors appeared on television to talk about the risk to epilepsy suffers because of the bright flashing primary colours in the London logo. Some 85 per cent of the public voting on the BBC online news poll said they hated the design. Fewer than four per cent of BBC readers liked the new design. Even the Wall Street Journal turned over a whole page to describing the mess.

Personally I thought it was not bad. But then again, I've got prints by Banksy hanging up in my living room at home. I think the designers did a good job of not pandering to the usual desire for a cute cartoon character (World Cup Willie anyone?).

But think about it for a moment: could it actually have been a deliberate ruse to get the public involved in designing a logo? Perhaps the largest ever outsourcing programme for a marketing project? Was the intention all along to annoy as many people as possible with a Tiswas-like logo, so that the public would then come up with dozens of great ideas, one of which might bubble to the surface as the best of the bunch. It's viral marketing, but it also looks like outsourcing the marketing of the London Olympics to a lot of people who are working for nothing. What's new?

Friday, 08 June 2007

Posted at 09:14

Financial firms lead the way in outsourcing

N ew research out this week from the outsourcing advisory firm Equaterra has concluded that financial services organisations plan to expand their outsourcing initiatives into new geographies, business units and emerging processes more than other industries. The financial service industry is extremely bullish about the prospects for the use of outsourcing in their business domain. The Equaterra research also found that organisations in this industry are among the heaviest users of IT outsourcing (ITO) and business process outsourcing (BPO).

According to the new research, IT itself is the process most commonly outsourced by financial services organisations, followed by call centres and then human resources. Other industry specific processes commonly outsourced include claims, transactions (such as credit cards or equity trading) and cheque processing. Some emerging trends identified in financial services outsourcing include an increase in the outsourcing of content and document management, as well as "knowledge process outsourcing" or KPO.

KPO, a relatively new area that I have blogged about in the past, continues to gather momentum and encompasses a broad array of processes such as market research, financial analysis, merger and acquisition (M&A) due diligence and related M&A legal work. Equaterra comment that the Indian market is particularly well suited to KPO not only due to its lower costs, but also because of its reservoir of highly educated workers albeit with limited experience and context around some of the business processes they support.

Larger financial services companies are at the forefront in establishing captive operations to perform KPO and related work. The new report also found that financial services firms have greater future outsourcing investment plans than do other industries. For instance, 36 per cent of financial services respondents whose firm had outsourced one or more of the defined process areas planned to expand outsourcing into new geographies or business units, as compared to 30 per cent overall in the study. Twenty eight per cent planned to expand outsourcing into new process areas. Financial services firms will continue to invest in multiple forms of service delivery models including shared services operations, captive centres and the use of outsourcing providers.

Financial services remains a very complex business sector, but as we have seen in the past, the sector leads the way in exploring blended service delivery models using strategies such as outsourcing.

Monday, 11 June 2007

Posted at 14:34

Protecting data

India has finally bowed to international pressure and has set up a new body to oversee data protection in the IT and business process outsourcing (BPO) industries. The new body, named the Data Security Council of India (DSCI), is a self-regulating member organisation. It has been instigated by the IT trade association Nasscom, and will be managed at arms-length by them – I would guess until it is of a sufficient size to manage as a completely independent association in its own right.

Nasscom has been instrumental in addressing the perceived threat to data processed in India. They recently set up the National Skills Registry (NSR), which aims to certify the background of individuals working in the industry – in much the same way that bankers in London need to have their CV checked out by the Financial Services Authority before taking on a senior role. Nasscom has applied the same principles to the entire outsourcing services industry in India, and they are getting a very good take-up from the companies and individuals there.

As I have mentioned before in this blog, I do believe that data security is partially dependent on the processes used, and partially dependent on the local legislation available to prosecute any errant companies or individuals. There is a lot to be said though for companies that go beyond these prescribed measures and apply their own standards. This is what most of the Indian suppliers have been doing – going far beyond what is required to give reassurance to the customer. What we all need to be asking of India though, is how long before DSCI can actually put some proposals together that end up on the statue book – so India can at least claim to have some thorough laws in place for the protection of data.

Wednesday, 13 June 2007

Posted at 12:32

Go green or your customers will make you

I had lunch yesterday with Hardeep Garewal, the European head of ITC Infotech. Though the company is not really that well known outside the outsourcing community, it often ends up competing with bigger IT players because it has the muscle of the ITC conglomerate as a parent. Larger parent companies always give a sense of comfort to service buyers in any industry. ITC is a $4bn-revenue group with a diverse range of interests including tobacco, paper, hotels, and foods. The Infotech division Hardeep manages functions as a separate company, providing IT and BPO services to some well-known European companies including Danske Bank, Finnair, and Abbey.

I actually met Hardeep just to catch up on a few things, and to swap cricket news. Amid our theorising over the inept handling of the Pakistan coach Bob Woolmer's death/murder he mentioned something about his company that really interested me: it is carbon positive.

That's really interesting. Only a few days earlier I had raised the issue of carbon neutrality with a much larger IT supplier and the managers I talked to were fairly ignorant of the issues. In fact when I suggested that customer requests were likely to start demanding that suppliers are carbon neutral as a condition of doing business they were shocked at the suggestion – the implication being that if it happens then they might address the issue. Or basically, head in the sand management.

Although I was just predicting this as a change in the market, Hardeep actually gave me a few examples of companies that are already demanding this of their suppliers – mainly from Scandinavia at present, but the trend is bound to spread across Europe and when it does every IT supplier needs to be ready to go green or go bust.

Thursday, 14 June 2007
Posted at 09:00
How not to market your company

Some outsourcing service providers, such as Asia Web Media, are now spamming this blog. These dodgy suppliers seem to think that by spamming the comments section of the blog with their URL they might create enough international goodwill to win them some lucrative business.

I might direct the managers of this company to an article I wrote about outsourcing suppliers over four years ago on the bpoindia.org web site, as they seem to fail some of the most basic tests I outlined back then for how best to present your public face to customers.

I tried calling the people at Asia Web Media to ask why they keep spamming the blog and what they think they might get from it. First I tried the London telephone number, only to hear a message 'this number does not receive incoming calls…' That's quite strange, so I called the Indian number. The only number given was a mobile and the person who answered sounded as if he was taking a ride on the back of an auto-rickshaw. Hardly a slick way to answer the phone, considering the way its web site spins some elaborate lies about 'quality' services.

I said I was calling from Computing and wanted to talk to one of the management team about their views on blogs and how they can be used to share information on best practice in the outsourcing industry. The guy on the auto-rickshaw (maybe he is also the driver?) told me that he could not talk at the moment, but that he was online and if I wanted to login to MSN then I could have an instant message chat with him.

I was wondering how he could refuse to take a call on the mobile phone and yet was available to chat on MSN, but I didn't let my mind mull over the problem for too long. The office address in Mumbai is listed on the web site, so when I am over there in a few weeks I might just take a taxi over to ask them in person, though I half expect to find myself in front of a cinema or shop when I search for the listed address. Anyone who buys any service from a company as immature as this is more stupid than the executives who think that spamming a blog is an effective marketing tool. I don't often express any ill will on anyone, but in this case I'll make an exception. I hope these spammers suffer a protracted period of poor business that costs them so much they even need to sell their auto-rickshaw and company mobile phone.

July 2007

Wednesday, 04 July 2007

Posted at 18:31

The Indian success story rolls on

The Indian technology industry association Nasscom has released its annual survey – giving some insight into what is going on in the Indian technology sector at present, and it is particularly interesting for those interested in outsourcing as Nasscom represents around 95 per cent of the Indian IT companies.

As we have experienced over the past few years, the numbers look good for India. The Indian technology sector will generate $50bn in revenues during this present 2007-08 financial year, which takes the industry closer and closer to the Nasscom target of $60bn by 2009-10.

In fact, at present growth rates it would not be a surprise to see that target achieved at some point in the next financial year. Revenues last year increased by 30 per cent, so the technology industry is still going through tremendous growth, despite the present short-term issues. There is no obvious sign of a slowdown and the industry now employs 1.6 million people in India, with at least six million other jobs supporting those in IT.

What of those short-term issues? Well some are shorter term than others, but they are all important. The appreciation of the rupee is hurting all those Indian tech companies that price services in dollars, but pay most of their people in rupees. There isn't a lot suppliers can do about this beyond praying the market moves in their favour and using some elaborate hedging to mitigate exchange rate exposure.

The government could speed up some changes to the law so international data protection measures are codified in Indian law. It seems like one of those things that Nasscom asked the government to do a long time ago and yet the urgency has gone so it's slipped by the wayside – until the next data protection disaster.

Physical infrastructure still needs to be improved in India. Traffic can be appalling in the major metropolitan areas and the airports are a disgrace, but the most important of the short- to mid-term issues is the supply/demand gap for talented graduates. Nasscom is particularly worried about this and has predicted a shortfall that could drive up the price of talent, but I'm generally not so concerned about this issue. I still believe that there is a lot of talent in India that is not being used effectively, so I think the talent pool crunch is more like a contraction in the market that will be corrected before too long.

India is like a super tanker where the captain has a foot hard on the accelerator. It's hard to change course quickly, but the ship is already heading in the right direction, and getting faster.

Thursday, 05 July 2007

Posted at 16:39

A novel look at business

I was travelling on a train from Birmingham to London this morning and I pulled out a copy of the new book I just finished writing, with the intention of doing a final read-through before the publisher gets their hands on it. I was smiling as I was reading the 'book' – it's fun to read something I have written once it is at the point at which I think it's ready to be published, even if my wife thinks it borders on the insane to be smiling at my own writing. I have a short memory, so I can laugh at my own jokes.

It made me think a little about business writing though, because I wrote this book as a short story. You could even call it a parable, a story about border collies with a message about globalisation and outsourcing (I know, you will have to read it to understand).

Whatever my plans were when I sat down to write it, I think the main thing I was trying to do was to write something about outsourcing that is not a formal management or academic textbook. It's a book about business that might even be featured on Blue Peter - though that's more because I'd like to get a badge from the lovely Konnie Huq before she steps down. The book I published earlier this year has been entered for the FT Business Book of the Year award. I don't know how it will do in the competition. It describes the globalisation of services in great detail, but how will the Arctic Monkeys and Snakes on a Plane globalisation case studies go down with the cerebral judging panel of business experts?

There are some who continuously poke fun at the whole genre of management and business literature. Lucy Kellaway in the FT is possibly the most consistent lobber of brickbats at books on 'leveraging core competence' and 'team values'. Charles Handy – who was educated in the Classics – bemoaned management literature and used to give his London Business School students a copy of 'Antigone' on the first day of term. No doubt that caused some confusion amongst the students expecting a weighty management tome from Peter Drucker and finding themselves considering the most ancient of Catch-22 moral dilemmas. I do agree with commentators such as these that there is a lot to be learned, perhaps far more, from literature. Business books can't teach what we already have within the entire canon of classic English literature.

I have a good friend, Mahesh Ramachandran; we sit on a couple of company boards together, including FXAworld [2009 note: I no longer have any interest in this company]. Mahesh is from a fairly small town in south India called Thanjavur, which is a 12-hour train ride from Chennai or Bangalore. He took me there once to meet his family and I was astounded to see his father's collection of over 40,000 books – all in the house. It was like living inside a branch of Waterstone's. As we walked around together looking at the books I was pointing out some that I knew and loved, George Orwell, James Joyce, Oscar Wilde, Aldous Huxley, JD Salinger, Graham Greene... after a few conversations about classic books Mahesh's father turned to his son and said something along the lines of: 'Son, with all these great books at home, how come you grew up only ever reading that business rubbish?'

It was a funny moment, but it's something I have observed in a number of the places where I have taught. Students working hard on their MBA seem to think that time spent reading the latest novel from Ian McEwan or Haruki Murakami is time they could be devouring another company case study or the latest book on corporate governance.

The classic book everyone talks about when thinking of corporate strategy is the ancient Art of War by Sun Tzu. I even know a guy here in London who wrote a book decoding this for the modern day manager – David Hawkins at PSL, which is an organisation set up by the now-defunct Department of Trade and Industry and the CBI and focused on promoting corporate partnership.

But what of outsourcing in classic literature? I'm not sure if there is a single classic novel or story that reflects company partnerships, and the good or bad in organising a company structure in this way. The classic beat novel Post Office by Charles Bukowski is a textbook (and shocking) story of how companies treat 'permie' and 'agency' staff completely differently. Perhaps Joseph Heller's Catch-22 is a great example of organisations in chaos. Or Oscar Wilde's Dorian Gray a warning for alpha-male business process outsourcing chief executives, but I'm afraid I am racking my brain here trying to think of a better example. Any ideas?

Thursday, 12 July 2007

Posted at 18:21

Taking account of offshoring

International accounting firm Ernst & Young (E&Y) has announced a move to handling UK tax compliance work offshore. It is going to hire 200 bright young graduates to handle the work in Bangalore.

E&Y has stated that the move is not about cost reductions and there will not be any redundancies. It certainly looks like a classic case of offshoring. The company can utilise the offshore centre for some of the lower-end tax compliance work, freeing the UK teams to focus on higher-end, more interesting and challenging work.

What I find quite interesting about the E & Y move is that the firms doesn't plan to use accountants in India – though one of the positive legacies of the British Empire is a well-established set of agreed accounting principles in India, that remain similar to those in use here. E&Y will hire graduates with some proven intelligence and then put them through a seven-week accountancy boot camp to get them up to speed on the new skills they will need to service UK clients.

Now I can't think of many things worse than a seven-week accountancy boot camp – perhaps it could only get worse if it was accountancy in a jungle with Ant & Dec as hosts. More seriously though, India has plenty of real accountants at all levels so one might ask if the profession itself is being dumbed down by this move? Would non-accountants be processing this information if it were being handled locally?

Friday, 13 July 2007

Posted at 09:00

It's not the pitching, it's the taking part

Each year, the National Outsourcing Association (NOA) holds a day-long focus on offshoring. This year it was hosted in central London at the magnificent South Africa House, thanks to the kind people at the South African High Commission who donated the use of their cinema for several talks about globalisation and outsourcing.

I was the chair for the event this year, along with my fellow NOA director Paul Morrison, who in his day job is a managing consultant at advisory firm Alsbridge.

The day featured a really interesting talk from Tony Virdi of Atos Origin. I have interviewed and done a podcast with Tony before so I have heard some of his views on this industry, but it was still interesting to hear it again. He has some strong views on the lessons of the manufacturing industry being applied to IT and services – he calls it industrialisation. Later in the day, JP Rangaswami, the CIO of BT Global Services was a bit dismissive of the terminology – preferring 'commoditisation' – but they essentially agreed on the direction we are headed.

Atos Origin was funding the food and drinks so they had a chance to get up and talk about some actual projects as case studies. The company chose to detail the technology being used for the Olympic Games, which is one of its major contracts. It was an impressive project and really demonstrates a very strict approach to global sourcing, with deadlines that cannot be shifted.

As an observer of the various talks through the day I would congratulate Atos Origin on its approach to the event. Even though it was sponsoring the bottles of wine, the firm never once stood up and did a sales pitch. It was either a case study of a real project or some industry supplier-agnostic thought leadership. A lot of IT vendors could learn from this approach – it makes them look like a far more mature supplier than someone who says 'buy from me!'

Monday, 16 July 2007

Posted at 16:00

Indian IT workers are in the driving seat not the sweatshop

The Guardian ran a story today featuring the result of an investigation into the clothes industry, particularly the outsourcing of clothes production in Bangladesh. The paper found that well-known retail chains such as Asda, Primark, and Tesco are purchasing from suppliers in Bangladesh that are paying workers rates as low as 4p an hour for 80-hour weeks. Understandably, the clothes retailers have all expressed their outrage and Asda has even pledged to undertake a complete review of all its offshore sourcing arrangements.

This story is reminiscent of a furore that broke out at the beginning of this decade. Fresh from the anti-globalisation protests at the 1999 WTO conference in Seattle – later to be termed the 'battle in Seattle' – the Canadian writer Naomi Klein published No Logo. The book remains a seminal document of that Millennial period and is still probably the best book on brands and branding, crossing seamlessly between the rigorous world of the academic and the fast and loose world of the journalist. No Logo picked apart the world of manufacturing outsourcing, with particular targets including branded leisurewear – the trainers that are designed in the USA and then assembled in a low-wage factory in China.

Suddenly the consumer was aware that those cheap basketball boots kept on getting cheaper because there was some poor soul in Asia stitching them together for less pay than the proud owner of the new boots might spend on a packet of chewing gum. A new wave of righteousness swept the world, with consumers realising they have the power to influence how and where manufacturers operate – and the standards they adhere to.

Within reason. Consumers still want stuff to be cheap. Anyone who can recall the opening of the Primark store on Oxford Street in London in April knows that a £2 bikini is extremely alluring. So the news that major UK retail chains are in trouble again for sourcing from Bangladesh sweatshops just demonstrates the difficulty in creating cheap products at the same time as defining labour standards that are acceptable to European consumers.

The question for those of us in the IT industry is really, are services any different? Bangladesh can offer IT services as well as manufacturing and the region is making a bit of a name for itself in animation, created these days using complex design software. Anyone with kids who has tuned into the many TV channels placating their offspring on a Saturday morning has probably experienced the output of Bangladeshi artists without ever realising it.

Basis, the hi-tech trade association in Dhaka has been quite vocal in promoting the region for IT outsourcing, despite the political strife of the past year causing some uncertainty for foreign investors. Indeed, the very thought of a military-backed emergency government is enough to prevent most people visiting the region, let alone outsourcing critical parts of the supply chain there.

Bangladesh is rather different to many regions because of the present political uncertainties, but in other locations where foreign investors are more comfortable, such as its larger neighbour India, wage inflation continues and most IT companies still talk about a 'war for talent'. Although some UK trade unions have talked about trying to join together with their brothers in India to demand a better deal, the simple fact is that in IT services the slave labour conditions of manufacturing just don't exist.

The fast market growth in IT services and continued demand for skilled labour means that employees have a great deal of power in naming their terms and expecting constant reviews and training. If they don't get a good deal, they jump ship. The idea of a global trade union for IT staff just seems a bit quaint in an environment where the service companies are so desperate for good people. Don't expect those Indian software engineers to be singing 'the red flag' anytime soon.

Wednesday, 18 July 2007

Posted at 10:54

Outsourcing to me (and please find my bike!)

I bought a new bicycle last Thursday. I use a bike to get around London most of the time, so if you meet me and wonder why I am wearing a hoodie rather than a suit and tie then this is the explanation in advance. I took the bike out on a couple of long rides at the weekend and found that I really liked it – we got along well together. Then, the first time I took it into central London, commuting to a meeting on Monday, someone stole it. I felt completely violated – it felt almost as bad as when a thief swiped my Apple Mac in the airport at Moscow last year. They even stole the locks – or that might be how professional thieves work, taking evidence along with the bike.

After the upset, I needed to consider an insurance claim. Anyone who has been a victim of crime knows that the first step is to ensure a police report is filed and a crime reference number produced for the insurance company. Any time this has happened in the past I have had to wander into a local police station, avoiding the stare of the characters loitering around outside, queued up, given all my details to a disinterested desk officer, and left with the thought that I always leave a police station feeling guilty about something, even if I was the victim reporting a crime.

This time I checked out the web site of the Metropolitan Police and found that they have automated this entire process for a whole raft of crimes, mainly theft without violence, such as my bike theft. It's now possible to sit at home with a coffee and to enter all the details directly, with the Met system immediately despatching the details to the nearest police station – just in case there is any chance of following up on the crime. They have reduced the effort required on the reception desk in local police stations and outsourced much of that effort to the crime victims. Outsourcing really does crop up in all manner of unusual places.

This is becoming a lot more common now - the outsourcing of tasks to the client of a service. Just think of how shops worked a few decades ago. You would call in with your shopping list, chat to the grocer and maybe have a cup of tea as he fetched the items you need – and if you didn't have time to collect in person then the delivery boy would drop them at your home. Now we all drive to stores the size of aircraft hangers and spend hours selecting from a dozen different types of potato – we are now doing the work of the grocer.

This concept has been used in business extensively for supply chain improvement. Companies with extensive buying power have found that they can improve their efficiency by standardising their purchasing systems – and forcing the suppliers to interact with that system if they want to continue receiving orders. Retailers now have such buying power that even established well-known companies would be taking a chance if they questioned the way they need to interact with the buyer. The launch of the new Harry Potter book is a case in point. UK supermarkets are offering the book to customers at a lower price than the book trade wholesalers are offering it to small independent bookstores – expect your local bookstore manager to be filling his trolley with Harry in Tesco's sometime soon.

The rise of peer-to-peer (P2P) services just encourages this trend even further. By eliminating a bank or retailer in the middle of a transaction a world is created where we are now happy to spend time buying and selling products online, packaging them, shipping them, offering refund policies. It's a whole new world where the services of companies have been outsourced to the consumer. As you package up your latest eBay purchase just remember to call Crimestoppers if a bloke in a pub offers you an almost new Genesis Day 03 in silver with flat handlebars...

Thursday, 19 July 2007

Posted at 17:57

Going mobile (in Warwick)

Indian technology supplier Tata Consulting Services (TCS) hosted an event last week at the Heritage Motor Centre near Warwick. It was an interesting venue, packed full of British motoring history, though it's not all that easy to get to unless you are using a car, which was a shame as I took the train from Marylebone. Arriving at Warwick I expected to find a line of taxis, only to find that Warwick station is a lot smaller than I had expected. The operator behind the window at a small mini-cab office told me it would be at least an hour before I could get a car. "It's that time of day innit..." I wasn't sure whether to agree or not – I never realised it was that hard to get a cab at nine in the morning.

Having got there in the end (someone else cancelled a car, so one was available earlier than they expected) I actually enjoyed quite an interesting event. TCS is making quite a play for major enterprise solutions, such as ERP, CRM, business intelligence, and so on – the big ticket systems that can often result in big ticket failure, or tremendous success. Obviously they feel like they need to escape the 'Indian offshoring' tag and so this event focused in on a single topic – the mobile workforce - and on some of the issues around it.

The consultant Steve Downton gave a talk on "improving profitability through efficient mobile workforce management" followed by some talks from TCS experts, followed by a nice lunch. Sometimes these events can be a bit self-serving and salesy, but this was useful for a couple of reasons. First, Steve seems to have been given a free rein to just talk about anything he wanted. In fact, it was interesting to observe that he didn't really talk about mobile workforce technology at all; he talked about organisational psychology and the issues of getting people in a company to behave in a new way.

I'm no expert on the topic so I was learning as well, but what I found really interesting was how the mobile workforce has changed in stature over the years. Many enlightened companies have finally realised that their fleet of service engineers is the main contact they have with their customers, and to treat them poorly or to direct and micro-manage them is not a smart move. Treat the guys on the frontline with some respect and it pays off a dozen times over. It's common sense really, but how many people treat their frontline staff more as an irritation than an asset?

A lot of companies that have outsourced the management of their mobile workforce have come unstuck because one of the first efficiency drives that is often used is GPS control – to track and direct the location of your mobile workforce. In an untrusting environment, introducing this kind of technology makes most of the van drivers run for the hills screaming 'Big Brother!'

Although it's clear that technology is making the mobile workforce a lot more efficient, and so it is an area that is easy for the outsourcing suppliers to sell into, TCS did a decent job of putting together an informative morning of talks. This allows them to bask in the glory of actually creating a useful event – rather than shoving their latest ERP solution in front of everyone and just hoping someone buys it. This is a topic that needs the people management to be as strong as the technology, so it was useful to see this covered in a thoughtful way by the speakers – drawing on quite extensive academic sources.

Monday, 30 July 2007

Posted at 12:07

Opportunities for Africa

In 2004, Tony Blair created the Commission for Africa. This was a task force dedicated to creating a future roadmap for Africa and it reported its findings in those heady days of 2005 – a time of white wristbands and Make Poverty History rhetoric.

In my view, one of the most disappointing aspects of the Commission for Africa report was the scant regard shown to the possibility of technology-enabled services to be delivered from African nations. There are many infrastructure issues that need to be addressed before a trade in services can truly explode, but that trade has already begun and the new era of trade across the internet removes many of the issues associated with trading in regions that most Europeans have never even visited.

It's only a few years ago that we saw the trade in services to countries such as India really take off, now outsourcing to India accounts for several percentage points of the entire GDP of that vast nation. Why not Africa?

Well, hi-tech business in Africa is on the agenda again, but this time it is the Commonwealth Secretariat organising the discussion. The Commonwealth Heads of Government Meeting – better known as CHOGM – is an event held every two years and collects together the leaders of all 53 Commonwealth nations. It is possibly the biggest scheduled gathering of Prime Ministers – and royalty - in the world. In November this year CHOGM will take place in Kampala, Uganda, and the conference associated with the event is giving some priority to various outsourcing-related topics. A huge technology park will be unveiled, offering modern office space to outsourcing suppliers, and the Ugandan government is engaging in an overhaul of its IT-related legislation, to ensure the region can support this type of international business.

Business process outsourcing (BPO) is still a fledging industry in east Africa, though the contact centre market in South Africa is very strong now. But it is growing. In Kenya alone, it is expected that 30,000 people will have BPO related jobs within two years and the government there is converting the Kenya College of Communications Technology to a specialised BPO centre to help increase the supply of educated young people into the industry.

Bandwidth cost and reliability remain the biggest issues for most service firms trying to operate from African countries, but this is surely just a matter for the communications techies to resolve. Many African nations have a large pool of educated people and entrepreneurs ready to tap into service opportunities. In the same way that technology outsourcing to India has provided far more to the region than just jobs for computer programmers, I think we will see global services offering huge development opportunities for Africa. Outsourcing could turn out to be of more value to the continent than any coloured wristband.

Monday, 30 July 2007

Posted at 13:04

Steria announces Xansa buyout

European IT services group Steria has announced its intention to buy UK IT and outsourcing firm Xansa.

Xansa issued an announcement this morning stating:

"The directors of Xansa and Steria are pleased to announce that agreement has been reached on the terms of a recommended proposal whereby Steria will acquire the entire issued and to be issued share capital of Xansa. It is intended that the acquisition will be implemented by way of a Scheme of Arrangement and, subject to the satisfaction, or, where appropriate, waiver, of the Conditions, it is expected that the Acquisition will become effective by the end of October 2007."

Xansa's roots go back to 1962 when Dame Steve Shirley created the FI Group, originally offering IT industry opportunities to women. Nowadays Xansa is perhaps best known for its NHS finance and accounting contract, but it does also have some high-end IT contracts, such as managing the technical systems supporting the ING Renault F1 team.

There are some synergies in this deal. Xansa is known for its offshoring expertise. It has delivery centres in several Indian cities and has many years' experience of the offshoring delivery model, along with a blended service from its UK centres. Steria doesn't have any of this offshoring experience, or a business process outsourcing (BPO) service line. However, Steria is a much stronger brand in Europe – Xansa decided to focus on its home market a few years ago and reined in sales teams from Europe and the US to focus on the UK.

It's a deal that has been coming for some time and there have been quite a few jitters recently around Xansa. Last month, the chief executive Alistair Cox moved on to head up the recruitment firm Hays, leaving chairman Bill Alexander to take up the operational management of the company until a new chief executive could be recruited.

In fact, Xansa shares have looked good value for some time considering the strength of the client base so it was only going to be a matter of time before someone came along and put a serious offer on the table. What is interesting is that it is not one of the offshoring giants from India trying to tap into the UK public sector business Xansa enjoys. This is more like two Europeans with different service lines joining together to be bigger and to fight harder in the market. It will be interesting to see how the new group manages to integrate the combined IT/BPO ethic of Xansa with the IT focus of Steria.

Tuesday, 31 July 2007

Posted at 13:06

Collaboration not comparison

Right now, the internet is filled with the buzz of consultants comparing different countries, testing their suitability for offshore outsourcing. The magazine BusinessWeek has been focusing on the upstarts – those nations out to take business from India, arguably wearing the offshoring crown at present.

I know that I have recently been writing about the potential for Africa in the offshore outsourcing market, but I wouldn't want to stoke the fire of a country vs country battle, where Uganda claims to be 'better' than India or Vietnam claims to be 'better' than Singapore. The debate is too difficult to generalise. Certain types of business process may work better in certain locations, but there are so many variables that involve the labour supply, legislation, foreign direct investment and taxation policy, quality of supplier, infrastructure and so on. It's really a political minefield to draw up direct country comparisons and fruitless to try to pronounce that contact centres work better in – say – South Africa than India.

This morning I had a conversation with JP Rangaswami, the chief information officer (CIO) of BT Global Services, and formerly global CIO of investment bank Dresdner Kleinwort – one of the real thought leaders on technology management here in the UK. It was part of my research for a forthcoming Computing project so I don't want to give away too much of what he said, but he did express some exasperation at the my-country-is-better-than-your-country approach to offshoring. In JP's world we are moving far away from the client-supplier model of outsourcing to a new collaborative model that is perhaps most easily imagined as something similar to the open source software community.

It's clear to me that the first legal expert that stops drafting all those soon-forgotten outsourcing contracts and starts working out a better way for clients and suppliers to relate to each other in a way that implies commitment and collaborative freedom simultaneously will make even more money than London lawyers already enjoy.

August 2007

Thursday, 09 August 2007
Posted at 18:00
Taking yourself captive

Market rumours suggest that financial services group Prudential is exploring how to sell off its back-office operations in India, to create a new business process outsourcing organisation focused on the insurance and pensions sector. The Prudential operation is in its office in Mumbai. These offshore, but internal, teams are often referred to as 'captive' as they are all employees of the parent company – to distinguish them from resource that is outsourced to a third party. It's a route that has been taken in the past by organisations such as British Airways, who set up operations in India and spun that off as WNS, or GE who spun off its Indian back office to create GenPact.

Just think of the business advantages in doing this. First the companies can make the most of the cost savings involved in going to a lower-cost location. Then, they can save further by improving processes and making the back-office more efficient. Then they industrialise the process so the back-office can operate as an autonomous unit – so much so that they can talk to investment banks about spinning the offshore unit off – a process that means they will earn millions by selling the company to established service companies, or other investors. Then, even once the companies are separate entities, they can still enjoy further benefits through preferential service pricing or keeping an equity stake in the new organisation, and making that company more valuable by creating a steady stream of work for it to process.

What is interesting though is that Prudential is not the only major company with offshore operations now considering this route; Citibank appears to be considering this option too. It's interesting because after the creation of Genpact in 2004 many considered that the days of the large offshore back-office would be numbered. Everyone in the industry was talking then about the boost this would give to outsourcing suppliers. If GE was opting to use outsourcing rather than its own offshore resource then it has to be the right business model. Yet, there were never really any other comparable examples of an internal captive department being spun off again in the same way, until now. At least, if the rumours are true.

If these sales really do go ahead soon then it will lead us to the same debate all over again. How big does your offshore operation have to be to justify going it alone or working with a partner? I think the jury is out at present because all conventional wisdom said that you work with a partner up to a certain size, then do it yourself to cut the supplier margins out of the equation. Now it's all changed, again.

Monday, 20 August 2007

Posted at 17:35

Going global

The global delivery model is something of a Holy Grail for most IT service companies. Everyone wants to be considered a global player, yet being able to offer global delivery is not just a function of how many offices a company opens around the world, so it's interesting to see a new paper from outsourcing advisory firm Equaterra on how to design a global delivery model. Equaterra makes some interesting observations in the opening section of the paper, including:

• An Economist Intelligence Unit survey of 300 executives worldwide found that when asked what country would be the best overall location for their firms' R&D work, outside of their home country, India was the country most frequently cited, followed by the US and China.

• Organisations also continue to tap into offshore resources via the captive route. Equaterra counts over 300 major captive operations of Western firms in India alone. Use of captive operations are sometimes transitional, as over time, the parents of the captives (for example, General Electric, British Airways and Citigroup) opt to spin them off to not only make a profit but also to rid themselves of the challenges and operating overhead.

• A 2006 Offshoring Research Network survey (led by Duke University and supported by Archstone Consulting and Booz Allen Hamilton) of 537 buyers in the US and Europe, 70 per cent of which were Fortune1000 and larger firms, found that over 50 per cent of respondents have now undertaken offshore outsourcing.

• The same study found that while IT outsourcing remains the leading offshore functional area, product development, general and administration, and call centre/helpdesk have also been outsourced offshore by 25 per cent or more of the survey respondents. Procurement, a functional area less frequently outsourced to date, is one of the leading areas targeted going forward.

The Equaterra commentary is useful and worth reading because it synthesises a lot of key commentary into a single short paper. It is a fact that business process and IT outsourcing has become far more global in the past decade – just look at the regions now trying to enter this market from all corners of the world.

The real key to success in global sourcing is addressing service delivery in a continuum – or thinking of the outsourcing value chain in much the same way as a product is assembled from raw goods on a production line. Though we have not really seen it yet, as sourcing becomes more global and more fragmented into smaller 'best of breed' contracts – rather than the big single-supplier deals – it is likely that users who excel at outsourcing can start considering this skill a competitive advantage in their industry.

Tuesday, 21 August 2007

Posted at 11:00

Don't toy with outsourcing

The world's largest toy maker, Mattel, was in trouble last week over allegations that some of its products contain harmful quantities of lead paint and dodgy magnets. The latest product recall involved 18 million toys. Only two weeks ago, 1.5 million Fisher Price toys were also recalled.

The problem stems from the manufacturing process in China. It seems that Mattel has not been completely on top of what its outsourced manufacturing partners in China have been doing and so standards have slipped.

I asked my father about this story over lunch last weekend and he had a more sanguine view than most: "We used to eat lead soldiers when I was a kid and it never did me any harm," he said.

However, most parents are a little more concerned about the safety of their kids when playing with Mattel toys.

This blog doesn't normally look at manufacturing, but a product recall nearly 20 million-strong that is triggered by faults in an outsourcing relationship can't be ignored. Some might also argue that most IT services are not as critical as the safety of children, but given that every organisation today is powered by IT in some form or other it's easy to see that airlines, railways, hospitals, all have safety-critical systems.

The lesson to be learned is that even the most basic processes affect the relationship you have with your customer. It might be assumed that painting toys is a pretty simple process, but here is a case study in how it can go disastrously wrong.

With IT services we often talk about the non-core elements of the company being outsourced and that term is often used as a synonym for less important – or even non-important. That's a big mistake, because it's those simple processes that are outsourced to a third party that make up the service you offer to your customer. If those processes were not important then they would not be part of your corporate supply chain - outsourced or not. It's worth remembering this as we read about how something as simple as contracting a company to paint your products can cause a corporate nightmare.

Wednesday, 22 August 2007

Posted at 11:00

Putting outsourcing on expenses

Back when I worked in a City bank I used to travel around the world quite a lot, which meant I had a major job tracking expenses and booking them all into a claims system. One of the good things my company did was to publish some guideline figures, so the process could be streamlined to a certain extent.

Basically, there were guidelines such as 'no more than £50 per person for dinner' or 'no more than £150 for a hotel room' – below these limits you could essentially zip through the expenses claim very quickly. More formal approvals were only required if you broke any of the suggested limits, in which case the boss would need to take a look and authorise the claim.

It all worked quite well. I suppose by offering this level of trust in the employee there was scope for fraudulently claiming for the odd cab fare here and there, but on the whole the costs saved by streamlining the process must have been worth more than the odd crooked claim by bankers who should know better. But my company was not perfect. The procedures I followed applied in London only. My colleagues in Singapore would have claims for single cups of coffee scrutinised in detail. Who were you with? What was the business purpose of that cup of coffee? An army of clerks crawled all over their receipts in complete contrast to the exception-handling bliss in London.

So I was interested to see that supermarket chain Asda has outsourced its expense claims to a partner called GlobalExpense and is trumpeting the fact that the firm estimates a future saving of £200,000 thanks to the new arrangement.

GlobalExpense saves companies money by insisting that claims fall within the corporate policy. According to GlobalExpense statistics, managers approve claims 99 per cent of the time, yet at least 15 per cent of expenses are outside policy - no doubt those receipts that come back from conferences in Las Vegas will now be scrutinised a bit more closely. It's not clear if any of these statistics apply to Asda, but as they are moving from a 100 per cent paper-based system for expenses to this new arrangement, it is clear to see how expenses will be paid faster, and will be within corporate policy guidelines more often.

Expenses management is not something that we often think of when talking about outsourcing, but it is clearly a discrete finance function where a return on better controls can be visibly achieved in a very short time – much to the dismay of bar owners the world over.

Thursday, 23 August 2007

Posted at 08:00

Business networks are best for small business

I've picked up on a couple of surveys by Datamonitor recently, as the researcher seem to be focusing a lot of attention on outsourcing. A recent study of 500 UK small to medium-sized enterprises (SMEs) found that only 25 per cent of smaller businesses have embraced outsourcing as a strategy that works for them.

Almost 60 per cent of the SMEs surveyed said they could never imagine their IT function will be fully outsourced. One of the interesting observations made by Datamonitor in this study was that there is nothing close to a dominant player in IT services for the SME market. Of those 500 companies surveyed, they had over 100 companies managing network services.

I have commented on this before in this blog, but it's worth reiterating. I don't really think we will reach a position where one or two IT suppliers becomes the outsourcing partner of choice for all SMEs. By their very nature SMEs are smaller and more fragmented, harder to reach, harder to sell to, and often have specific needs that don't quite fit the normal solution.

What we really need is a more established SME-to-SME capability – a business network. This would encourage smaller companies here to engage with smaller companies in Russia, India, China, as well as locally, rather than assuming the big players will now scoop up SME business because they are running out of steam with the big contracts.

Thursday, 23 August 2007

Posted at 18:00

Some thoughts on IT infrastructure outsourcing

Research firm Datamonitor published a report recently that looked at the question of offshoring technical infrastructure. Most of the 150 CIOs and senior IT managers that were questioned said they would rather offshore their infrastructure to Eastern Europe than India. They also indicated a preference for an established Western supplier, rather than an overseas supplier.

This was positioned in much of the media as an anti-India story, or a pro-Eastern Europe story, or just a plain old anti-offshoring story, but isn't this really like teaching your grandmother to suck eggs. Think about it for a moment. Infrastructure has always been important, but in an era that is becoming dominated by virtualisation, services-oriented architecture, Web 2.0, software as a service, and any other acronym that basically means you need immense business flexibility, infrastructure is now absolutely critical.

The key drivers for a successful IT infrastructure site will be all around the quality of the facilities, reliability of the power and cooling systems, telecoms connectivity and so on, and none of these things are linked to labour arbitrage at all so I find it a bit odd that we keep on reading about offshoring and infrastructure in the same sentence. Should we expect the huge server farms in California to be going offshore anytime soon? I don't think so.

Friday, 24 August 2007

Posted at 09:01

The legal ins and outs of outsourcing

It's always nice to be involved in some way in a new book. I am familiar with writing for the internet and communicating through podcasts or super-fast SMS, but I do still enjoy reading books – and writing them. I even collect George Orwell first editions.

So I was pleasantly surprised to be contacted by Bharat Vagadia, who has written Outsourcing to India: A Legal Handbook, because he wanted me to contribute a foreword introducing the book. I reminded Bharat that I am not a lawyer and have no specialist legal knowledge beyond that I get from talking to people in the legal community about the contracting process. Most of my legal knowledge has been gleaned from Inspector Morse or The Bill.

However, he insisted that I write the introduction to the book because he wanted it to appeal to those interested in the legal process of outsourcing to India, but who are not necessarily from the legal profession. So I was pleased to recently receive a copy of the book in the post with my foreword included, but I still think that most of it is a bit too legal for me to understand! But it is well worth a look if you are involved in contracting with Indian firms.

Tuesday, 28 August 2007

Posted at 11:02

Never mind the quality, feel the spam

Now and again dubious service providers, who seem to believe that adding useless comments to my blog will result in heaps of new business, spam this blog. Let's just think about that for a moment. I have not noticed BT or British Airways or Reuters or Virgin Atlantic spamming the blog. It's always some miserable little firm that even the owner's mother has never heard of, spamming away in the failed belief that any publicity is good publicity.

Well, it may have been a genius of the calibre of Oscar Wilde who claimed that 'there is only one thing in life worse than being talked about, and that is not being talked about', but in this case I would have to disagree with the great raconteur. Getting your company talked about because they spam blogs, or Myspace profiles, or YouTube videos is not really a very positive way to drum up publicity.

In fact, it affects the entire outsourcing industry. The seasoned service providers are focused on service – even the major offshore players have stopped crowing about their rates. Everyone has started to accept that for outsourcing to work as a viable long-term business strategy, it has to be through the creation of a genuine partnership between two companies. The nature of that partnership is something that academics have been writing about for years, yet most companies in the industry have paid lip service to the notion – talking of partnership only as part of a sales pitch that relies on slashing costs.

Cost remains a key driver in all aspects of business, but it's good to see the major service providers talking more about risk and expertise these days. I had a chat with a senior IBM executive recently and one of the key things he said was that its customers can get new servers configured and up on their network within 20 minutes. Try achieving that with your old in-house IT department. These are the true measures of flexibility that make it worthwhile to consider outsourcing as a strategy that can take the business somewhere new.

Thursday, 30 August 2007

Posted at 17:01

The NOA awards

This is a quick call to all of you in the industry who have yet to enter the National Outsourcing Association (NOA) annual awards for 2007. The entry closes on 7 September so there is only a week left now.

The NOA insists on people entering for the awards, rather than just having a panel of experts create a shortlist from whatever is going on in the industry. It doesn't cost anything to enter any of the 15 categories and there is no requirement to be a member of the NOA, so there is no reason to not enter – even the application form is pretty simple so it doesn't take long. This whole process is focused on finding and rewarding the best in the industry and it has been steadily getting bigger each year.

The NOA is expecting more than 500 people to turn up in person for the awards ceremony on 18 October and of course there is all the usual media publicity for the winners. I'm a judge and a board member of the NOA, so it might be only natural for me to support and promote the awards, but I would say that this is one of the most 'honest' awards in the entire outsourcing arena.

The whole process is run with a focus on rewarding best practice in outsourcing and not merely as a money-making exercise – all too often some 'industry awards' need you to pay hundreds of dollars for an entry form and then you are hounded to sponsor the gala prizegiving event. The NOA does seek sponsors for the final award ceremony, but that is because feeding and watering 500+ people does not come cheap. If we cover costs then we are happy. The board directors give up a lot of time voluntarily to judge and rank all the entries, and there are some real gems that crop up in this process.

In short, in the outsourcing game this is an award worth getting, but if you don't fill out a form in the next week then you won't even get considered, so go and have a look at the information on the NOA web site for details of how to enter.

Thursday, 30 August 2007

Posted at 17:59

Out(source) of Africa

Africa has yet to make much of an impact in the list of offshore outsourcing destinations, and it's no surprise given the reputation for civil unrest and poor governance in many African nations, but with a total of 53 different countries and growing enthusiasm for hi-tech global services this might all change.

I asked Richard Mwangi, managing director of NorthWest Offshore in Kenya, a few questions about what is going on at present in his part of the world. First, I asked about the lack of exposure and credibility given to Africa, to which he gave quite a pragmatic response.

Mwangi said: 'Remember that an average business process outsourcing (BPO) project in India has 2000 seats, while the whole of Kenya has less than 2000 seats. Instead of trying to change this perception [of poor infrastructure in Africa] the best thing to do is to address the problem and a number of projects in East Africa are at different stages of being realised. However, talking of perceptions my personal experience has been that this changes once people make a personal visit – what you see in the press and what you see in real life tend to be different.'

Mwangi explained to me that Ghana and South Africa are now starting to take off as popular destinations for BPO work – of course he also said that Kenya is the next place to watch. In fact, South Africa is becoming an extremely popular destination for voice-based work due to reduced issues with accent compared to Asian destinations such as India, along with a time zone far closer to that in Europe.

One issue that does need to be rectified is the lack of a trade body to represent the region for IT-enabled services, such as BPO. Nasscom does this well for India and though Africa is of course a collection of many countries, it would serve them well to have some form of unified trade body working in the interests of the region.

When I asked Mwangi about the issue of human resources and the steady stream of graduates we often hear about in India and China, he said: 'African countries might not have the numbers you will find in India and China, but African professionals are as good as the best anywhere else in the world. Many African universities are making a conscious effort to train students for BPO. However, in the African context it's also important to look at productivity and not just absolute labour cost. The cost of internet connectivity and lack of access to capital is a barrier especially when you take into account the educated workforce that is unemployed.'

I really do believe that we are on the cusp of an African services revolution and it will be entrepreneurs such as Richard Mwangi who steer a course for many African nations in the 21st century.

September 2007

Monday, 03 September 2007

Posted at 15:27

A purchase to India

There was news of an interesting acquisition just before the weekend when Indian business process outsourcing firm FirstSource (formerly know as ICICIoneSource) bought MedAssist, a healthcare revenue management firm (debt collector for doctors and hospitals) based in the US. Firstsource spent $330m on the acquisition, once again demonstrating that there are Indian service companies out there that are now prepared to start finding niche service companies in the US or Europe and to secure a pipeline of business by acquisition.

Firstsource can now lay claim to being a provider of healthcare BPO from the US, as it doesn't intend to lay off any of the 1,400 US employees, clearly an extension of its growing global delivery model. The company has already been hiring thousands of Brits in Northern Ireland for contact centre work and importing its methods of managing call centres back to the UK – because its standards are higher than those generally used in Northern Ireland. We are witnessing some extremely rapid growth in the global services marketplace and the money available for acquisition by Indian companies is remarkable.

I predict that it won't be too long before we stop being all that concerned about where a company was founded. It's true that there is still a natural bias against companies from Asia, particularly South Asia. We don't prefix IBM or EDS with 'American', Xansa with 'British' or Capgemini with 'French' all that often – they are accepted as global service companies. As their business brands strengthen and they hire more overseas resource it really will be the same for Firstsource, and Infosys, and Wipro… if they are the best in the business then who cares where they were founded? After all, wasn't HP started in a garage?

Tuesday, 25 September 2007

Posted at 08:00

Rewarding green excellence

I thought it was worth giving a shout of congratulations to IBM for an award it won last night.

It was at a rival to the Computing Awards for Excellence, for which I am a judge this year, but the technology press in London is really just one big happy family so I'm sure Computing won't mind me mentioning the Cnet UK Business Technology Awards, for which I was also a judge.

Unlike the Computing awards there was no specific category focused on outsourcing, but IBM won the Green IT award for its Project Big Green. I've recently had a couple of conversations with Bruce Ross over at the IBM South Bank office and I also interviewed him for a Computing project where he talked a lot about IBM's green initiatives.

I have an issue with most IT green initiatives. Often they seem to involve jetting journalists all over the world on alcohol-fuelled junkets to remote data centres so we can write about how 'green' the tech company really is. Well I think those days are drawing to a close and not a moment too soon, but it's always worth keeping an eye on blogs such as BusinessGreen and Greenbang for all the juicy non-green green stories.

What strikes me as different with IBM is that it really is going through the organisation at a very detailed level and creating a greener company. It's a bit like root canal surgery because there is no area of the company that is not being examined as a part of Project Big Green. The great thing about this for IBM is not that it wins awards or gets press coverage saying how green it is (though I am sure the marketing people don't mind that), but the company becomes the best in the world at taking an organisation and reducing its carbon footprint. That expertise leads to juicy contracts as other major corporations want help in going green, and joy for IBM shareholders as it wins new contracts that are not just focused on how good the company is at delivering IT services, but how good it is at delivering green IT services.

Tuesday, 25 September 2007

Posted at 10:37

More opportunities for government outsourcing?

A new study just out from Kable, the public sector research and events company, shows that UK government spend on IT outsourcing is expected to increase from £74bn in 2007–08 to £100bn in 2012–13. Most of this (£56bn) will be spent on citizen services in 2012–13 as compared to £41bn in 2007–08, while £44bn will be spent on government services in 2012–13 as compared to £33bn in 2007–08.

The study outlines the need for reform and efficiency as the main driver of government outsourcing and a need to reduce ongoing cost. In addition, local government and NHS are expected to continue as the largest spenders on outsourced services, while the education sector is expected to provide the strongest growth to the IT outsourcing spending, primarily due to the Building Schools for the Future programme.

It would be interesting to understand what the figures are for the retained organisation across all government services. I understand that there are some highly sensitive or classified areas of the government IT network that would never be handed off to a supplier, but the growth highlighted by Kable does not seem astonishing to me when put in the context of growth over a five- or six-year period. Anyone would expect the government to be outsourcing more and this seems like a modest increase. What is still contained within the civil service and how the interaction with suppliers might be streamlined might be of more interest.

(Thanks to http://www.globalsourcingnow.com for the tip off).

Tuesday, 25 September 2007

Posted at 15:00

What can the iPod teach us about outsourcing?

Protecting intellectual property (IP) has become a key part of the outsourcing debate, especially as service providers are now offering more valued knowledge services that potentially create value outside the established physical walls of the organisation. Digitised content ends up everywhere and even in our non-work role as consumers, the rules around digital content are unclear. I mean, is it still really illegal to rip a CD that you have bought and paid for to an iPod or have they changed that rule yet?

Though most outsourcing contracts draw up some form of IP protection on a case-by-case basis is it also useful to be aware of what is going on in digital rights management (DRM) – which tends to focus more on the ownership of content such as music or literature. I believe that as we advance more and more into knowledge process outsourcing (KPO) in our part of the business, all the cross-border intellectual property arguments we hear about involving Apple and iTunes will become more relevant to what we are doing in sourcing services, because we are talking about services that create knowledge and content.

A guy I know from my local BCS branch in north London, Jude Umeh, has just written a book about the whole debate over DRM and IP protection and he is going to give a talk about the subject in central London on 23 October (details here). I plan to go and hear what he has to say and to see if there is anything we can learn in our part of the industry from what is going on in the music and entertainment sector. In any case, it will be a good opportunity for a bunch of IT people to see who has got the biggest iPod song list.

Wednesday, 26 September 2007

Posted at 12:59

The Buffalo stance on offshoring

G iven that I live in London, and not New York, The Buffalo News is not often part of my daily reading matter, but I was drawn to a story about Senator Hillary Clinton today because of the links to Indian technology firm Tata Consultancy Services (TCS).

Clinton has been criticised by anti-globalisation and anti-offshoring supporters because four years ago she assisted TCS in coming to the town of Buffalo and opening a local office. The spin at the time was about economic regeneration and how Tata would be employing up to 100 local people from the Buffalo area within two years.

Unfortunately The Buffalo News has reported that TCS currently has only 10 people, with plans to hire around five more. Clearly that's not exactly the economic regeneration promised by the marketing people, but there is another side to the story. When the newspaper asked TCS to explain why it had not created the promised local jobs the company confessed that the biggest problem has been luring people with the right level of skills to Buffalo.

For those without an intimate knowledge of US geography, Buffalo sits on the wind-swept coast of Lake Erie in northern New York State. It's about 400 miles from the lights of New York City and in terms of population it's about the same size as Belfast. So we are not talking about a one-horse town, but even Leeds is twice as large.

So I can understand what TCS is saying and a quick look at the web site does indicate that it has over 50 offices in the US, employing over 10,000 people in well-paid consulting jobs. So it would seem that a lot of the negative briefing is politically motivated, rather than just objective criticism of Clinton. In fact, it seems the TCS story has come to light because another hopeful for the Democrat's presidential campaign nomination, Barack Obama, was briefed that Clinton's 'support for offshoring' could be an issue worth focusing on in the forthcoming campaign.

It takes me back to the presidential campaign of 2004. Offshoring is bad. No, it's good for the economy. No, it takes US jobs away to India and China... here we go again.

October 2007

Thursday, 11 October 2007
Posted at 10:00
The UK economy and globalisation

Macro-economic policy is not something that usually excites me. Though I write about globalisation I am personally more interested in the dynamics of work flowing across borders and people migrating more easily towards work, and especially in the way that my industry – IT – enables and contributes to this change. This concept of a network society is fascinating and truly exciting, it's something that our industry is enabling for every other possible industry and something we should be proud of.

But globalisation – and outsourcing across borders is one component of that process – scares a lot of people. Not just the petrol-bomb wielding protestors who show up at every meeting of the World Trade Organisation (WTO), but normal people who are not as excited about the prospect of a global talent pool.

Firstly the change process means everything is different and less stable that it used to be - who considers they are getting a job for life these days? - and also there is a strong sense of how unfair it is to have to compete with low-cost workers in far-flung locations. We have seen offshoring demonised by many commentators, especially those with a 'patriotic' or local job protection agenda.

So it's interesting to see a new report from the OECD that tries to look at the big picture of the UK economy in the light of how globalisation is changing our nation – including such topics as the real effect of offshoring.

I'm not going to detail the full report on this blog because you have a link here that lets you read it for yourself, but to quickly summarise some of the most important points raised by the report:

- The United Kingdom's welcoming approach to globalisation has contributed to a strong growth performance. GDP per capita is now the third highest in the G7, compared with the lowest 10 years earlier.

- GDP growth has been close to its trend rate of around 2.75 per cent for a number of years, suggesting that the amplitude of the economic cycle is smaller now than in previous decades.

- This strong performance is not only due to the willingness to embrace the opportunities offered by globalisation, but also to sound institutional arrangements for setting monetary and fiscal policy as well as a period of robust trading partner growth.

- Despite offshoring, employment has grown steadily and unemployment is low.

- But the labour market position of many low-skilled workers needs to be further improved. The participation rate of some groups is low and others suffer from poor incentives to progress in work.

The implications are clear to me, and I'm not a student of the dismal science. The economy itself is in reasonable shape, but there are implications for the workforce. People need to be more flexible about work to compete in a more global environment and this can be a particular problem at the lower end of the pay scale, where locals may well pass on low-paid jobs encouraging the migration of those who are prepared to do them. This can create structural unemployment where job vacancies exist, but they are in the wrong place or just no one wants the work on offer.

There is a complex picture emerging of a work environment that will be very different by the time I retire (if I ever can), and the next generation at school today will have no conceptual understanding of the old rules of corporate loyalty – entering a company after graduation and working your way up the ranks. Outsourcing is a process that is facilitating a lot of this change and as that change accelerates it is an exciting place to be involved and focused, but scary too as the sand shifts everyday in this industry – I don't even know what I will be working on in 2008, liberating or terrifying?

Thursday, 11 October 2007

Posted at 12:19

Are you ready?

That bastion of corporate advice, Forbes, just published a great article titled Eight Signs You're Not Ready For Outsourcing. I think it's a really good snapshot of some of the key issues in outsourcing today, and in particular some of the recurring problems I keep hearing over and over again.

Forbes mentions the problem of suppliers not being interested in smaller contracts – even though we know the theory of relationship building, all too often the idea of starting small with plans to grow just doesn't work. The reality can be a supplier that is inflexible, unresponsive, and the account management faces changing all the time.

I've heard about this exact problem last week when someone came to me for advice on supplier selection. They wanted quality and first-class delivery, but the contract size was not going to be enough to interest any of the major IT service companies. The solution is generally to work with some of the second-tier Indian suppliers – they have an excellent quality ethic, but are still hungry for the work.

Forbes also mentions another couple of really important points that often get missed. Your own house needs to be in order before outsourcing and if you want to move fast then you might not want a supplier that is going to follow every single step on the CMM process.

A lot of the processes around quality have been designed using the production line paradigm – eliminating errors on the line to fix errors while it is still reasonable to do so. In rapid iteration agile environments, where you want to get to market quick through a process of trial and error, putting all these robust standards in place can put a block on progress.

I have to confess I don't usually look at Forbes for their outsourcing coverage. In fact I have not read it much at all since I stopped working in the City, but this was an excellent feature with a very clear focus on some real problems in the market at present.

Friday, 12 October 2007

Posted at 11:52

Taking education online

I saw Professor Sadagopan of the International Institute of Information Technology at the Assessment Tomorrow conference in Bangalore giving a lecture today on the future of education and assessment of students in particular. I have known Sadagopan for a few years and I recall visiting the campus of his university on the day it opened. The building was modelled on Stanford in the US and sits directly across the road from the well-known Infosys campus in Bangalore.

It has often been commented on within the outsourcing community that although India has nearly three million graduates entering industry each year, perhaps only 500,000 are ready to be considered for multinational companies. That's because of a combination of English language skills and other communication abilities, in addition to basic academic achievement – there are just a lot of graduates who are not really ready for work. Though this is a problem we also see in the UK, it's on a far greater scale in India.

Professor Sadagopan highlighted some of the key problems faced by India, namely that faculty is leaving education for better-paid opportunities elsewhere just as more students are entering higher education. To say that the Indian education system is getting squeezed is somewhat of an understatement, but he had some interesting ideas on a resolution that doesn't involve the normal government programmes for change.

Sadagopan suggested a much stronger link between the IT industry and He pointed out that Indians are known across the world as teachers. From Alaska to Brazil to the UK, he said that Indians are often viewed as either teachers or IT professionals – so why not link the professions further? The education opportunities are enormous if assessment and testing using technology can move beyond just multi-choice questions and the opportunities for IT are also enormous – just look at the millions of students wanting a better way to engage in India alone.

This idea that education and assessment of students can be delivered remotely and online is one of the golden opportunities for outsourcing over the next decade or so and Professor Sadagopan has put his finger on a key point – India has such a dynamic IT industry and also millions of students. Will India become the global online education hub for the 21st century?

Saturday, 13 October 2007

Posted at 08:00

A little savoir faire

D o you remember studying a language at school? I certainly remember having to study French and being forced to attempt to take oral tests of my linguistic ability by lining up with other students and having to converse with my teacher at a time that suited her. That's pretty much the normal way oral tests are performed – there is always a bottleneck with many more students than teachers and a requirement to conduct the test at exactly the same time – with all the problems of keeping students who have completed the test away from those who are still waiting in line.

So I was interested to talk to Gavin Cooney, chief executive of Irish firm Learnosity, this week at the Assessment Tomorrow conference in Bangalore and learned that there is a completely new way that companies such as his can process oral tests that works far better for both student and teacher.

Learnosity uses a very innovative system that works using mobile phones and instant messaging (IM) tools such as Jabber. Kids can call a special number on the mobile phone and go through a security process to identify who they are before answering a series of questions, which are recorded and analysed. Similarly they can login to the IM system and chat on various topics, with moderators viewing the conversation and advising in real-time, to keep them in the target language. Though the system doesn't use biometric security at present, that kind of voice recognition technology is in the pipeline.

Students can then podcast their own response to how the test went so there is some immediate feedback from the student, followed by a rapid analysis of how they actually performed in the test. In Ireland, the system is used to test Irish language skills at school and students and teachers there report that the use of IT and mobile phone makes the whole process easier and with a far higher level of interaction – though in some cases Learnosity has found that the teachers need a bit of guidance on some of the technology! On an additional plus side for Learnosity, Gavin found that his own Irish has improved since he started delivering these tests for the Irish government.

Learnosity is running high-school exams in this way for several governments now in Ireland and other European countries and as I spoke to Gavin he was en route to Australia to work on a series of tests there. It's a nice time of year to be going down under.

In Australia they offer online testing for many more subjects than just languages and the New South Wales schools board has a very interactive web site that allows students to practice and test themselves in advance of the real exams. More than four million students have tried the practice tests on this web site and Learnosity found that the experience of building the practice environment allowed them to build an even more robust infrastructure for the live testing environment.

One of the amusing aspects of this is that Gavin's company can observe when and how students are practising for tests. It's obvious that most students cram for hours the day before an exam and relax through the weekends immediately prior to exams. We all know this, because we did it ourselves, but it's funny to see the hard data produced by the system.

This whole idea of outsourcing the assessment of students whether for languages or other subjects is certainly a growth area. Computer-based testing has moved a long way from the days of multiple choice tests and given the advantages of this style of testing such as reliability, equality, and transparency, most schools in Australia now prefer testing in this way.

Learnosity has clearly thought about the entire process of testing in great detail. They can cope with visually-impaired kids, physically-disabled kids, dyslexic kids, and even high-school kids who need to take a break from the test to breast-feed! Their environment is very impressive – Gavin claims that they designed it to work for "completely blind Linux lovers", the aim being that if they can get their system working perfectly for such demanding users then able-bodied Windows users are easy to please. The issue of inclusiveness is a serious one though. All kids need access to the exams and so it is not possible to build a system that only caters for 95 per cent of users – it has to work for everyone.

Education and assessment is an area of strong growth in outsourcing and the normal issues of quality delivery are of far greater importance than in regular BPO. When a firm is delivering exams to kids it is absolutely critical that the service works every time – to fail could not only cause a problem for the child taking the exam, but it would probably blow up into a political issue as irate parents call radio talk shows to berate the government for saving a few dollars with online exams. It goes to show that outsourcing could become a political issue in many more ways that just the argument of 'vanishing jobs' alone.

Monday, 15 October 2007

Posted at 13:51

R&D is changing fast

T he conventional wisdom on outsourcing, at least for the past 10 or 15 years, has been that of the core competence theory. In general, stick to what your company does best and outsource the rest. This theory tends to favour keeping high-end activities such as research and development (R&D) local, but a new study just published by US research group Battelle indicates that the R&D market is changing fast.

In terms of effort, funding, and activity – however you measure it – R&D is shifting away from being a US-dominated activity. Even within a decade from now it is far more likely to be split into three geographic distributions; the US, the EU, and India+China (or that awful term Chindia some people insist on using).

Battelle highlights a number of significant reasons why this might be taking place, though one of the most interesting is market access. Companies from the West want to access China and India as markets, not just as sources of cheap labour. One way of doing this is to set up shop in the region and create high-value R&D jobs there, leading to a much more favourable environment when going on to the process of selling in that region.

In fact, it can even be observed that many Indian and Chinese companies are now wealthy enough to be commissioning R&D from the US, giving them credibility when they export their own products to those markets. So the hard and fast concept of national borders preventing the export of higher-value work such as R&D is rapidly disintegrating.

This challenges many of ideas on core competence and the idea that we in the West can continue outsourcing small well-defined parcels of work, while we keep all the R&D for ourselves. In fact, many of these views are linked to some of our general preconceptions about regions in Asia such as India or China. For an excellent factual view on some of these misconceptions, take a look at this video on YouTube of Professor Hans Rosling debunking some 'third world' myths. I just love it early on in the presentation when the professor notes that even chimpanzees could score better than his students.

Monday, 22 October 2007

Posted at 12:39

Is outsourcing recession proof?

With the current economic volatility still ongoing some commentators have been mentioning that dreaded word - recession. In fact, there is probably someone out there counting how many times "recession" is mentioned on blogs like they used to do in newspapers back in the day, so here are six more notches for the recession blog-counter.

Is it possible to not be worried about any future recession? A new survey from EquaTerra indicates that while the recent turmoil in the financial services industry could slow some outsourcing efforts in the short-term, and continue to negatively impact some providers, the longer-term expectation is that outsourcing in this industry will grow as buyers seek to reduce operating costs, avoid investments into new systems and capabilities, shift focus to more strategic activities, and leverage their growing supply of skilled global resources.

Equaterra believes that this trend in financial services illustrates that outsourcing as an industry has become "recession-proof", and that outsourcing is a tool buyers use in "up markets" to improve performance and in "down markets" to reduce costs and remain competitive.

EquaTerra expects this trend to be replicated in other industries that are negatively impacted by economic and demographic factors such as ageing workforces and weak local labour pools. These industries include consumer packaged goods, healthcare, public sector and retail.

This dual-benefit is something that has been long suspected, but it strikes me as a little bit disingenuous. After all, in good market conditions outsourcing is marketed as partnership, reaching out and buying-in expertise. To say it is all about slashing costs is anathema to most service buyers and providers. But perhaps, if the chips are down and a recession is on the way then are cost-reduction measures the only way to go? And if so, then is it really the only reason to outsource?

Monday, 22 October 2007

Posted at 16:00

Congratulations to the winners

The other day I put on my tux and bow tie and headed off to the Brewery in the City for the annual National Outsourcing Association awards for best practice. I hate wearing a bow tie, so I have avoided many awards ceremonies in the past, but this year I have a surfeit of invitations to black tie events. Either I had to buy a new suit and tie or I would develop a new reputation for being about as sociable as a hermit crab.

I won't list all the winners as you can see a list by clicking here. It was a fantastic evening and very well organised by the team at Buffalo Communications, especially Emma Pocock and Kam Perera who both worked really hard to make this event work well. The MC, comedian and radio presenter Fred Macaulay, controlled and humoured the corporate audience very well and the process of giving out the awards went on just long enough to give them the reverence they deserve, but not so long that everyone got bored of hearing yet another list of nominees.

I'd like to give a quick shout of congratulations to the people at the Philippines Embassy in London for winning the award for best offshoring destination. That's one over on the Indians! Also, Stephen Page from the Sapphire Group and his project with Betbrokers (something I wrote about on this blog recently) won the award for being the best outsourcing project of the year – congratulations to everyone at Sapphire for beating off some larger competitors in that category.

Congratulations to everyone who was shortlisted and especially the winners – on to next year when I expect these awards will be even bigger and even better!

Monday, 22 October 2007

Posted at 16:00

Look outside India's big three

It's nice to see that the Indian tech company Patni has just signed a $200m deal with Carphone Warehouse to provide systems integration and technical support services. Patni was already one of Carphone Warehouse's IT suppliers with present functions including legacy systems and CRM, but this is quite a big vote of confidence.

Patni is a good company with capable people. It has hovered around the edge of the mega-suppliers in India for some time, up there with most of the rest, but not getting the general industry recognition of some who have played the branding game better. Let's hope that the very public recognition that a deal of this size with a marque such as Carphone Warehouse means that a lot more people realise there are choices outside the Indian top three – and quite often they are very capable companies that are hungry for the work.

Tuesday, 23 October 2007

Posted at 08:00

Thought leadership in a flat world

You might remember Thomas Friedman's book The World is Flat, published in 2005 and showered with praise ever since. When I wrote Global Services with Richard Sykes earlier this year it was with Friedman in mind – we focused on the practical application of his flat-world theories and how this applied to the IT industry.

Yet, Stephanie Overby has stuck a pin into the flat world bubble in her latest CIO blog by claiming that the world is not flat after all – it is in fact quite complex and we are making it even more so.

The basis of Overby's argument is that instead of life becoming easier and simpler as the flat world encourages services to be traded across borders, we are actually making service delivery more complex.

I have to say I've got some sympathy with her views and here is an observation on why.

When is the last time you went to a conference in London or New York and were completely blown away by a conference presentation or the ideas coming from a non-local service company? We all know they can deliver, the "safe pair of hands" is essential for offshore delivery, but the ability to lead thoughts and ideas is something that's not really possible without a deeper connection than that offered by a contract alone.

I've been in meetings and events recently where people from Capgemini, BT or IBM have said some really interesting things – thinking beyond what they do on a day-to-day basis and forward to what their clients might want next year. It's still quite rare to find yourself in front of a presentation from an Indian or Chinese service provider that does not discard all the stuff about how much money they are making, how many people they employ, who their best customers are and so on. If it happens then do let me know.

Tuesday, 23 October 2007

Posted at 13:00

The value of knowledge

Cognizant Technology Solutions has acquired marketRx, a provider of analytics and related software services, for $135m in cash. Like Cognizant, marketRx is headquartered in the US, though with the majority of its staff based in India. MarketRx focuses on providing services to life science companies in the pharmaceutical, biotechnology and medical devices segments.

This is a good example of a major IT player trying to enter the ever-growing knowledge process outsourcing (KPO) sector, as Cognizant is a 49,000 strong technology company currently getting around half its revenue from financial services. MarketRx was only founded in 2000 and has just 430 employees, with 260 of those in India. Considering most of the value in an analytics company really does lie in the heads of those employed by the company it is interesting to observe that the company has been valued at over $300,000 per employee.

The revenue multiple used for this deal seems quite modest at 3.4, or perhaps it is just modest compared to some of the other hi-tech service companies in India, but I wonder how easy it is to value a KPO company? Should it be by revenue alone or is there some magic sauce that values the potential for knowledge to sell?

Nonetheless, it was a hotly contested auction with others companies from India bidding – including Infosys and Wipro, proving that every IT player sees a future in selling knowledge services.

November 2007

Monday, 05 November 2007

Posted at 11:31

The psychology of outsourcing

Organisational psychology is a subject I find fascinating, ever since I found that the best grades I received in my MBA were for the organisational behaviour module. If sociology is the study of groups of people or society in general and psychology is focused more on the individual, organisational psychology bridges the gap between the disciplines – focusing on the way individuals behave within organisations.

This is an important subject in our present environment. We all know that things are moving faster these days. Everyone is under more pressure at work, and there are those who claim that outsourcing is having a direct impact on the health and wellbeing of some employees.

No, I don't mean the wellbeing of those workers in the UK who fret over the possibility of their job being transferred to a far-flung location. I mean the fact that outsourcing encourages an explicit measurement of service delivery and so the workers delivering the service are suddenly under more pressure than ever – every moment at work can be measured.

This is not news to those in the contact centre industry. I can remember a campaign lead by Channel 4 News about 10 years ago, where they referred to call centres in the UK as 'dark satanic mills'. There were tales of toilet breaks not being allowed, long hours, constant performance checks. This was back in the 1990s well before the present boom in offshore contact centres had begun.

So I found it interesting when I had a chat recently with Payal Shah from the Irish organisational psychology experts Inicio. Inicio has recently started focusing more attention on India and it is using the experience of working in outsourced service centres in Ireland in the high-pressure Indian environment.

Anyone with any experience of human resources in India might be doubtful of what an organisational psychologist can do to make an outsourced team more effective – or less stressed. A typical view is that this is all just woolly fluff geared to making the organisation look like a better place to work, without really improving anything at all.

I asked Payal all these questions and I was impressed by the approach Inicio has taken, which is to take the expertise of a similar industrial environment in Ireland and to apply that to India, where directors of the firm have personal experience. The firm does focus on the individual, but its main concern appears to be in reducing sources of stress or conflict in the working environment. Personal stress from issues such as relationship troubles or addictions may actually be beyond the control of the company, though many employers are starting to help in these areas too.

Inicio's help with planning how to look after human resources by eliminating stress created by the working environment is certainly needed and Payal explained to me how the firm genuinely feels it can quantify what it brings to an outsourcing firm. In short, whatever the services cost will be more than saved through the improvement to the workplace, and given that the biggest problem in the sector is securing the right people and then hanging on to them, I think she might just be right.

Thursday, 08 November 2007

Posted at 13:15

A personal invitation

Last month I mentioned in this blog that I had a new book about to come out - Building a Future with BRICs: The Next Decade for Offshoring. Well, I'm happy to say that it is out in the shops now and also that there is a launch party planned in London for later this month. I'd love it if some readers of this Computing blog could come along to say hello.

It's going to be at 6pm on November 30th at the Nehru centre in Mayfair. I'll be talking about the book and there will be a couple of other speakers there, including the chief executive of Indian technology firm NIIT. We won't drone on for too long though – no more than an hour of chat and discussion about the book before we open the bar and enjoy some drinks and networking.

If you are interested in finding out more and registering for the event then go to this web site. I hope to see you there!

Thursday, 08 November 2007

Posted at 13:19

So here it is, Merry Christmas (well, almost...)

The early bird catches the worm – so the old saying goes. So here we are with two months of the year left to run and already the advisory firm Equaterra (now incorporating Morgan Chambers since the acquisition in September) has started sending out its predictions for outsourcing in 2008. It's the first of the 2008 lists I have seen, but I am expecting them to flood in over the coming weeks.

Anyway, the full list of predictions from Equaterra of the important trends for 2008 is:

• Outsourcing is recession-proof. IT outsourcing Demand in North America will improve in 2008.

• Europe will experience more growth than the US, perhaps because it is at an earlier stage of the outsourcing evolutionary cycle.

• Public sector demand will continue to grow as baby boomers retire and the sector struggles with attracting talent. Shared services and internal transformation in this sector will get stronger.

• Recent turmoil in credit markets will slow outsourcing in the financial services sector in the short term but drive more IT outsourcing in the longer term. Financial services firms will also continue to pursue offshore captives but often within the region rather than in India or China for various regulatory and risk reasons.

• Global multi-shore and multi-provider outsourcing will become more the norm than the exception. This could mean several providers in several regions around the world.

• Indian service providers will set up more local delivery services centres in US and Europe as the Indian market gets impacted by wage inflation; talent attrition; stronger rupee and infrastructure strain.

• Canada's appeal as a near-shore destination will lessen due to currency appreciation.

• A confluence of factors will lead to the expansion of service-delivery capabilities beyond India to regions like Central/South America, Central/Eastern Europe and China.

• Governance of outsourcing deals will become paramount as buyers seek to maximise value and minimise value leakage.

This is a good and broad list of trends, and I believe that they are all important, but it is interesting to observe a few that seem to be missing in action. Almost every IT supplier I talk to at present is also talking about:

• Innovation; how suppliers can work in partnership to drive innovation to their clients

• Green Agenda; how the IT industry has to start taking notice of the corporate carbon footprint and how suppliers are going to have to start dancing to the tune of green service buyers pretty soon

• Web 2.0; how the tools that every teenager is already using are transferring into corporate life and the IT suppliers are at the vanguard of trying to sell this expertise

By the end of the year I'll think of a comprehensive list of my own trend observations to write up for this blog.

Friday, 09 November 2007

Posted at 14:01

A great night out

On Wednesday evening I was out at the Computing Awards for Excellence ceremony. It was a great evening, with Sanjeev Bhaskar cracking jokes about the local tandoori in Battersea and nearly 1,200 people from the IT industry all gathered together for dinner and drinks.

I had a chat to the competitiveness minister, Stephen Timms MP, when I saw him sitting nearby. The minister was there to collect a special award granted by the editor of Computing, Bryan Glick, for his outstanding contribution to the UK IT industry.

Timms is in the right job. With a background before politics of working for companies such as Logica and Ovum, he is well suited to his present role and over the years he has held the IT or ecommerce portfolio – but in politics people change jobs all the time depending on what the party leader requires. It's good to see him coming back to IT now. I reminded him about an interview we had done together in Mumbai back in 2004. That interview was at the Nasscom conference, the big event every February where the entire Indian technology industry all gets together to plan the year ahead.

Timms told me that he had really enjoyed seeing India that time and that he would love to return, especially now he has a focus on the IT industry again, so if the Nasscom conference planners are reading this you know who to invite for 2008.

And on this Indian theme today, happy Diwali to readers over there – enjoy the fireworks!

Friday, 09 November 2007

Posted at 16:00

The green agenda will drive IT offshore

Thomas Friedman writes a regular column in the New York Times (NYT) and is well known throughout the outsourcing community for his book The World is Flat – an exploration of globalisation that takes in offshoring, outsourcing, and a new wave of services along the way.

His NYT column yesterday addressed the questions of the green agenda and how so much IT work is going to be needed to change IT systems so they are all carbon neutral, it should be obvious that a load of offshoring is going to take place. He suggests that India is the natural best destination for that offshoring to take place – for the combination of brains and value.

I agree entirely with his sentiments. It's a fact that customers are going to soon be demanding carbon neutral IT suppliers. Any IT company today that is blundering along not thinking about this is going to be dead in the water when their biggest client calls them up one day and says we can only continue working with carbon neutral suppliers. This is even more important for IT companies with clients that are in energy hungry sectors, such as airlines, utility companies, or transport.

What I'm a bit doubtful of is holding up companies such as Infosys and Satyam as exemplars of this new breed of green company. I have nothing against either of them and I've done lots of things with both of these companies before, but it seems a bit forward to suggest that putting up a few solar panels is expressing leadership towards carbon neutrality.

IBM seems to only get a fleeting mention in the NYT article, yet IBM has very publicly announced its 'Project Big Green' which aims to turn the company inside out – not only going carbon neutral itself, but explicitly learning the best way of being able to advise others because the company has done it itself. The only Indian player I can think of that is actually carbon neutral is ITC Infotech. It is a mid-size organisation, owned by the massive ITC Group. It is already carbon neutral, so how come the company doesn't get a mention?

Friedman is right, but we shouldn't forget that the green agenda can be tapped for media coverage and the 'feel good factor'. It's not good enough to say that your company is green - it needs to be proven.

Monday, 19 November 2007

Posted at 10:06

Innovative habits can improve data centre costs

I attended the 2007 Innovation Forum hosted by Indian tech giant, Tata Consultancy Services today. It was a forum focused on the connection between IT, outsourcing, and innovation – particularly how an IT services group such as TCS can be involved in helping their clients engage with more innovative technologies, rather than just low-cost outsourcing.

TCS has started a collaboration with the London School of Economics to explore how outsourcing can stimulate innovation and professor Jonathan Liebenau from the LSE talked to the forum about some new research he has performed on creating innovation 'habitats'.

I found the presentation by a fairly small company called Cassatt really interesting though. Cassatt has a really exciting system that can control power use in data centres. They are partnering up with TCS to give them the scale to reach out across the world, and TCS clearly gets access to the innovative nature of the Cassatt solution so it looks like a good partnership.

Steve Oberlin, Chief Scientist at Cassatt, described some stats that set the scene for those who still doubt that efforts to explore data centre efficiency are worthwhile. He said that about $7.2bn was spent on running data centres in 2005 and the power requirements are going up by about 8-20% per year. A really interesting fact though is that the present 3-year cost of powering a server is now more than the cost of a server itself. That kind of fact does emphasise how important this can be – not just for creating a green 'image' for the company, but for the possibility to explore the creation of extensive new efficiencies.

Essentially, idle servers use a lot of power. We pay to heat them up and we pay to cool them down again, so active power management through the use of a service such as Cassatt makes a lot of sense. By outsourcing the power management of a data centre to a company such as theirs you can introduce business rules that ensure servers are switched off when not needed for any business activity, switched off when idle, switched off when power emergencies occur, and all the requirements for applications to be closed down gracefully can all be handled – of course servers can't just be shut down like the lights in an office!

Services like that offered by Cassatt are clearly making the issue of how to explore green infrastructure a lot easier to manage and the great thing is that by actively taking some time to look at the efficiency of your infrastructure footprint, you will probably end up saving money and making what you have in the data centre perform better.

Wednesday, 21 November 2007

Posted at 15:52

Outsourcing is more than a cost-cutting strategy

One of those dirty little secrets about outsourcing has finally been challenged. The slash 'n' burn strategy.

Although everyone in the industry hates to admit it, the reason most executives have historically considered outsourcing is to reduce or control cost. That's pretty much it. Yes, every IT supplier has a suite of research to indicate how the outsourcing model gives access to a global resource pool of better educated people with up to date skills and the immediacy of being able to scale up and down the resource requirement as needed. But regardless of all these strategic reasons for using outsourcing as a business model, most executives would still summarise it as a cost reduction exercise.

However, the latest research from recruitment firm Harvey Nash indicates that the theory and potential for outsourcing may finally have caught up with the reality. Three-quarters of the 650 UK-based CIOs surveyed by Harvey Nash indicate that flexibility and responsiveness are the key benefits they are looking for when outsourcing. This is a strong demonstration of outsourcing kicking away from the cut-cost approach to an access-to-experts strategy.

In fact, half of the surveyed CIOs indicated that more than ten per cent of their entire budget would be spent on IT outsourcing, so it's becoming a serious chunk of the entire IT industry. It cannot be denied that a lot of companies explore outsourcing when they need to reduce cost, but to see a survey like this with quite a large sample of CIOs who – in the majority – are focused on flexibility rather than cost demonstrates that outsourcing is really maturing as a strategy.

December 2007

Monday, 03 December 2007

Posted at 09:34

They shoot, they score...

"**C**ome on, you Satyam!" No, I haven't got 'Villa fever', that well known scourge of Computing reporters. Instead, something interesting has happened in the world of sports sponsorship. Indian technology giant Satyam has been appointed the IT service provider to the FIFA 2010 and 2014 football world cups.

I almost feel in two minds about the messaging the deal sends out. On one hand, it's a great thing to see one of the Indian technology companies raising their visibility as the technology partner to a major international sporting event. Who can forget the little IBM logo whenever the Wimbledon scores pop up? No doubt Satyam will be doing the same with their logo all over the results in South Africa 2010 and Brazil 2014.

It does show a growing maturity from one of the Indian companies. It's no longer good enough for a major global company to just take out a few adverts in The Economist and expect business to fall at your feet, you need to create a sense of empathy and trust – which is even more important as the Indian companies are still breaking away from the cheap offshoring destination tag. Being as visible as the technology partner for the World Cup will give a huge boost to Satyam's reputation in the market and will probably be the first slide on all of their business development slide packs for years to come – in much the same way that Atos Origin talks about their Olympic games contract.

So on the whole, I think it's a great thing to see this happening. The barbarians really are at the gate for the established IT players if they can no longer claim that they are worth more money because they have that certain 'X factor' – Satyam will no doubt be flying clients down to South Africa to watch that 'X factor' for themselves, though it might be 'XXX factor' if John Terry is involved.

But then on the other hand, this is football. When board level people do sport it's usually golf, cricket, tennis, rugby... all those sports where it's possible to get a nice box and do some work as the game takes place, without needing to join in the jeers against the blind referee. It's a class thing isn't it? Perhaps the world cup might be different, but I doubt it.

Tuesday, 04 December 2007

Posted at 09:04

The real cost of the Pru's outsourcing deal with Capita

So after all the kerfuffle earlier this year when it became clear that some cost saving was essential, but it was not really defined where, UK insurance giant Prudential has now announced a major deal with Capita.

The aim is to initially hit some quite short-term cost reduction targets all focused around 2010 and it will involve the transfer of 3,000 people to Capita, with some of them working for the Pru in the UK and some in India. It's not quite the disaster scenario we might expect the tabloids to write about.

First, Prudential has already got extensive operations offshore in Mumbai and so the processes are already shared between the UK and India, so the outsourcing process here will actually see staff in both countries shift to become employees of Capita.

The deal with Capita is worth £722m over a 15-year period and the carrot for the Pru is an immediate £60m a year saving, helping to deliver all the savings that had been promised back in March.

I've been to the Prudential centre in Mumbai and I was impressed by what I saw, so it's clear that Capita have got themselves quite an asset from Prudential at a time when the Pru just wanted to restructure and start saving some cash. It seems interesting that with their own deep experience of offshoring processes to India and their own internal team, Prudential could not make their own operations work more effectively and now finds the need to outsource everything.

They appeared to be one of the insurance companies with good experience of delivering internal services from offshore, so are they just struggling to get someone to shake up the internal processes or are they just so out of control it's easier to get a third party to take over?

Wednesday, 05 December 2007

Posted at 16:03

The future of outsourcing is just around the corner

LogicaCMG have been continuing their research relationship with the London School of Economics and in particular Professor Leslie Willcocks. Willcocks is well known to all of us in the outsourcing business as he is a prolific author, with something like 25 books on sourcing strategy to his name and he still holds down a day job as professor of technology work and globalisation at the LSE.

'Building Core Retained Capabilities' is the title of the new research paper published this week. It investigates one of the key longer-term issues of outsourcing, what happens to your own company and the retained skills if you always buy in expertise from outside?

Willcocks believes that senior managers must identify and retain key skills and core competencies in their in-house teams if they are to truly benefit from the relationship with their outsourcing supplier. The research shows that organisations are currently prioritising short term cost reductions over an "invest to save" strategy, resulting in a number of outsourcing projects developing problems such as loss of control, inadequate service, and constant renegotiation due to a lack of strong internal leadership and project management.

As organisations outsource more and more to achieve strategic advantage [by 2012 about 58 per cent of the average corporation's IT budget will be with outsourcing suppliers], it is crucial that they resource properly internally. The research identifies nine core capabilities that must be equally applied to ensure long-term business performance and strategic advantage from IT and business outsourcing. These capabilities include leadership, business systems thinking, relationship building, architectural planning and design and informed buying, which lean towards softer business skills.

It's worth listening to voices such as this. When the benefits of outsourcing are only ever considered over the life of a business plan it ignores the longer-term effects on the organisation, but as Willcocks demonstrates with his research, the future can arrive a lot sooner than you expect if you don't plan for it.

Friday, 07 December 2007

Posted at 10:05

Offshoring can help boost research & development

The giant US-based pharmaceutical company Pfizer has announced that they are considering a major shift of their manufacturing processes to India and China. At present, the plans are just on the drawing board, but as the exploration of these ideas has been made public to investors it is clear that it is more a case of when and where, rather than if.

The proposals suggest that at least 30 per cent of their drugs could be contract produced in offshore locations, up from about 15 per cent that is presently outsourced. Pfizer is seeking to rein in costs at present as they are also reducing the size of its workforce as well as announcing this intention to increase the scale of their outsourced manufacturing operations.

The only real question is why they don't just go for an almost entirely offshore manufacturing operation? The real value in a company like Pfizer lies in their ability to research and develop new drugs that improve medical treatment or enhance quality of life in some way. If they can't go on achieving success by researching and creating new drugs then they will cease to exist.

The process of manufacturing the pills is pretty mundane in comparison to the R&D operation, so if the company is in need of some financial prudence at present then why not fire all the big guns at research and get the manufacturing up to 95 per cent outsourced?

Monday, 10 December 2007

Posted at 11:09

Managing economic and social development

A week last Friday in Mayfair, there was a crowd assembled to hear me talk about my new book 'Building a Future with BRICs: The Next Decade for Offshoring'. They had gathered at the Nehru Centre for the official launch of the new book and to hear me talking about the book, along with Arvind Thakur talking about the knowledge century.

Arvind is CEO of NIIT Technologies and they stumped up for the cost of organising the book launch – so thanks go to them for ensuring everyone was fed and watered. The launch event went really well and I had a lot of people asking me questions about the book and the topic.

What became very clear is that there is an immense gulf between economic and social development. Any development expert can tell you this, and it's often why some states appear to be economically powerful, but remain quite immature and authoritarian at a social level. Countries with a single dominant political party such as Japan or Singapore immediately spring to mind, though of course these are not the only examples.

Just about all the questions I was asked at the reception after the book launch was how a country like India can continue its immense economic growth when there are social issues affecting hundreds of millions of people not really being addressed. India has a mature democracy – often quoted as the largest in the world – yet a large proportion of the economy is agrarian, leading to a huge dependence on the monsoon for wealth each year.

In addition, this agrarian economy is extremely poor when contrasted to the hi-tech metro-based people we might interact with in the IT industry. The IT industry has also been pretty agnostic about the caste system and gender equality, but other areas of society are not so liberal. How on earth can the economic changes proposed within the BRICs thesis affect people who have never even heard of it?

Everyone who bombarded these questions at me had valid points, and with slight modifications they could also be asked of the other BRICs nations. These nation states are grouped together because of their former developing status and their desire to embrace global capitalism and to grow and enrich their people. Unfortunately, there is no easy answer to how to deal with social change and tradition as a country becomes richer.

Political scientists across the world are still grappling with the problem of how authoritarian a state can be while still granting democratic freedom to its citizens. India has been on a remarkable journey since economic liberalisation in the early 1990s. Changing a social structure developed over centuries or millennia will be difficult, but if it can happen anywhere then it will happen in India.

Wednesday, 12 December 2007

Posted at 11:26

When outsourcing is just plain stupid

This blog is generally supportive of outsourcing as a strategy, but I like to be objective when organisations do outsource - because it is not always appropriate. Sometimes it's just plain stupid.

Charnwood Borough Council in Loughborough has come under fire from unions such as Unison recently for its plans to outsource services such as HR and benefits to third-party companies. There have even been noisy protests outside the local town hall.

I have to confess some sympathy for the union this time. The council openly confesses that its objective is to cut costs without cutting services – the old chestnut trotted out by elected officials the world over. The target is just a 10 per cent reduction; not so much a great leap forward, more like a timid step.

First, handing all your services over to the third party just to slash costs is entirely the wrong approach to take anyway, not least because it sends a message to the supplier that cost of service – rather than service quality – is your primary driver. Second, how much time, effort, and risk is involved in the outsourcing process and is it worth taking that risk for a potential 10 per cent reduction, that is only a target anyway?

It seems a shame to listen to council leaders talking of outsourcing as a panacea for their service provision. We all know how bureaucratic and unfocused some local authorities can be, so it is true that outsourcing to specialist providers really can work well for councils, but if this council takes such a simplistic approach to planning the way it delivers services then it deserves to suffer at the ballot box come the next election.

Thursday, 13 December 2007
Posted at 08:00
Down the pub

Take a look at these points and think for a moment:

- India remains the most popular destination for offshore outsourcing.
- But, there are some other credible destinations offering high-tech services such as Russia, Brazil and China.
- Spending on offshoring continues to rise and the US is probably the highest spending nation in the world.
- Companies are considering the use of globally diverse delivery rather than just using an outsourced service from one location only (spreading it around a bit).

Do these gems look like the kind of insights you might pay through the nose for, or just the common knowledge of anyone with a passing interest in outsourcing? Well, as you might have guessed, these are the headline insights from the latest report on offshoring by analyst Gartner.

I don't really have anything against Gartner. I have quoted from its research myself in the past, but if an analyst is going to launch a major new research report and charge a hefty fee for access to the detailed research then don't you think you might expect the findings to be a bit more than could be gleaned from a pub conversation with any call centre agent?

Tuesday, 18 December 2007

Posted at 10:23

What suppliers want

The outsourcing advisory firm Alsbridge just published an interesting research note that takes the view of the supplier rather than buyer.

As anyone who reads any outsourcing research knows, most advice is geared to the buyer – how to get the best deal, what supplier to select, how to exit a contract, and so on. Everything seems to be designed for the buyer and I guess that's understandable as they hold the purse strings. Who cares about the poor old supplier?

Well Alsbridge went out and spoke to a whole bunch of suppliers about some of their issues in the marketplace at present and they got some interesting results. You can read the research note for yourself here, but I want to just flag up one comment they made as I think it is very perspicacious.

When asked what suppliers want most from the relationships with their clients, the key issue they responded with was that the client and supplier should have both mutual respect and mutual responsibility.

These comments are important and worth focusing on. The typical 'hardball' approach to vendor selection does not encourage respect. In fact, the selection process is more often than not adversarial rather than respectful. The question of a client having to take some responsibility for the quality of their own programme management is another critical comment. How many times has outsourcing gone wrong, not because of a hopeless supplier, but because the company buying the service just can't interact with the supplier?

I hope Alsbridge take some time to focus on this single issue alone in their next supplier research project because it is an area worth exploring in more detail.

January 2008

Monday, 07 January 2008

Posted at 09:59

The year ahead in outsourcing

First, I'd like to wish all my blog readers a happy new year. I've been away over the Christmas period and I'm now back in action so the blog will spring to life once more for 2008. What better way to start the year than to take a look at some of the outsourcing trends that might be making the news in 2008?

Some commentators have noted that the biggest trend in outsourcing this year is that there is no change, a steady-as-she-goes approach. In some ways that is true because the market is maturing, with both buyers and suppliers getting better at what they do and creating fewer surprises, but there are a few changes I predict this year.

First, let's look at some of those 'no changes' to kick off the predictions. The US dollar exchange rate will continue to be an issue for many service companies billing in dollars and with costs in another currency. More mergers or acquisition activity can be expected – maybe this is the year one of the Indian majors will buy into the big league as rumours continue to suggest? The Indian technology firms will certainly continue their exploration of the consulting territory and buyers will insist on more flexible contracts.

So far, so similar to 2007. There are some new developments such as remote infrastructure management starting to grow and develop in importance now many of the offshore players are developing in stature, but I think the real story in outsourcing for this year will be the impact of the green agenda.

In most cases, companies that are overtly going green and examining the impact of their organisation on the environment are dealing directly with consumers. Consumers are becoming more concerned about the environment and those companies are responding to this consumer demand. The retailer Marks & Spencer has pledged to be carbon neutral by 2012. The supermarket Tesco plans to include carbon footprint labelling on all its products soon. Online bank First Direct installed new technology to reduce its use of electricity.

And looking beyond retailers and banks, the travel sector has the most to lose by not being seen as green by consumers. Airlines such as EasyJet are working hard to convince passengers that they can still fly and have a clear conscience.

The consumer is demanding these measures and pledges by socially aware companies. So how does that affect the outsourcing market? It's very simple, because Marks & Spencer buys services from other companies, as Tesco does, as First Direct does. Every company sits in a supply chain, but where outsourcing contracts are involved it is becoming more common now for these socially responsible companies to insist on the same behaviour from their suppliers. If suppliers have not seen a request for proposal yet insisting on a statement of their green credential yet then they certainly will in 2008.

One trend that I foresee stalling in 2008 is the fledging African outsourcing story. I have talked about the opportunities in Africa before and though nothing has fundamentally changed, when stories such as the crisis of democracy in Kenya sit at the top of the news agenda it does not give foreign investors confidence to try out a new market for services. I was talking to The Times last month about opportunities for Kenya and frankly it looks a bit optimistic now. I mean, if you were exploring regions to work with right now and your job depended on getting it right then would Kenya still be on your list of places to visit?

Friday, 11 January 2008

Posted at 16:05

Get your value outsourcing deals here...

A new survey from the business process outsourcing (BPO) company Syntel reveals that more than half (53 per cent to be precise) of companies plan to increase outsourcing spending in 2008, up from 38 per cent in 2006 and 48 per cent in 2007. This was a survey of 250 IT professionals, presumably in the US as that's where Syntel is based.

Commenting on the new survey, Bharat Desai, chief executive of Syntel, said: "In a weak or uncertain economy, companies look for technology solutions that will increase productivity, efficiency and savings."

We all know what he is getting at. You can't pick up a newspaper or listen to the business news on the radio these days without finding some concern that we are about to enter a global economic slowdown.

The credit crunch in the US that leaped the Atlantic and subsequently caused a run on our very own Northern Rock bank is contributing to fears that a global recession is on the way.

Yet, the outsourcing suppliers seem to be rubbing their hands together. When times are good, big companies engage in strategic outsourcing largesse to improve their service offering and when times are hard they use outsourcing to cut costs to the bone, so the suppliers might argue that it's a case of "heads I win, tails you lose" as far as they are concerned.

This feels like is has to be a step backwards for the industry in general. How many times have we all listened to the supplier community tell us vehemently that outsourcing is not about cost control, it's about flexibility, access to improved services etc, etc... If a recession really is on the way then it would seem that there should be a new boom in offshoring, as companies that are still shy about the process decide to explore it just to save money. Which torpedoes the notion that offshoring can really be about anything more than just labour cost arbitrage.

So does that mean that the marketing efforts, advertising, and attempts to build credibility by the offshore suppliers are all wasted? Only time will tell, but it remains a fact that the original strategy of Tesco supermarkets, as defined by its founder Sir Jack Cohen, was "pile 'em high and sell 'em cheap". It worked for Tesco, but are we really heading into a world of nothing more than "value" outsourcing?

Wednesday, 16 January 2008

Posted at 15:36

I will buy with you, sell with you, outsource with you

We focus a lot of time on justifying the various reasons for outsourcing in a defensive way, as if it is a strategy that needs to be defended from critics, yet there are many examples of outsourcing that have improved the business model for an organisation completely. These examples show that by working in partnership with an expert, you can improve your business – not just cut costs.

Take that bastion of the English arts, the Royal Shakespeare Company (RSC); the world-famous theatre company focused on plays produced by the bard of Stratford. The outward-facing image of an organisation with its focus on literature that is 400 years old hardly seems like a good place to find best practice in outsourcing, but think again.

Accenture has been using specialist data-mining software from KXEN to help boost audience numbers for the RSC at its base in Stratford-upon-Avon and for its London shows. Accenture has been able to create a system that segments the potential audience for different shows, allowing the RSC to target the audience better when tickets go on sale. The improved booking patterns are impressive with a 50 per cent rise in ticket buyers at the Stratford-upon-Avon theatre, a more than 70 per cent increase in regular attendees and significantly earlier sell-outs for London bookings.

Since asking Accenture to help, the RSC has even found it easier to plan future performances – as it understands the potential audience better than before. The audiences the RSC can target are now more clear-cut, and it has become possible to tell exactly when to communicate with different groups to maximise the response.

The RSC employs more than 700 people and sells more than a million tickets a year for shows produced by the company, so it is an arts juggernaut that depends on big sales for investment in future productions. Thanks to interesting and innovative projects like this, the company can hopefully keep any tragedy on the stage.

Friday, 18 January 2008

Posted at 10:03

Some things you can't outsource (Computing editor says: "I agree")

Shock news from the US for journalists the world over. Shocking enough perhaps to make the hacks in the Computing office choke over a pint in their local Soho pub. The Miami Herald, a newspaper with no less than 19 Pulitzer prizes to its name, has considered offshoring journalist jobs to India.

It's true that India has a lot of skilled journalists that use English in their professional life and I'm sure they are generally cheaper than those employed in Miami, but what's the deal? The Herald felt that offshore journalists could edit some of the more formulaic pages in the newspaper, such as the classified ads and community news. This would then leave the local stringers to focus on local stories.

In theory it sounds like a good idea. After all, Reuters already use this model for some of their own journalism. Many – admittedly quite formulaic – news stories about corporate results are churned out by their news team in India for consumption the world over. However, could it work for a community newspaper?

After consideration the Herald decided it wouldn't work, even on a limited basis. It's obvious why. The more local and community focused those pages are, the more essential it becomes to be closer to the community – otherwise how on earth can the editor understand if information is right or wrong? Offshoring just can't work in this type of scenario – though there may be some scope for certain types of editing or typesetting within the industry.

Additionally, style is a funny thing and does not travel well. Anyone who has read a business newspaper in India will know this. Contrast the use of English in the Economic Times in India with the Financial Times in the UK. Perhaps it is just my own personal preference (because I am English), but I hate reading news stories that are punctuated with constant acronyms and unexplained jargon. Give me the self-deprecation of Jonathan Guthrie any day please.

Friday, 18 January 2008

Posted at 16:00

Thinking small

Interesting to observe that as all the Indian IT companies set their sights on the big boys in the technology service sector, CSC is looking the other way. Last year, CSC launched a new programme called Project Accelerate aimed at competing head on with the Indian firms on smaller deals, focused on the $50m to $350m range. They see this mid-market focus as now being of increasing importance as the days of the mega-deal wither away.

As we know, the big players who might consider themselves ready for the huge multibillion-dollar deal have probably already explored that option - try finding a Fortune 100 company that is not already outsourcing now - so it's true that the mid-market is ready for growth. CSC might be onto something.

Tuesday, 22 January 2008

Posted at 10:03

Not a Mickey Mouse issue

I'm staying at Disney World in Florida right now and looking out of my hotel window at some gorgeous January sunshine. Now this really is a good place to be in the middle of winter. The reason for being here is that the annual Lotusphere conference is taking place here in Orlando – a gathering of over 5,000 industry experts and techies, all with an interest in what Lotus is up to for the coming year.

My own experience with tools such as Notes has left me with mixed views on Lotus. It's always felt a bit clunky to me, a bit too much of the "fat client" that we should have left behind ages ago, but though I am still only in the first day of the conference I can see that the company is changing fast.

I'll write some more on this in detail over the next few days where it's relevant to this blog, but the key message I'm seeing is that Lotus is trying to stake out a place for itself as the corporate partner of choice for anyone interested in collaborative and global work environments – clearly that's an important message for anyone involved in global IT services

I know that this used to be the case ages ago with tools such as Notes and Sametime, but new tools are being constructed and released at a pretty fast pace now, with Notes as the framework that holds everything together. My view is that Lotus sees a new generation of users that are going to build their own solutions anyway using publicly available tools on the internet – like using Facebook when at work for social networking. Having thousands of employees all building their own solutions doesn't help anyone, even if their intentions are good, so it seems like the Lotus mantra is to take the open tools of the teenager and to get them inside the corporate environment.

It's an important place to aim for and could certainly give the company an entirely new relevance in a Web 2.0-enabled global services environment. As companies outsource more and therefore collaborate on projects across company borders and national borders, we all need better tools – this stuff can't be managed by email alone for much longer. It's not possible to get anything done when managers are fighting off hundreds of irrelevant emails per day.

Tuesday, 22 January 2008

Posted at 15:00

A very expensive consultant

Indian IT services supplier Satyam has purchased Bridge Strategy Group, a Chicago-based management consulting firm. It's a $35m all-cash deal that adds 36 management consultants to the ranks of Satyam, boosting its ability to deliver high-end management consultancy in the US.

Satyam has announced this purchase with the usual platitudes: enhancing leadership capabilities, strengthening the brand, adding higher value service offerings, but perhaps I'm missing something?

This is an all-cash deal. So that means the company just paid about a million dollars for each new employee. I appreciate that given the nature of management consulting most of the value lies in the head of each one of those consultants, but that is also the danger in purchasing this type of company. What happens if those guys and girls don't like working for Satyam and they walk?

Satyam plans to continue using the Bridge brand in the US, but anyone who is an existing or potential customer will know that the company is really just a subsidiary of Satyam now. That can be seen as a positive - access to a large resource pool, proven expertise etc - or a negative - they can no longer give an impartial recommendation about the best place to get some IT work done.

It seems like the team at Bridge has negotiated a great deal, but I'm not sure how this helps Satyam to start competing with the likes of Infosys and TCS – who are both well down the road of developing their consulting offering, but in a more organic fashion. If they can afford to throw a few million around here and there then why not go for some big name hires and develop the consulting service more organically? It takes guts to do it because there will be a long lead before the business rolls in, but in the long term surely that is where the real value lies, building your own brand to be a trusted source of advice.

Wednesday, 30 January 2008

Posted at 09:48

Testing, testing

I recently helped the British Computer Society (BCS) put together an event that will take place at the BCS offices in Covent Garden, London, on 11 February. It's focused on the globalisation of software testing and should be an interesting exploration of whether you really can outsource testing to an offshore location.

This is an area that the offshore players are all now exploring and so I brought together the BCS to provide their expertise of the industry, with the Indian technology firm Tata Consultancy Services, to provide some case studies of what is possible through offshoring. The head of testing from Carphone Warehouse will be there to talk about his own experience of offshoring and whether it can really work for testing.

It should be an interesting debate, with all sides of the debate represented and plenty of time for audience participation. It is free so please do come along and take part.

February 2008

Monday, 11 February 2008

Posted at 12:03

Good morning Madam President

I'm sitting in the Sofitel hotel in Manila right now enjoying some fresh mango at 4am – because I'm jet-lagged. I only got in last night and within minutes of arriving at the hotel I was already whisked off to a welcome reception for speakers at the e-Services conference, taking place here in Manila for the next two days.

The cold drinks were certainly welcome and it was good to meet everyone who will be sharing the speaker platform, but I was feeling incredibly tired – travelling from Saturday morning in London to Sunday evening in Manila. Then, just as I was going to slope off to my room to get some sleep, one of the hosts came over to me: "We have seated you with the Philippines president in the morning. So you can talk to her about how to make the region more attractive for outsourcing."

That's nice. Although, my name badge actually highlights that I am from the UK National Outsourcing Association, reminding me that I really should write a book called the Outsourcer's Apprentice at some point.

It will be a pleasure to meet the president in the morning, but given my present frame of mind, I might be half asleep by 10am.

Thursday, 14 February 2008

Posted at 09:10

A big thank you

As you might recall from an earlier blog, I left the UK without a visa to enter India and still I have managed to get into Mumbai so I can report from the Nasscom conference here. I just wanted to ensure that the team at Tholons in the Philippines got a big thank you on the blog for making sure that this was possible.

They took my passport away and with the help of the commercial team at the embassy of India in Manila, they managed to get my visa turned around within 24 hours. This is a process that usually takes six days and requires a personal visit to the embassy, yet I managed to carry on working at the conference in Manila while the Tholons team did all the running around for me.

Maybe I should forget to renew my visa more often, as it ended up to be a far easier process than usual!

Thursday, 14 February 2008

Posted at 11:07

A buzz about the Philippines

I just flew into Mumbai in India, after a journey involving four countries in one day. I had breakfast in the Philippines, lunch in Hong Kong then my plane to India stopped to pick up more people at Bangkok in Thailand. That's pretty good going even for me and I've done a fair few air miles in my time. I'm going to be really pleased to get back home and to have a pint at the Castle Inn in Ealing without having to remember what flight I am on the next morning and where I put the ticket. In fact, I could not even find my air ticket this morning, but given that everything is electronic these days I could at least show the security guard at Manila airport an Apple Macbook screen image showing my ticket. Luckily she believed me.

The annual Nasscom show launched this evening in Mumbai. I missed the opening party because I was travelling today, but the meat of the conference is across the next two days anyway. I'm getting ready to record a lot of interviews and to capture some thoughts on what is really going on in India at present. I've already had some text messages from people at the opening ceremony though so I know the Indian tech firm NIIT has 6ft high posters of my image on their stand! That's because they were mentioned a few times in the book I wrote last year with Dr

Richard Sykes. It will be nice to get my photo taken by these posters, I guess!

I want to mention a few words on the Philippines before I switch entirely to what is going on at Nasscom. I have some interviews and notes that I'm going to refer back to at the weekend so I'll blog a bit more once I review my notes, but as a quick and initial observation I am leaving the place very impressed by what they are doing there. The government is incredibly supportive of the technology and hi-tech services industry. They see it going from a standing start at the millennium to being worth 11 per cent of GDP by the end of this decade so it's no wonder they are rolling out the red carpet for anyone ready to invest there.

The physical infrastructure in the Philippines is a lot better than India; the city streets are covered with smooth asphalt rather than the craters you bounce across on the way to an Indian hotel. It's also quite a bit more inviting to the western visitor. Starbucks branches can be found on most city corners and other little cultural connections crop up making the place feel very inviting. Over the past few days I've found loads of people just coming to chat to me about England – quite often about things like the Premier League, or the girl on the Sofitel hotel reception desk telling me about her holiday in London last year. To be honest I think the only place I have ever felt the people being similarly friendly to foreign visitors and investors was Thailand.

And it's not just about the people being friendly - the companies are getting serious too. Captive centres – multinationals opening their own local facilities – dominate the Philippines at present, so there are no well-known home-grown companies yet, but they are trying. I spoke to several companies working on both software and services and some were doing really interesting work, often for well-known clients in Europe and the US. What they really need to do is just boost their own brand and the brand of the region itself – something India has been phenomenally successful at doing over the past decade.

I think they will get there. There is a buzz in the air about what they are doing in the Philippines and the government really has a strong plan in place to help support the industry, from working with universities to improving infrastructure in dozens of smaller cities so the work can be spread throughout the county – about 80 per cent of this business is in Manila right now. I'm looking forward to returning soon if I can find some projects out there that are interesting for me to work on.

Friday, 15 February 2008

Posted at 10:19

Toilet trouble

L ast night Nasscom made various awards to the great and good around the world, for their contribution to the Indian technology and service industry over the past year. Various international business leaders such as Willie Walsh of British Airways, and John Chambers of Cisco received awards, along with local heroes such as Ratan Tata.

These awards are well respected and the recipients are certainly worthy. These are people generating thousands of jobs in India, and investing hundreds of millions of dollars (or even billions in some cases) in the country.

When Willie Walsh appeared on screen to accept his award - he couldn't make it in person, but the BA chief information officer Paul Coby did come and accept it on his behalf - the chatter in the crowd turned to the amazing efforts of the BA flight crew who recently managed to avert disaster by crash-landing their Boeing 777 on a Heathrow runway, even though the engines had failed several miles from the airport. Hundreds of tons of steel should not glide – in my personal view those pilots are incredible.

The Indian people around me at the awards thought that the crew were absolute heroes. When I mentioned that it looks like some of the passengers might be trying to sue BA for compensation, they could not comprehend it – they felt the passengers should be grateful to be alive. Certainly an interesting cultural difference and perhaps a sorry example of Britain coasting down the US path to ambulance-chasing litigation.

On a lighter note though, I noticed a couple of differences about the awards this year, and you could say they are connected. The bar stayed open during the award ceremony itself. In past years, the moment people start accepting their awards the bar has closed and opened again once the awards are all handed out. Presumably, this is to ensure everyone takes a seat and watches the show, rather than hanging around at the back with the barflies and reprobates.

I was hanging around chatting to the Xansa team, now owned by Steria and being rebranded to Steria soon. Hilary Robertson and I made several runs to the bar prior to the awards starting, scooping up enough wine and beer to last the table through the awards, only to find that the bar did not actually close this year so we had to work our way through an entire table full of drinks. It's a hard life, but we managed it.

Now for the connected item, usually there are more than enough toilets available at this event. This is a dinner for about two thousand people and with the bar being open for longer, one might assume an increased need for toilets this year, but it seemed that they reduced them. I only found six, in total, for boys and girls. Perhaps I just missed the others, but the lines of men with crossed legs made me think that the organisers should have exercised some joined-up thinking. More beer is always welcome, but make sure the number of cubicles also increases in future please!

Friday, 15 February 2008

Posted at 10:24

India gets the jitters over Western economic problems

So here we are at the Nasscom conference once again. I've been going to this conference for the past six years, watching each year as the entire Indian technology industry rails against some injustice, or just enjoys the moment. My earlier visits to this conference were against a backdrop of violent anti-offshoring protests in the UK and US. How times change.

Something I noticed last year was that there seems to be less of a unifying theme at the conference, possibly as the industry matures. This is even more obvious to me this year, although some people have insisted to me that innovation is the theme for 2008, but I'm afraid that's a bit too nebulous. I don't mean the theme on the programme, I mean what everyone is talking about in the coffee shops and bars around the conference venue.

I walked into this event thinking that the general theme might be quite negative this year. Stock prices in the sector have been struggling as margins have been eroded by the unfavourable dollar to rupee exchange rate. Add that to a general fear of economic slowdown in the West and you might expect a cloud or two to be hanging over some of the participants, but in general the mood has been upbeat. Companies either see a downturn in the US as an opportunity to get out there and use the low-cost-India calling card once more (something they had just about managed to discard in a quest for acceptance as strategic partners), or they just see new opportunities on the horizon.

I had a cup of tea with one of my mates from London, Paul Morrison from the consulting and research firm Alsbridge. He acknowledged some of the difficulties, but he felt that some of the industry voices fearing the future are protesting too much.

Paul said: "I would challenge a lot of these general concerns running across the Indian technology industry because I don't think those problems are really so deep. I think that in fact, the real discussion here is more about the next set of growth opportunities. Knowledge process outsourcing (KPO) for example. KPO is not new, but we are now seeing real case studies coming through, rather than just talk. I think there is a lot of discussion about where captives [foreign companies with their back office or delivery centres in India; HSBC for example] are going to go. Some of the captives in India are bigger than some service providers. The domestic Indian market is also rising up the agenda and so the main question is really, where is the balance going to be struck between any potential slowdown and all of these different opportunities for growth?"

Paul is absolutely right. What's the point in talking vaguely about a wave of innovation on the horizon, when there is a list of very real and tangible industry opportunities right there and ready to be grasped by whoever wants to go for it? In fact, it makes the concern over recent share price performance seem incredibly short-sighted. Yes, we all know that public companies need to justify their performance to external shareholders – who start getting jittery as margins are eroded, but the only company I can think of in this sector that has really taken leadership and stuck a flag (rather than their head) in the sand is Cognizant. It has talked up the market opportunities and told the market analysts that results are going to be higher than market predictions. Brave words. So let's hope Francisco D'Souza, Cognizant's chief executive, achieves his numbers and proves the industry doubters wrong.

Tuesday, 19 February 2008

Posted at 15:32

The world is going to India

I travelled home from the Nasscom conference in Mumbai at the weekend, suffering a taxi with a puncture on the way to the airport. Still, I did manage to get there on time and thanks to the great online check-in system on ba.com I was all set to go when I arrived at the airport, though the Mumbai international airport version of a fast bag drop is rather more pedestrian than that on offer at Heathrow.

The BA chief information officer Paul Coby was speaking at Nasscom so I guess any BA complaints could be directed to him personally, but after taking too many flights over the past week I really liked my BA homecoming experience. Not least the fact that 26-year-old episodes of *Only Fools and Horses* are on the entertainment system, welcoming the weary British traveller back to Peckham.

I'm going to write up some comments from people I spoke to at Nasscom over the next few days, but I wanted to immediately comment on something that struck me while I was there. It's something that I spoke to a few people about and everyone seemed to agree with me – that the Nasscom annual conference is becoming less about India and more about the business of global outsourcing and IT services in general. India is just where Nasscom is based, but the conference itself is starting to become a focal point for regions across the world promoting their outsourcing services.

For example, consider this: The pre-conference discussions were dominated by International Business Wales, the government body that promotes investment into Wales. Similar pre-conference discussions featured representatives of the hi-tech sector in Pakistan, Malaysia, and China. The evening reception on the first day of the conference was sponsored by Nova Scotia, Canada. Canadian delegates were handing out newspapers extolling the virtues of investing in their country. Lunch on day two was sponsored by Costa Rica, and dinner that evening was thanks to the Egyptians. The keynote sessions on day three featured representatives of Egypt, China, and Australia and then the lunch was funded by our very own Think London. The final session of the conference examined software innovation in India, China, and Israel.

This international involvement in what used to be an India-focused technology conference underlines a couple of points. India has become the centre of the international IT service industry – this really is where a lot of the thinking is taking place. Also, it does demonstrate that the industry in India is far more mature than even just a few years ago. Many of these international trade bodies are partnering with India because they want to capture a little piece of the magic dust for their own IT services industry.

Nasscom is becoming the central reference point for the global IT services industry and it would not surprise me if they even dropped 'India' from the title of the conference in 2009.

Wednesday, 20 February 2008

Posted at 16:05

Indian acquisition rumours could be more than speculation

I was recently chatting on the sidelines of the Nasscom conference in India to Alex Blues, a partner at PA Consulting. Alex is known to just about everyone in this business, as he is one of the leading global advisors with a long track record on some major deals.

Alex was on his honeymoon, with his new wife enjoying the pleasures of Mumbai as he went from meeting to meeting at the conference. That's real dedication to your work... well, in fact he was actually on holiday nearby and timed his return home so he could spend time at the conference, but he was still technically on his honeymoon.

Alex said something really interesting to me while we were chatting that could reignite the debate over potential mergers and acquisitions in the outsourcing supplier marketplace. I had asked Alex when he thought that we could drop the prefix "Indian" from the names of the Indian technology suppliers – in the same way as we never prefix a country in front of IBM, Capgemini, EDS, or Atos Origin. Basically, I wanted to know when will they grow up and be considered global players?

He said: "I think that there will soon be a Indian supplier making a significant purchase in the UK. There have been a lot of market rumours and some of those were pure rumours, but some were serious bids. I think that in the next 12 months there will be a huge surprise in the market and somebody with very deep pockets will make a major purchase. That company will be the one that moves from being considered a major player in India to being a true global player. It will be really interesting to watch this over the next 12 months."

No matter how much they deny it, industry insiders know that the Indian slide rule has been run over several European service companies. If Alex Blues says we should be watching for something to happen in 2008 then I think it's a serious insight and not just the further propagation of market rumours.

Thursday, 21 February 2008

Posted at 11:51

Is there anything you cannot outsource?

I was chatting to Egidio (Edge) Zarrella, global head of IT advisory for KPMG, at the Nasscom conference in Mumbai last week and he mentioned something to me that was a bit off the beaten track. We had been talking about the development of the international knowledge process outsourcing (KPO) market because he just published a new research report with some useful insights on the growth in this sector, but then he said that we were now going to start seeing the 'core' being outsourced.

The 'core' in this context is what we have spent years defining as the part of a company that can't be outsourced. Everyone who has been to business school has spent ages trying to define what is the core of a company, and what are the services that can be purchased in from someone who can perform the service better.

Every academic with an interest in this area, from Charles Handy to Gary Hamel, has written reams on defining that boundary between the organisation and the hired help. Entire university courses look at defining the retained organisation, yet here is Edge saying that the structure of the company itself is about to be radically overhauled.

Edge gave me some examples, such as several companies he advises that have outsourced their own chief executive. They just buy in the best gunslinger that is available on the market. It was an off-the-cuff conversation, but based on some of the comments he had presented to the conference and I thought it was fascinating. Where does the core sit if you can even hire in the head of the company through an outsourcing deal?

Edge sponsored the Bollywood Dreams dinner at the Nasscom conference and he ended up getting hauled up on stage in front of a couple of thousand people for some Bollywood dance lessons. Given that performance though, he might have wanted to outsource the dancing to someone else in KPMG.

Tuesday, 26 February 2008

Posted at 14:56

The damaging aspects of offshore outsourcing

I went to the London School of Economics last night to listen to a lecture by Professor Joseph Stiglitz, a Nobel laureate and one of the most-cited economists in the world today. He is well known as a critic of many aspects of globalisation, though the lecture last night was actually about the immense cost of the war in Iraq – as Stiglitz has just published a new book on the topic.

I've been thinking a lot over the past few days about some of the more damaging aspects of offshore outsourcing. First, a student emailed me asking for some help with a dissertation that explores the pros and cons of outsourcing, then I had to think about it once more as I am putting together a TV documentary and it will include some analysis of both sides of the coin.

Of course, going to see Stiglitz speak just galvanised some of my thoughts and I've got a lunch planned this week with fellow blogger Peter Skyte, at the union Unite. An interesting thing regarding Stiglitz's new book though – and considering that he is usually viewed as pretty much left-of-centre and critical of everything – is that the military veterans of the Iraq war are very supportive of his analysis. That fact alone does make it sound like a lot more than just left wing tub-thumping.

For all the arguments that developed nations can enrich developing nations by purchasing goods or services, there are many counter-arguments from the detractors. I was in India recently and I was sitting on a bus next a guy from Belgium who worked in the IT sector in Europe, but had never been to India before.

He was completely shocked at the absolute poverty in the streets of Mumbai. It brought me back to my own reaction the first time I took a taxi from Mumbai airport to my hotel – I couldn't get into the hotel fast enough after seeing the slums. My Belgian friend had internalised a vision of India as the technology companies present it; gleaming offices, smart well-paid staff all with phone-book length CVs, opulent hotels.

The reality is far from what we see on the corporate web sites, like the old holiday brochures that failed to mention your holiday resort is still under construction. And in a sense that is a good analogy, because a place like India is still under construction, and things are still a mess around the edges of the more developed industries.

When I was in the Philippines a couple of weeks ago, they were talking about IT outsourcing being worth 11 per cent of GDP within the next 2 years. It's clear that our industry is of phenomenal importance to developing regions. All you need is a broadband link, some reliable electricity, some smart people and you are in business. This means that the opportunities for enriching the lives of billions of people is a genuine reality – because every industry now relies on IT – so demand for IT services can only increase.

But in our rush to advance economic enrichment and the redistribution of wealth from the north to the south, it's worth also considering some of the genuine social issues. We know about the fears on our side of the equation, people fear their jobs will all vanish offshore, junior roles will all be offshored leading to a problem with the career path as people can't gain experience on a real career ladder, constant uncertainty about the future.

What about on the other side of the offshoring story too? Taking India just as an example, the newspapers are full of stories of sordid scenes at nightclubs, rape, murder, drugs, drinking, and the arrogance of very young people earning far more than their parents. It's not directly the fault of the outsourcing industry, but by default we have created immense clusters of young well-paid people with markedly different values to the generation that preceded them.

If we can export values such as gender equality then that's great, but a problem of exporting cultural values is that you don't have much control over which ones are exported and adopted. India has such a rich and diverse national cuisine, yet the kids at most call centres seem to be wolfing down curried pizza from Pizza Hut, or lamb burgers from McDonald's...

I was asked to write a a book about this a couple of years ago and I just never had the time to put it together, but no one else seems to have written a book that looks at both the way our jobs are changing and the way work and society is changing in the places we work with. Maybe I need to think again about the offer from that publisher.

On the whole, I'd suggest that it is of extreme value to work with those regions that are less wealthy and less developed. It's almost a moral imperative these days, and the moment some serious technology-related work starts getting outsourced to African nations then we will really start being aware of what is possible. However, we need to keep our eyes open to the social as well as the economic changes, in our own countries along with those we choose to work with.

Thursday, 28 February 2008

Posted at 14:33

Protecting employees should be a priority

In 1961, the Indian state of Karnataka (where Bangalore is located) created a new law banning women from working at night. In 2002, this law was amended to give special dispensation to the IT and IT-enabled service sector, provided the employer offers adequate protection to any women working at night, including safe transport to and from home.

On December 13, 2005, a female employee of Hewlett Packard Globalsoft in Bangalore was raped and murdered by her cab driver when she was on her way in to work a nightshift. The police filed a complaint to the labour commissioner who then filed the complaint before magistrates, claiming that the managing director of HP Globalsoft had been negligent in not providing secure transport. At that time, the MD of HP Globalsoft was Som Mittal, the new President of Nasscom and now the figurehead of the Indian IT industry.

Mittal has fought to quash the complaint, but the Indian Supreme Court has just quashed his final chance of appeal, so it looks like the police are going to get their way and will be able to convict him of not providing adequate security for female employees. The maximum penalty is a fine of 1,000 rupees. That's approximately £12 or $25.

The whole affair is quite pointless and rather demeaning to the memory of Pratibha Murthy, the murdered employee. If HP was negligent in not screening the background of cab drivers employed to collect their female employees late at night, then a proper penalty should be applied. If they could not have prevented the situation then there is a no case to answer. However, the outcome that the Indian legal authorities appear to have reached after much legal wrangling between the Karnataka High Court and Supreme Court is that the former managing director may have to pony up an amount that is equivalent to lunch in a London sandwich bar.

It's really a waste of time, tax rupees, and legal effort and appears to be driven by over-zealous bureaucrats more concerned with the application of the law to the letter, rather than in any pragmatic fashion. Let's hope Som Mittal can put it behind him and get on with the job of leading Nasscom.

The Indian regulatory authorities pursuing this type of case ought to be asking the question why it is unsafe for women after dark in India. Surely this is the underlying question? Why should private sector companies be responsible for running their own fleet of taxis because the cities and states can't provide good enough local infrastructure for employees to safely travel to and from work, whatever the time?

March 2008

Thursday, 06 March 2008

Posted at 13:07

Of leaky taps, plumbers, and Indian IT suppliers

I was in Starbucks yesterday with a guy I know from the sourcing industry. He is a consultant who often works on supplier comparison, helping companies to looks at the strengths and weaknesses of different suppliers, and hopefully helping them to pick the right one for their project.

He said something interesting to me that chimed with some news I read in the Indian press this week about TCS starting a new unit focused on small to medium sized enterprises – with an expectation of earning $100m a year for at least the next five years from this new unit.

My coffee companion recently had a client with a fairly small project. Not millions at all, but probably about £50,000 a year of work. That's about $100,000 per year to a supplier, so it is comparatively small, but the client was interesting and so the potential was clearly there for the relationship to grow bigger. It was a helpdesk project that could expand into support for several languages. He had called one of the top 10 Indian suppliers to ask if they would be interested in the project. His call was not returned. He tried calling again. He got nothing but voicemail. After three days of getting voicemail he gave up on them, thinking that if that's the way they organise their own customer service then how are they going to organise it better for the client?

It's not even as if they were just avoiding him because the project was too small to deal with. He was calling the switchboard of their London office and getting this reaction. Even if the project was too small to be of interest, the very least someone could have done is given him a call to let him know.

No, this was not TCS, but it was certainly one of the well-known Indian suppliers and it does demonstrate once again the old adage that a plumber never has time to fix the leaking tap in his own bathroom.

Friday, 07 March 2008

Posted at 15:44

Is China slipping behind?

I was just called by a financial journalist based in the City. She wanted to ask me about the news that JP Morgan plans to scale up its operations in the Philippines from around 5,000 people to 8,000 – quite an increase.

As so often happens when someone calls asking for an off-the-cuff comment, I had not read the news myself and I was sitting on a train from London to Nottingham with no access to the internet, other than through the tiny screen on my phone. So I gave some general comments on the situation in the Philippines and why a company like JP Morgan might want to invest further in the region.

It is clear to me that something interesting has developed in the marketplace, where everyone is usually comparing the relative merits of one country compared to another – even though these comparisons are usually too simplistic to be of much use. The thing is – and whisper this – everyone seems to have finally stopped comparing India to China.

I had a meeting earlier this week with some representatives of the Suzhou industrial park in China (an industrial park that is 288 square km!) and I mentioned this to them. They seemed to be quite upset, as I was implying that China is potentially slipping off the radar of western buyers interested in knowledge-based services. Then they slipped into the same mistake that everyone seems to make when promoting their region, trotting out statistics on tax breaks, office space, the graduate population, the number of golf courses, and just about everything except the weather and attractiveness of local women - though believe me, some investment agencies have actually spun that line with me.

It should be fairly obvious why JP Morgan is expanding in the Philippines. They have a considerable operation there already and the location offers everything a foreign investor might want – all those great things the Chinese were telling me about. So, with all those benefits and an incumbent operation, it is not likely that JP Morgan would hire 3,000 people in another location unless it was for a reason such as business continuity management.

I don't want to sound flippant, but most senior executives I meet and talk to are really much more focused on the capabilities of partner companies, regardless of where that company is registered.

Can they do the job? I don't care if they are based in California, Cornwall, or Korea. Yes, when companies are planning an offshore captive facility they will need to examine the fundamentals of that region, but I would argue that outsourcing is a lot more common than offshoring and creating a major captive for services.

Companies offering IT or IT-enabled services from regions such as China and the Philippines might want to work harder at developing their own reputation as a company, rather than supporting government-led initiatives and trade missions that do little more than present a sea of statistics and images of golf courses. I hate golf anyway. When someone uses a golf course as a way of selling a location to me it just makes me think of Bruce Forsyth in funny trousers. Not an attractive thought, even if he does deserve to be knighted for services to tap dancing and games shows.

The India and China debate is a serious point though. Go back a couple of years and every analyst and conference debate was about the question of who is going to win the outsourcing race – India or China? Today, the environment is much more open and it is clear that Chinese technology service firms are opening up to exports, but they are still really busy with the booming domestic market. Indian firms have just got better and better, but it is new players in countries such as the Philippines and Vietnam that are really going to be making the news in Asia.

Monday, 10 March 2008

Posted at 16:03

Hello? Hello? The problem with call centres

It's amazing what you read in the papers sometimes. I've just been looking at a story in The Guardian today about how some voice-based contact centres are shifting projects back to local agents rather than using an offshore business model.

Hello? I've been talking about that trend for at least the past couple of years at business conferences and to my MBA students. Clearly there was a page free in the business section today and they had to call up that well-known journalist 'Phil Space' to get something together.

The offshoring backlash reached a peak in the UK in 2003. There was a significant international public backlash caused by the 2004 US presidential election, and since that time many voice-based customer service centres have explored how best to improve their service. In some cases, that resulted in a focus on local agents for some services, but we have an interesting situation in the UK. Our local contact centre industry continues to grow even as the amount that is sent offshore also grows, because the use of contact centres by all businesses continues to increase.

I was explaining the tendency to focus on voice-based contact centre work to MBA students at London South Bank University last week (and apologies to the evening MBA students as I should be talking to them today, but I am away in Prague), and one of the students questioned my logic.

"The problem is not accents, or local people in a call centre. If you get a local British person and they can't help you then you still get frustrated. The problem is that call centres are just not designed very well and you always end up feeling angry after calling one, regardless of where they pick up the phone," she said.

She had a valid point that's hard to argue against.

Tuesday, 11 March 2008

Posted at 10:15

Czech-ing in

I am speaking today at a conference in Prague. I'm not on until just after 1pm, but I thought I would arrive promptly at 8am so I could follow the talks in the morning. So I got up and had breakfast early, listening to BBC Radio 5 in my hotel and was pleased to hear my editor at Computing, Bryan Glick, talking about broadband use in the UK while I was munching on my toast in the Czech Republic, thanks to the wonders of the BBC iPlayer – exactly the thing Bryan was talking about.

I walked to the Czech National Bank, avoiding the morning traffic, and took my place in the audience. Then the lectures started and I discovered that the entire morning is going to be in Czech and only switches to English once I am involved later in the day!

I'm certainly not a little Englander, insisting on the use of business English everywhere I go, but I have to confess that I only know a few words of Czech. At least if it was French then I could follow most of the debate, but I am afraid that I am reduced to blogging while people speak right now...

Wednesday, 12 March 2008

Posted at 18:23

The contentious issue of overseas IT workers

There was some news this week in Computing about foreign IT workers entering the UK that could certainly be seen as alarming for those on both sides of the offshoring debate.

Atsco, the Association of Technology Staffing Companies, put a Freedom of Information request to Work Permits UK, the section of the Home Office responsible for issuing work visas.

Atsco found that 38,450 work permits were handed to non-EU IT workers last year. Of those visas, 82 per cent went to Indian nationals and there were about 5,000 more visas issued than the year before.

So what is Atsco worried about? There must be almost a million people employed in IT or IT services in the UK – at least that was the magnitude of the industry when I was doing research into offshoring from the UK for the BCS. A few thousand people sounds like small beer, doesn't it?

Atsco's concern is over what it terms 'onshore offshoring', where an offshore IT company wins a contract and then staffs the project with people from that remote location. Given that four out of five people getting these visas are Indian, let's assume we are talking mostly about the big Indian IT companies here. So the allegation is that once TCS, Infosys, or Wipro wins a big UK contract and requires resource locally in the UK, they don't go on a hiring spree over here, they just bus everyone in by filling the economy class seats on Air India and renting some cheap apartments.

No doubt those companies will retort that if they win a major contract and suddenly need to launch a major UK-based programme of work that involves auditing systems, benchmarking, and probably a knowledge transfer, then it's only natural to get the people over from India – because when the systems are transferred they are the people who are going to have to manage them.

In addition, there is also the question of ramping up to meet demand. If I'm a CIO and I am choosing IT suppliers and I notice that one says it will take six months to hire the required people for the project and the other says they can have knowledgeable people on the ground in two weeks, then what would you expect me to do?

CIOs are not hired for their altruistic nature. They need to support the business and the business expects results, so let's try to cut some of the quasi-patriotic crocodile tears from the way Atsco is presenting this reality.

In its new report, Atsco also talks about the long-term danger of bringing in foreign workers to handle low to middle-ranking IT jobs – creating a lack of opportunity for graduates here. I'm not sure I accept all of their arguments, but there is an issue. Again though, the CIO will be faced with the reality check of hiring fairly low-cost but completely inexperienced employees from UK campuses or experienced staff for a similar cost from offshore.

However, I'm not such an ardent capitalist that these concerns do not worry me. Greed is not necessarily good. I think that there is an issue with the way work visas are issued for IT projects in the UK, but we have to inject the debate with a sense of pragmatism and business reality.

I would ask the Home Office to review its conditions for granting visas and the longevity of those visas. I do believe that there is something wrong when a "knowledge transfer" programme can take two years or more – and so people can be expatriated from India to work on that project for several years, continuing to earn an Indian salary, rather than being hired locally in the UK.

There must be a way to use the flexibility of outsourcing or offshoring work partially to other regions, but also maintaining a commitment to local workers through the visa programme. If a job is going to take more than a year then surely that's not really a task where someone should be brought in to the UK is it? What we need is a fresh debate and consultation that involves the key players with the Home Office. We can't close down the borders entirely because domain experts are needed wherever they are, but if IT companies are just using the weaknesses of the visa system to bring lower-paid workers into the UK then there has to be a review in the near future.

Tuesday, 18 March 2008

Posted at 10:20

Czeching out the European information age

I had an interesting visit to the Czech Republic last week. I was speaking at a conference focused on the business of information technology in the country and it covered a multitude of areas, focusing a lot on legislative changes for most of the morning session.

What struck me, when the deputy prime minister (DPM) was speaking in the afternoon, was the directness of someone so senior in the political machine. He confessed that the IT industry should not expect too much from the forthcoming Czech presidency of the European Union. In fact he even confessed that he was not sure what anyone could expect from the presidency, but he did vouch to be working hard on ensuring the country would get as much as possible from the EU presidency.

The Lisbon Strategy is due to be reviewed soon and from what the DPM was saying, it looks like the UK and Czech Republic are the most progressive nations in the union, pushing for real measures to drag Europe into the information age – particularly in the area of IT-enabled services. Given the nature of the EU and the requirement for 27 nations to debate these matters it might be some time before we see much action.

Tuesday, 18 March 2008

Posted at 15:25

Vietnam calling

I had a chat on the phone the other day with Paul Smith, managing director of Harvey Nash outsourcing. Of course, Harvey Nash is well known as one of the world's leading staff recruitment companies, but it also offers outsourced services. The company recently signed a new contract with Prudential in Vietnam, extending an existing relationship, and so I gave him a call to ask about Vietnam.

First I asked Paul, why Vietnam? He said: "We had a lot of feedback from clients saying that they were experiencing staff churn in India, as well as the right quality. So we wanted to influence the quality of staff in our centre by becoming the first choice – we wanted to be the elephant rather than the flea"

That's understandable and it sidesteps many of the staffing issue faced by India at present. Paul added: "We are now expanding here by 300 per cent per annum, we get the top graduates coming out of the major cities, we have influence on the universities and we even have our own university in Hanoi. And you don't get 'Delhi belly' in Vietnam."

To be fair, I know that I've eaten everywhere from street-side vendors to five-star hotels in India and very rarely suffered the dreaded Delhi belly, but I do know of some people who still pack their bag full of British snacks to keep them going with risking the local tiffin.

Paul believes that the demand in India is causing a major problem when staffing projects.

"You have so much demand pushing into India now," he said. "People like Oracle, IBM, and Microsoft are creating such huge demand at the universities that people are prepared to hop job for just a dollar more. Your domain knowledge and the ability to create long-term relationships with teams will be affected in that environment."

I asked Paul about the move to using local call centres for dealing with local staff and he agreed entirely. In fact, he outlined that the staff at the call centre in Vietnam are actually dealing with consumers in Vietnam, not offering a far-flung service to punters here in Britain.

"Prudential is very confident about using staff in a call centre in Vietnam because they use English people to speak to English customers and Vietnamese people to speak to Vietnamese customers," he said.

"As with Prudential, companies like HSBC and Standard Chartered also see Vietnam as a massive consumer market that is developing very fast. We do not recommend voice outsourcing into the UK market from Vietnam, though that is more of a general rule that customer service staff should be local."

So there you have it. I mentioned this on a blog the other day because of a news story talking about this as a recent trend. I believe Harvey Nash has been working to build up its Vietnam centre over the past eight years and Paul is one of the best-known commentators in the industry, so I'm inclined to believe what he says as a fairer picture of what is really going on.

Tuesday, 18 March 2008

Posted at 18:00

US troubles are the least of India's worries

I recently asked Deepak Khosla, senior vice president of marketing at Patni, about the economic slowdown in the US and the potential for recession – which some commentators say has already happened. The news from the US is looking ever more bleak now as even stalwarts of Wall Street, such as Bear Stearns, are getting into trouble.

Khosla acknowledged the US turmoil as an issue, but he listed a number of more local issues in the Indian outsourcing industry that are presently the focus of the IT players there.

"I think there are a few challenges that we had not really thought of," he said.

"Who would have expected the dollar to go down as it did? Also, look at recruitment. Earlier we were interviewing six people for every person we recruited. Now we need to interview about 16 for each person we hire. We have to manage something like 70,000 interviews in 220 working days."

Khosla said the entire industry is changing in India and there are some larger, more mature, companies capable of riding the change and some who will fall by the wayside.

"We previously had the models, but the environment is changing," he said. "I am not surprised as the industry is going through an evolution. We are looking to the long term and trying to plan for the future, but it's true that some companies are just struggling to keep their people, let alone acquire new business."

Khosla actually highlighted that the IT service players in India are now differentiating their approach – it's no longer a one-size-fits-all industry.

"Some are taking the mass-production factory approach, but some are going into specific niche areas," he said.

"At Patni, we are looking very much into embedded systems and there is very strong growth in this market. Some companies are looking at business domains, some are looking at industrialisation, and some are looking at these niches. There are some benefits for us too by doing this - after all, an engineering drawing is an engineering drawing wherever you are and whatever language you use."

It seems that the domestic issues in the Indian IT industry remain higher up the agenda than any worries about the US, but the market is changing and there are still some opportunities to thrive – provided the service providers know their market and can focus.

Wednesday, 26 March 2008

Posted at 12:16

Tata takeovers are good for everyone

It's exciting to hear that the Tata Group in India is purchasing Land Rover and Jaguar from Ford. Jaguar might be losing cash, but as a combined unit the two marques are generating a healthy profit for Ford, so it looks like a good purchase for Tata. The difference in strategy is the investment for the long-term, which Ford seems to be shying away from - perhaps wanting to cut free after years of trying to make Jaguar work.

With a five-year commitment to the business, this deal is good for British car manufacturing – securing jobs in Land Rover and Jaguar as well as Ford in the UK, as part of the deal involves sourcing parts from Ford.

Tata is becoming the poster-child of rapid industrial development in India – and Asia in general. In the UK we have seen them in the news a number of times in recent years. Tata now owns Tetley tea, and the purchase of Corus (formerly British Steel) by Tata Steel was one of the big business stories of last year.

The group also happens to run Tata Consultancy Services (TCS), the biggest player in the Indian technology services market. TCS made more than $4bn in revenue last year and it is safe to predict that they will be north of $5bn when this financial year ends.

TCS is about to completely restructure the organisation around business domains. My impression of the new strategy is that it is breaking the company up in a virtual way, so the retail IT part of TCS becomes entirely responsible for sales and growth in that part of the business, as does the public sector part of the organisation. It is like creating a number of virtual IT companies all within the TCS banner and each with their own revenue and growth targets.

I'm sure that they have always analysed where the money is coming in and who is generating growth, but it looks like some business autonomy is being passed down to the domain heads. That's a good thing and in theory a good strategy. The buyers in the market that I have already spoken to about this (some of them TCS customers) are keen on the idea because it gives them better access to TCS and more flexibility.

I wonder how this impacts the second-tier suppliers though? They sell themselves as being smaller, quicker to react and more focused on particular industries when compared to the IT giants. Now TCS is acknowledging that the way forward is to specialise on the businesses they serve and to know those industries as well as their clients do. Where does that leave the smaller IT shops?

Friday, 28 March 2008

Posted at 14:29

Terminal 5 - The insider's view

O h dear. The opening of Heathrow Terminal 5 (T5) has been a disaster. British Airways chief executive Willie Walsh must be in the running for understatement of the year for describing the mess as "not really our finest hour." In this situation it might have been better to search for a quote from the Queen Mother, rather than alluding to Churchill – the poor passengers must have a touch of the Blitz spirit in T5 right now.

I've been talking to a number of IT companies about the T5 migration and they were all holding their breath. Both NIIT and TCS count BA as a major customer and even though it looks like the technology is not to blame, no IT supplier wants to see a good customer and business partner flailing around like a fish out of water.

I was a passenger on the first Eurostar service from St Pancras International station to Paris. Eurostar managed to operate services from Waterloo one day and to switch everything overnight to St Pancras without a hitch – apart from the fact that on opening day there were still no shops at St Pancras so it was impossible to even get a coffee, but the train service ran smoothly.

I appreciate that T5 is on a far grander scale than a train station, but there is no denying that the Eurostar project was a huge overnight transition too – and it worked. BA and BAA need to come up with some answers about what went wrong soon and especially whether it was really just a lack of burly baggage handlers or some fundamental design problems in the new technology commissioned for the terminal.

I want to end this blog post by featuring a long quote, basically an entire email straight from the BlackBerry of friend of mine who is a very senior UK-based executive in a major IT services company - that shall remain nameless. I received this last night, so it's an excellent view from the coalface of the T5 experience on opening day:

"Sadly the UK hasn't covered itself in glory today. I say the UK because that's how important the success of T5 is for the country.

I'm currently on Eurostar to Paris, while my bag wanders round T5's state of the art baggage system lonely as a... well actually I expect it has quite a few disgruntled baggy friends this evening as it circumnavigates the underground rubber runways.

T5 looks nice, nice artwork, high tech and you can see the concept the designers are aiming for, but today it had lots of teething problems, not just the kind of fundamental shortage of flying opportunities. Check-in luggage conveyers were working intermittently, security operations slow. Information provision via the IT systems slow - slower than BA's internet updates which at least confirmed my flight was cancelled, rather than the suggestion chez T5 to queue up and enquire (such a polite term – 'I say, would you mind awfully telling me if my plane might leave today?') Yes, please speak to a warm and fluffy human. Sadly the ratio of query-ers to query-ees was unmanageable.

I guess they'll show the queues that BA staff had to cope with on the news. By now I'm expecting at least one murder to have occurred, mentally - not, one hopes, physically. Many were stoic - at least when I left. But it could get ugly. I predict a riot?

Arrivals was fun. First you can't actually leave departures - by any means. So we had to queue again until security could escort us out. Then once you've managed to leave, so to speak, you have to arrive. 'Do you have your landing card?' 'I haven't taken off yet.' 'Oh!'

I guess I'll go through the 'arrivals from the EU" channel at customs.

As I looked through the glass back into check-in on my way out, the seething queues suggested even check-in was pushing up the daisies.

Abandoning my bag after being told I could look for it online, rather than join the next one-hour queue at arrivals baggage claims customer services, I headed for St Pancras station.

I did have a nice opportunity to share some views - and mine were very positive - with the very nice BAA customer service man I met on the Heathrow Express back. I know he's going to think about these.

I hope Willie Walsh commends the fortitude of the BA staff for the sheer drain on their emotional skills today. They are the easiest to blame - because they are there - and I sometimes despair at the amount of vitriol fellow passengers are prepared to deploy. For BA and BAA this really is a nightmare, and I have to say that I sympathise. It's all too easy now to be smug and suggest more testing or a phased approach. But it really will be a fantastic feat when it does come together (could I propose tomorrow night - when I return from Paris?). And I have to say even today; my T5 experience was a whole magnitude better than that received at Delhi airport last month – twice.

The difference is that we don't expect this standard from the UK's flagship airport. And you're always leaving Delhi at about 3am.

I feel a case study coming on.

I missed the first Eurostar in favour of buying a toothbrush, hairbrush and a few other essentials at the station. I 'was' a big fan of M&S's new railway station stores - until today when it dawned on me that 'simply food' really did sell what it says on the tin, to mix business straplines. So I couldn't rely on M&S in my time of greatest need. Thank you Accessorize.

I now have a G&T in my hot and bothered hand, but sadly relaxation won't come. There's an unhappy child in the adjacent seat who'd like to share his frustration with us all. Carpets are stained and it's looking jaded. I expected a sit-down buffet-car meal where some may have even dressed for dinner and with a sporting chance of a murder or a chase or a disappearance. The pasta forestiere eaten at my seat had no romance, but wasn't bad. And it's now turned peaceful across the aisle.

Off to brush up on my business French. Hmmn, wonder if Nicolas Sarkozy and Carla Bruni are on board?

Bonsoir et Bon Voyage. "

April 2008

Monday, 14 April 2008

Posted at 10:53

UBS feels the crunch

The news that UBS has apparently ditched a programme to outsource some of its human resources (HR) function, might send shivers down the spine of every outsourcing provider. Is the runaway train of outsourcing growth about to run off the tracks?

Well, I think it is worth putting the issue in context. UBS recently had to write off more than £19bn thanks to the global credit crunch sweeping the banking industry. That's an enormous figure. It's no surprise that UBS is now reining in any possible expense.

A major outsourcing programme such as that proposed by UBS would have long-term benefits. It could improve the provision of staff training and HR services and reduce overall running costs, however the transition would be expensive. There is already some existing method of managing staff and there is some existing programme for staff training, so if you were running the bank right now then what would you do?

I have not spoken to anyone at UBS to form this opinion, but I'm assuming it's not far off the mark. Major change programmes, such as the proposed one for HR, will be put on ice and thawed out when we know (and or least have an idea) how bad this credit crunch is going to be.

Thursday, 17 April 2008

Posted at 11:46

A marathon session

I was the first speaker at the Outsource World conference at the eXcel centre in London yesterday. I was really sweating as I was approaching the eXcel because the place is so remote. I live in west London and the eXcel is deep into the docklands of the east end.

I think the last time I went there was to collect my running number for the London marathon, and I drove that time from north London so I didn't get such a sense of how far out it is. The centre is a beacon of modernity on the Royal Victoria Dock, still an iconic place in my mind, with the majestic cranes still punctuating the skyline. But the only time I have really had a good look around this dock was 20 years ago when Jean-Michel Jarre performed one of his laser and music shows right there.

Things have changed in 20 years. Now there are apartment blocks all over, and the eXcel itself. I was arriving there with about five minutes to spare before I was due to speak. Fortunately I was only planning to speak (I mean, no complex audio-visual kit required) about some of the present issues in outsourcing I felt the audience should be thinking of (knowledge process outsourcing, the green agenda, remote infrastructure management, the present macro-economic concerns, and small businesses). I had all my notes ready and printed in my bag so I was all set.

Then I found out that I was supposed to chair the conference for the entire morning. I was under the impression that it was just going to be for the session I was involved in, so I would speak and then I would introduce a few other speakers - who in the event were from Forrester, Capgemini, Skandia, and Logica. In fact, I would normally have not minded chairing the whole morning, but I was getting concerned about a flight I needed to catch in the afternoon to Kolkata in India.

Fortunately, Frank Casale who runs the Outsourcing Institute, was there and took over the chairman duties after the coffee break, so thanks for that Frank. We have corresponded by email quite often, but never met before as Frank is based in the US. When we finally got to meet I was worried about my flight and practically begging him to take my speaking slot at a conference!

Once Frank took over it meant I had a half hour free before I needed to leave, so I had a quick spin around the event to pick up some business cards. Outsource World has been criticised in the past. I know it really used to be a terrible event, rubbish venues, no meaningful agenda, useless sponsors touting cheap and cheerful offshoring... it was truly dreadful. Two years ago the organisers really started to turn it around. Roger Ellis, who I knew already from the BCS and some events he has hosted, started running the event in London and injected a lot of new professionalism. It looked like a new event, but the past two years never saw very many people attending - it was essentially still a tainted product.

So, it was good to see this year that the conference was packed. People were having to stand to listen to the talks in the morning and more kept coming in. For some reason unknown to me Roger is not running the event this year - which in my opinion looks a bit like he put the effort in to change the event format, but never got to see the time when people would start returning.

There is a lot of focus on regional outsourcing at this conference, so different regions of China were promoting their wares, alongside Mauritius and then dozens of individual firms. It was a pretty good event and is now starting to get legs again, especially for the small business market - it has a strong focus on serving smaller companies and that is something that is really needed in outsourcing today.

Friday, 18 April 2008

Posted at 06:00

Welcome to India

I have come here so many times before, but I was a bit fed up yesterday morning when I arrived at the international airport in Delhi. I needed to transfer immediately to a domestic flight to Kolkata (still better known as Calcutta), so I went immediately to the transfer lounge. Lounge is a euphemism as this is more like a holding pen full of flies and mosquitoes.

You might expect that the transfer between an international and domestic flight would be a fairly smooth procedure, but that's until you have experienced travel to India.

I arrived in the lounge at 7.01am only to find that the transfer bus leaves on the hour. Great. Another hour until the next bus. Nothing like a rapid transfer service here in Delhi. But what really annoyed me as I arrived was the fact that the security guard managing the entrance to the lounge asked to see my air ticket. It seemed like a reasonable security question, but he then took it and handed it to a guy in a dirty t-shirt who walked off and told me to follow him. I called after him and sure enough he was a taxi driver hoping to earn a few bucks by giving me a "fixed price transfer" to the domestic terminal in his cab.

Now, we all know cab drivers will hustle for business wherever they can, but the airport security being in on the game too is a bit much. I went up to the only member of staff wearing a suit and asked him what is going on when the security in the lounge transfer area - which is basically a waiting area for the free bus - are handing air tickets to cab drivers? He said he had no control over the cab drivers, who can come and go as they please walking in and out of the terminal building when the rest of us get harassed for tickets or passports to prove a reason for being there.

Then I sat around waiting for the 8am bus when the guy sitting on the next chair asked if I had my name on the list for the bus. What list? I've been to Delhi before and I can't remember ever having to get on a list to get access to a bus that just transfers you from one terminal to another! This guy insisted that I had to have my name on a list, so I wandered over to the same people I had earlier been asking about the bus timetable and they confirmed that I did indeed need to be on the list if I wanted to get the 8am transfer bus. I asked them why they did not take my name earlier when I was asking the time of the next bus - they just smiled at me.

Sometimes I feel so happy to arrive back in India, but today after a night flight with no sleep, no sound on the only movie I wanted to watch, my only reading material being A Short History of the Labour Party, and then all this hassle on arrival, I think I'd be quite happy to be waking up at home. The punch up when I went through security just added to the flavour of the morning...

Monday, 21 April 2008

Posted at 14:09

Indian IT is much more than the usual suspects

I made a short visit to Kolkata (Calcutta) in India last week. UK Trade & Investment (UKTI) had arranged a mission to West Bengal to examine how more links could be established between that area of India and the UK. I was speaking at a conference for a group of local Indian technology firms.

I had prepared a talk the day before leaving and then polished it off waiting in the bar at Heathrow airport. Things like a limited battery life can really create a strong incentive to get things finished. I arrived at the hotel where I was staying – and where the talk was due to take place – with very little time to spare. I basically arrived in India on Thursday, got a shower, had a shirt pressed, and then went downstairs to do the talk. Talk about hectic.

On the agenda it said I had 45 minutes. Just before I was going to start they said to me I should aim for 1hr 15 minutes instead, as the agenda had changed! Fortunately the extra time made it possible to turn the presentation into more of a dialogue with the audience. I asked them to interrupt and throw comments into the talk so we could bounce ideas around, rather than waiting for a Q&A session at the end.

My session went on for about 90 minutes and it was great. I was talking about some of the present issues in outsourcing generally and then more specifically how Kolkata could/should promote itself. The audience was full of comment and we had a great debate.

In the afternoon, a number of local companies were presenting to each other with me there as well to offer some tips on what UK service buyers might think of their pitch.

On Friday I went around Kolkata in a car in blazing heat – and with failing air conditioning. Each office we called at offered some respite from the heat and the traffic noise. I visited some of the major companies that have invested in the area such as HSBC, Cognizant, Capgemini, and IBM.

It was interesting to see the facilities these major firms had created in Kolkata. Each of them has recruited thousands of people locally and they kept on repeating some of the same reasons for investing in this part of India – primarily attrition is much lower here, there is a stronger sense of loyalty to the company and people don't job hop as easily as in some other locations. It's also slightly cheaper than locations such as Gurgaon or Bangalore. However I don't think the difference in cost outweighs the far greater benefit of being able to reduce the staff churn to someone more manageable.

I actually found some of the local home grown companies more interesting, perhaps because there were some stories and studies that I enjoyed hearing, from companies I have never heard of. Rebaca are working on better ways of pushing video around the Internet and creating streaming technologies that blend all sorts of existing technologies – I imagined it as something like a cross between Sky+, Joost, and Slingbox.

Brick and Click also impressed me with a number of product ideas, including a complete pharmacy management system that handles the entire prescription and dispensing process for pharmacy retailers. The NHS should really talk to these guys, given some of their difficulties in this area. The Brick and Click system has already been rolled out to a number of US states.

And let's not forget the humble contact centre. The COO of BNKe Solutions, Suresh Menon, was so keen to meet me he dragged himself into the office after major spine surgery. It was literally his first trip outside since the surgery and then the people from the West Bengal government who were arranging all my appointments hustled me in and out in something like 15 minutes, because we were running hopelessly late on the schedule! Suresh explained how his major advantage in the market was that he has an attrition rate of below 5 per cent. It's an incredibly low figure for a contact centre and does demonstrate that there are differences between different regions of India. That sort of figure would be almost impossible in Bangalore.

I hope to get back to Kolkata soon. Not just because I want to explore some more of the historic sites associated with Nobel laureate Rabindranath Tagore, but there is a lot taking place in India beyond the well-established metropolitan areas we are all familiar with. I'd like to see how fast this ancient city could develop a hi-tech future.

Wednesday, 23 April 2008

Posted at 11:49

Outsourcing creates security pluses and minuses

A new survey out today commissioned by PriceWaterhouseCoopers and the Department for Business Enterprise and Regulatory Reform (BERR), indicates that 13 per cent of Britain's large businesses have faced malicious network penetration by cybercriminals.

This is an interesting observation, not least because the survey took the views of over 1,000 companies, but also because the figure was a marked leap from the 2 per cent reported only two years ago, and could even underestimate the problem, given that many firms do not admit to successful attacks on their IT systems.

Malicious attacks are estimated to cost the UK economy several billion pounds a year. The same survey also revealed that despite falling victim to 94 serious data breaches in the past year, 90 per cent of businesses still let staff take sensitive information off site on USB sticks and in laptops – a disaster waiting to happen with various examples of pub laptop thefts proving the point.

Outsourcing can provide two sides to the coin. Sometimes it can be a benefit to get some standards written up, procedures in place, and relationships with a specialist IT company that understands the value of digital information. On the other hand, sometimes it means that company-to-company hand-offs of information need to take place where previously everything was internal, and that itself can cause issues.

Wednesday, 23 April 2008

Posted at 12:00

A loo brush with the stars

I was in the gents' toilet earlier today at the Washington Hotel in London's swish Mayfair district. "Who would have thought it? I cannot have imagined this 10 years ago," said the London-based correspondent of PTI – the Press Trust of India. We were sharing a toilet conversation about the past hour in which we had witnessed some of the great and good in British politics talk about the importance of the UK / India relationship.

The lunch was arranged for the Labour Friends of India by Saffron Chase, a PR and lobbying firm run by a friend of mine, Vikas Pota. Vikas is one of those movers and shakers in political society who knows everyone worth knowing. As I entered the room, Vikas wandered over and grabbed my arm; he guided me over to have a chat with the guy running one of the biggest hedge funds in London.

The MP for Ealing North, Steve Pound, who chairs the Labour Friends of India, gave a talk about the British relationship with India. He introduced the Prime Minister, who had been delayed trying to get through the crowded bar area of the hotel, much to the amusement of the guests – at least one peer was heard to mutter that this was not the first time the PM was delayed in the bar, though I'm sure it was in mirth and not in the literal sense of a Liberal Democrat leader.

The Mayor for London, Ken Livingstone, followed with a speech that included the sentiments that he could never disagree with anything the Prime Minister said. I bet Tony Blair wished for that kind of compliance back in the day.

Lord Kinnock, Chairman of the British Council and former leader of the Labour Party, was being presented with the Fenner Brockway medal for promoting better relations between the UK and India. He then made a rambling, but interesting speech. The hosts were getting worried as Kinnock was going on a bit. It was interesting to most of us, but clearly some people like the PM and Mayor had to get moving. Steve Pound attempted to sneak up alongside Kinnock to tell him to hurry up.

Kinnock immediately said that he knew he was running over and that he would finish soon. He then added that he was always careful when people approached from the side in case he would get stabbed in the back. He recalled a 1985 speech at the Labour Party Conference where Eric Heffer had tried approaching while Kinnock was speaking.

It may have been somewhat hagiographic because of the Indian audience, but the off the record view of many politicians is that India is a great friend and worth developing. A lot of those in power fear talking on the record about their concerns for China, and so the emphatic support for India can be taken as a vicarious way of saying that they will support a large democratic state over a large dictatorship any day – but the economics of the matter prevents them saying it openly...

Thursday, 24 April 2008

Posted at 10:55

TCS shoulders the cost of transition work

Roll up, roll up. Get your free outsourcing here! You know how we spent years trying to shift the perception of offshore outsourcing from the slash 'n' burn strategy, the race to the bottom, the exploitation of developing economies where everyone will work for pennies?

Remember how it gradually moved into the realm of being a strategic tool used by the management to access better, more flexible resource, with skills that were not previously found in the retained organisation?

It seems we are now reaching the ultimate in low cost offshoring though – free offshoring. Well, not really totally free, but Tata Consultancy Services (TCS) is using the loss leader concept to try stimulating some buying decisions. It's a bit like the supermarkets that will sell butter and eggs at a loss safe in the knowledge that once you are inside their four walls, you are probably going to buy something else.

TCS has started offering to shoulder the cost of transition work, the process of preparing a function to be moved from it's current location and into the new offshore location. Usually the client would pay for this, as it is their project, but this TCS 'special offer' looks like it is designed to spur on a few decisions that may be currently stalled due to the black clouds swirling over the economy.

Perhaps it is working for them, but it seems like a bit of a cheap shot that devalues the expertise of the supplier. Will they ever be able to charge for transition again now some clients get it for free?

Monday, 28 April 2008

Posted at 14:25

To offshore or not to offshore

One of the big debates around offshore is whether the US economic slowdown will encourage more investigation of offshoring by companies as a means to control costs, or will it just mean that all purchasing decisions are frozen? In a recent report, Offshoring IT Services Can Cut Costs: Options for a Potential Economic Downturn, analyst Gartner claimed that the slowdown will be an absolute boon for offshoring.

The Gartner prediction states that the US economic slowdown will lead buyers of IT services to consider increasing the percentage of their labour in offshore, lower-cost locations. India will remain the dominant location for IT offshore services for North American and European buyers as a result of its scale, quality of resources and strong presence of local and traditional service providers.

Gartner goes further to state that this will be the case whether we only see a mild slowdown or a more prolonged and deep recession. The analyst believes that in the best-case scenario – a mild slowdown – existing plans to use the offshore model will be accelerated and some companies who might not have previously considered offshoring will now think of it as a more feasible option.

In the worst-case scenario – a deep recession – we can expect to see a considerable amount of cost cutting through aggressive offshoring programmes.

On the surface it all sounds good for the offshore suppliers, but in my recent conversations with several of these companies I know they are starting to feel the pain because the uncertainty in the economy is making it harder for their clients to make a decision. Even companies that are considering offshoring programmes are taking a lot longer than usual to make decisions right now. Let's face it, if your firm has reined in business travel and put a freeze on new recruits then a major business decision such as outsourcing a process to the other side of the world is going to take longer to plan than usual.

Tuesday, 29 April 2008

Posted at 08:00

Restricting voices

I received an interesting email from a friend of mine, Gavin Cooney, who runs a company in Dublin called Learnosity. It is focused on using the telephone for tests and exams, such as taking an oral language test with the telephone instead of with the teacher in a school.

Gavin is trying to set up a call centre in India. It's designed to connect job candidates to people who can test their English language skills on the phone. Now, in most countries this would be a pretty easy thing to set up. There are plenty of virtual call centre services such as Voxbone that could be set up extremely quickly.

However he has a problem trying to get any service together because there are questions over the legality of some kinds of IP services using voice over IP (VoIP) in India. Take a look at this blog entry for an opinion - http://andyabramson.blogs.com/voipwatch/2004/08/india_cracks_do. html.

Isn't it strange that India presents such an advanced face in the contact centre industry, yet unrestricted VoIP is not an option?

Wednesday, 30 April 2008

Posted at 12:11

Feeling Blue

The Indian technology providers are offering services for free, cutting back on new hires, not replacing consultants as they leave firms – and let's face it with all the uncertainty and cutbacks going on – a lot of people are just choosing to walk.

And yet, what's going on at IBM? It just increased its dividend by 25 per cent. For the past four quarters shareholders in Big Blue have enjoyed a 40 cents per share dividend, yet in the latest payout IBM paid 50 cents per share.

Just two weeks ago IBM reported a 26 per cent increase in annual profits and earning forecasts were increased. In fact, IBM is even buying back $12bn of its own shares this year.

Has anyone told IBM there is supposed to be a global credit crunch that is causing some other IT service providers to weep into their masala tea?

May 2008

Friday, 02 May 2008

Posted at 09:58

...but Computing is still the best

I was out last night in Soho at a bar next door to the Computing office for the launch party of a new outsourcing magazine – Sourcing Focus.

Chris Middleton, an ex-Computing staffer, is editing the new magazine and it will feature outsourcing content from the National Outsourcing Association – along with news and blogs.

In theory it's competition I guess. People looking at the blogs on Sourcing Focus might not be here on Computing checking out our blogs, but I don't feel worried. The very nature of online content means people subscribe to a large number of news feeds and use what is useful now and then, rather than exclusively using one source of information as the Gospel version of the outsourcing truth.

There is still a real shortage of good quality information and writing on outsourcing. It's a huge topic affecting millions of people, yet much of the writing on the topic remains ill-informed or just plain dull. I'm involved in the industry and yet my eyes glaze over reading a lot of the information sent to me by marketing departments and eager PRs.

Tuesday, 06 May 2008

Posted at 10:21

White paper - white noise

Does anyone really read any of the white papers churned out by IT suppliers? I don't want to sound flippant because I know that there are some great publications produced by some organisations, but generally the quality is dire.

Let's face it, the role of most commercially-oriented (as opposed to academic) white papers is either to function as a marketing device – bits of paper to hand out at conferences – or as an ego boost to the consultants who write them.

I just received two white papers by email from one of the major international IT suppliers - take a look at a quote from one of them:

"Many IT organisations have a metrics handbook that suggests the set of metrics to be followed. If such a handbook prescribes a set of mandatory metrics, I would like such metrics to be rather small in number. A larger set of metrics can remain optional, leaving it to the discretion of the project. Now the question is - how can one decide what would be the right metric. It is the question of finding the right metric first before getting the metric right; the irony that comes out of Joseph Juran's adage do right things before doing things right."

Excuse me? Now, a paper on improving software quality is never going to be a gripping read, but it should be possible to read it without thinking you just wandered into one of the drug-taking sequences in a Hunter S. Thompson novel.

So what's the answer? In my view it's staring the IT companies in the face, the humble blog. If those consultants really are as smart as they claim then they should be able to produce short, regular comment that is far more interesting and useful than the dirge they presently produce. These are supposed to be IT companies, so how come they seem wedded to the idea of supporting the printing press forever more?

Tuesday, 13 May 2008

Posted at 04:05

Building business between UK and India

I facilitated a meeting the other day for the board of the UK India Business Council (UKIBC). This is the (fairly) new body created from the earlier Indo-British Partnership Network, the major difference being that the IBPN was essentially a networking group, yet the UKIBC is a well-funded body focused on the business relationship between India and the UK.

UK Trade and Investment, the government organisation that promotes British business overseas, has released £1m of funding into UKIBC. This is intended to create a raft of new research and services to British business, allowing an easier relationship with India.

Though the UKIBC covers all sectors, it has some areas of focus and the hi-tech and sourcing sectors are of great interest. Some of the services UKIBC can help with include helping British companies wanting to explore the offshore option in India. Although UKIBC has received funding from government, it operates as a private sector firm and the intention is to focus only on operating in the private sector – so it's a good place to go for real business advice.

I had not interacted with the council before, but as I looked around the room I recognised a number of faces from my own work on linking business between India and the UK. It's a great team they have assembled and I hope they do a good job.

Tuesday, 13 May 2008

Posted at 10:01

Merger mania to hit IT services?

Two giants of the international sourcing industry have joined forces. HP has revealed that it is to acquire EDS for $13.9bn. As EDS is the second largest IT services player in the world and HP is the fifth, this creates a new $40bn a year leviathan – a real challenge to the beast that is IBM.

The business press is excited about the deal, and the way the story seemed to play out in the press makes it look as if the story leaked before either company wanted it to be public.

Although in revenue terms this will create a giant IT services firm, there is one area where it would not excel – management consulting. As everyone knows, EDS sold off its management consulting arm AT Kearney two years ago and HP has no real expertise in that area either.

In her blog for CIO magazine, Stephanie Overby hints that Accenture might be next. And why not? The combined might of HP and EDS could probably consume Accenture and if the merger works then the new entity would be a genuine rival to IBM, both in size and range of services.

It looks like the predicated wave of mergers and acquisitions in IT services is not only going to be at the second tier of smaller companies.

Monday, 19 May 2008
Posted at 16:12
Lloyds TSB cuts are a sign of testing times...

It looks like a large number of IT jobs in Manchester might be under threat at high street bank Lloyds TSB. The company has announced that 250 jobs are to be cut from an IT division employing around 470 people. Expectations are that a software testing unit in Wythenshawe employing 132 people might be cut altogether taking the brunt of the cuts, though a large number of contract staff would also be released.

The unions expect that the testing work is going to be transferred to the facilities the bank has in India. Typical union statements such as 'kick in the teeth' pepper some of their statements about the intended move.

Though there is an emotional reaction to this news, there has to be some pragmatism too. Software testing is becoming a largely automated process. Even where it requires human intervention, the largest pool of testing experts is now on the subcontinent. It makes good business sense to do the work there for the expertise, let alone any reduction in cost.

The high street financial service companies have shown that there does not need to be a flight of all services to some remote offshore destination. Most consumers hate having their customer services call answered in a remote country. Regardless of the quality of service, they just don't like it. Most of the banks have taken this on board and so we have seen some of the more reckless offshoring of voice-based services coming back home. Companies have even used their local call centres as a form of competitive advantage.

But software testing? However much the union protests, it's not something that the man on the street is really aware of. And this ignorance is something that the banks are very aware of. So long as the people answering the calls are local, almost any other service can be sourced from any location. Software testing in India is just one example of this. Take any of those companies that trumpets their local British call centre and I can guarantee that significant sections of their business are performed using offshoring or offshore outsourcing – just it's not the bit the customer sees.

Wednesday, 21 May 2008

Posted at 16:17

Not in his back yard

I was just browsing some of the business news from India on the Sify web site when I ran into this story about municipal outsourcing. The author of the story writes about how it's a terrible idea for local authorities to be outsourcing jobs such as street sweeping or fixing electricity pylons to private sector suppliers. In fact, he even calls this trend "a disease".

When most workers across the world are considering how they can compete with workers from India and China, it's nice to see how people in India can champion outsourcing at one moment and then fear it the next. Perhaps it's an example of not-in-my-backyard syndrome.

In the UK it is now almost unimaginable for power supply to be handled by the government. I have distant memories of government-controlled power in my childhood: basically the memories consist of having to remember where the candles are located as another power cut loomed. Who can remember the last power cut they ever suffered in London? And not only service levels have improved. The retail energy sector in the UK allows consumers to change energy supplier at the click of a button. I showed the Uswitch web site once to a French friend of mine and his jaw hit the floor when he tried understanding the concept that there could be different companies competing for your electricity or gas bill.

Last summer, a guy who works for Veolia – a supplier subcontracted by Westminster Council to empty the bins and sweep the streets in central London – started swearing abuse at me. I took his photo with my camera phone and sent it to his company. The next day he was fired. Can you imagine that kind of reaction to a misbehaving municipal street sweeper?

I don't believe that municipal outsourcing is a panacea for all ills, but every time I have worked with public sector managers they have time and again argued that the greater transparency of service available with an outsourced contract helps them to deliver their public service, within an agreed time and budget. Perhaps India should try some of the medicine it dishes out to the rest of the world?

Wednesday, 21 May 2008

Posted at 18:00

A NIIT to remember

Congratulations to the Indian IT services and training company NIIT for winning the coveted Digital Opportunity Award for its path-breaking work in spreading computer literacy and improving the quality of education at grass root levels, by the World Information Technology and Services Alliance (WITSA).

WITSA is a consortium of over 60 IT industry associations from economies around the world. Phil Bond,president and chief executive, Information Technology Association of America (ITAA) gave the award to NIIT chief executive Vijay K Thadani at the 16th World Congress on IT (WCIT) 2008 Awards' Ceremony, the annual congregation of the world's leading technology companies and associations held at Kuala Lumpur, last evening.

I was talking to the UK head of NIIT technologies, Ravi Pandey, on Monday, so he will be the next guest on my Talking Outsourcing podcast – which is very timely.

NIIT won the award for its 'Hole in the wall' scheme. This is an experiment devised for putting computers in very poor villages, where kids would never normally have access to IT systems. There is no training provided. Part of the experiment was designed to see how children could interact with user interfaces and learn about IT without being guided. It has been an amazing success and NIIT has contributed not only to the knowledge of how children learn, but also to the wealth of these villages – it gives the next generation a chance of education and hope.

Thursday, 22 May 2008

Posted at 10:02

Outsourcing's coming home

Today is the annual conference of the European Outsourcing Association (EOA). It's been held in a number of European cities before including Frankfurt and Amsterdam in recent years, but this time it has come home to London.

I say come home, but there is not really a geographic home for the EOA. The organisation is modelled on the UK National Outsourcing Association, celebrating its 21st birthday next month. The NOA structures have been applied to other countries allowing a federal body to be created across Europe.

I'm presenting a completely interactive research session during the conference, where every delegate will have an electronic keypad allowing them to respond en masse to my questions. It should be fun, and as soon as I have some of that live feedback from every delegate in the room I will make sure I blog the results – watch this space.

Friday, 30 May 2008

Posted at 12:16

What the experts said about outsourcing

The European Outsourcing Association annual summit all went well. In the end people were being turned away so in terms of getting delegates out for the event, it was a great success. In fact it has taken me nearly a week to blog the research results, partly because the after conference party was so good...

I ran an interactive session at the event, where I used some electronic kit to get immediate feedback from the audience. I'll try summarising some of the feedback from the conference delegates.

To start with, delegates feel the globalisation of the outsourcing industry will soon see one of the major Indian players acquiring a large European or US provider. It's a rumour that keeps returning to the fore, but with everyone believing it, will it really happen?

Some 75 per cent of respondents believe that such an acquisition is imminent. Consolidation was earmarked as a rapidly increasing industry trend by 68 per cent of delegates, in light of the recent acquisition of EDS by HP. Some other key findings that came up during the session include:

• Continental Europe is no longer as protectionist about outsourcing and offshoring as it once was – it is now an accepted business practice across the continent. Only eight per cent of respondents believe that European countries such as France and Germany are far behind in accepting outsourcing as a useful business strategy.

• New nearshore locations, particularly Romania and Bulgaria thanks to their recent entrance into the European Union, have brought a new attractiveness to the European offshoring market. Some 59 per cent of respondents believed Romania and Bulgaria are now more attractive to work with, while only nine per cent believed the attraction had been reduced.

- The delegates realised that Eastern European nations do not have the scale of staff to resource huge outsourcing deals, with the majority (58 per cent) believing that different geographies are suited to different types of outsourcing projects. Only 17 per cent believed that Indian providers are leaps and bounds ahead of all other geographies.

I also asked some questions on the global credit crunch and the potential for recession. It's not specifically related to outsourcing, but it does affect outsourcing decisions so I wanted to gauge the mood of those present. The first surprise (considering the doom and gloom presented each day in the media) was that 64 per cent of delegates had not seen any impact on their business, so far.

I tried to check on perceptions, rather than actuals, by asking if delegates were worried. Even then, 43 per cent were not worried and 17 per cent were not sure – a lot more than the worried 40 per cent. Then I asked if a recession might even be a good thing for the global outsourcing market, encouraging people to explore outsourcing where they might not have before. Some 64 per cent agreed that it would be a good development with 19 per cent not sure – a huge majority that would actively like to see a recession!

So it's an interesting mix of results. Certainly the European market is maturing quickly, both as consumers of services and as providers, but the really interesting result for me was that no one in this industry appears to be worried about the credit crunch. Pass the Bollinger...

June 2008

Tuesday, 10 June 2008

Posted at 15:04

Don't write off the outsourcer

Interesting to note that although outsourcing is becoming more popular, the day of the megadeal with a single outsourcing partner appears to be over. Analyst firm Gartner defines a megadeal as a contract with a total value of more than $1bn – last year only 10 deals of this magnitude took place, down on 12 the year before.

Partly this is because more and more companies are using outsourcing as a business practice, so at all levels of the company it's more usual to work in this way. So it's more likely for smaller deals to be struck that don't end up reported as megadeals.

Also, there is an increasing trend to multisource and break up requirements across a basket of suppliers – offering access to best-in-breed services, rather than just going to a monolithic one-stop-shop.

The combination of multisourcing and increased automation of services is highly likely to result in reduced contract sizes – but it is likely there will be more contracts as these solutions become more and more popular. Don't write off the outsourcer just yet because megadeals are on the decline...

Tuesday, 10 June 2008

Posted at 18:00

The recession is a good business opportunity

Here is the news that everyone has been waiting for; economic slowdown is officially a good thing. Well, I'd better qualify that by saying that it's good if you are involved in offering global services to clients – particularly through offshore outsourcing.

A new study out today has highlighted this as a key finding. The study is titled 'Global BPO Market Forecast 2008-2012' and was undertaken by NelsonHall. Other observations from the research include a prediction that the global market for business process outsourcing (BPO) will be worth $450bn by 2012. That's a serious amount of cash.

In theory our economy is still growing, yet with studies like this predicting continued strong growth in the outsourcing market it looks like a good place to be if things do start getting rough in the year ahead. Recession, what recession?

Wednesday, 11 June 2008

Posted at 12:47

Obama bows to reality of globalisation

After all the excitement in the US regarding who is going to stand in the Presidential election this year as the Democratic nominee, it's only fair to wonder what the candidates might think about offshore outsourcing. After all, Hillary Clinton has long been on record as a strong supporter of investment in the US by Asian companies, but now she is out of the race.

The presumptive candidate for the Democrats, Barack Obama, talked on Monday to an audience in Raleigh, North Carolina, about the subject – so we have an idea what his side of the house feels about the subject.

The basic message from Obama is that you can't fight globalisation. You can't stop US companies working with people overseas.

"Revolutions in communication and technology have sent jobs wherever there's an internet connection; that have forced children in Raleigh and Boston to compete for those jobs with children in Bangalore and Beijing," he said.

So the internet takes most of the blame, but he has acknowledged that this access to global resource does increase competition – more than ever before, US workers need to compete with others.

Obama has a suggested short and long-term policy plan that involves training, education and equipping workers for the more competitive and innovative workplace of the future. He also savagely attacked the Republican candidate John McCain, suggesting that he had nothing to offer voters beyond an endorsement of the policies of the present Bush administration.

Clearly a political strategy that attaches McCain to the washed-up legacy of George Bush is something we are going to hear more of from Obama over the coming months, but to be fair to McCain I have yet to hear him talking on this subject. Perhaps he might make some statements this week now that Obama has chosen to fight him on the outsourcing and globalisation agenda.

I hope so, because this was a major campaign issue back in 2004. To hear Obama talking about changes to education, training plans, and support programmes demonstrates a greater maturity than the debate four years ago – where offshoring was something that the legislators believed could just be banned.

Obama is right to take a more pragmatic view. We aren't talking about offshoring anymore. The way companies do business has entirely changed because of global networks, and US companies are leading that change. Let's hope the Republican candidate takes a similar view so whoever becomes the next President of the USA will start focusing on the long-term issue of equipping US workers for the future.

Friday, 13 June 2008

Posted at 17:01

We want your views on outsourcing

My friend Dr Richard Sykes chairs the outsourcing and offshore group at UK hi-tech trade association Intellect. Last year, Richard and I wrote a book about Global Services and outsourcing for the BCS.

Richard's group is running a major survey of industry to try predicting some future trends in outsourcing and offshoring and so if you are checking out this blog then it might be useful for you to go and try filling in the survey.

If you participate then there are some benefits and prizes as well as the warm feeling that your views will help shape some research into where the industry is headed. You can take part in the Intellect survey by clicking here.

Friday, 13 June 2008

Posted at 17:05

It's not only about India

I was sitting watching the Austria v Poland football match last night trying to remember how on earth England failed to get into the Euro 2008 competition. Still, when I glanced at Fortune magazine today I saw some information that made me feel a certain pride in being English.

Good old British Telecom – now more correctly known at BT Group and driven globally by its BT Global Services division – is going great guns. In the last three months, BT signed more than $1bn of multi-year service management contracts with clients such as AT&T and Verizon. Just this week BT signed a $650m contract with Procter & Gamble to handle data, voice, and networks.

When we look at the use of outsourcing and offshoring by major companies, the detractors often assume it means nothing more than jobs are migrating to lower cost locations. The success of BT in transforming itself into one of the largest global operators in networks and IT services shows that the best technology suppliers are not necessarily in India.

Monday, 16 June 2008

Posted at 17:43

Outsourcing: It's just another day

A survey by the Management Consultancies Association of members of the British Bankers Association has found that 41 per cent plan to outsource more of their business.

Ninety per cent of respondents have already engaged in some outsourcing – quite impressive and demonstrative of how far entrenched the use of outsourcing is within financial services. More importantly, 89 per cent of respondents believe they have used outsourcing as a business tool without leading to a loss of jobs.

It's hardly likely that in this kind of survey the respondents would say something negative, but nine out of 10 bankers saying that they are using outsourcing - and it does not affect local jobs - is quite a statement of how companies are doing business today. Outsourcing has become just a regular day at work.

Wednesday, 18 June 2008

Posted at 10:29

Is India slowing down?

S. Ramadorai, the chief executive of Tata Consultancy Services (TCS), the biggest offshore outsourcing company in India, has told reporters at an OECD conference that the offshore outsourcing market is slowing down.

Ramadorai was talking to journalists at the OECD ministerial meeting on the future of the internet economy. He predicted that the industry in India would grow by 20-22 per cent this coming year – compared to about 25 per cent last year.

That's still not bad, but what I find interesting is that everyone in the industry seems to be talking up the opportunities for offshoring in a recession. Most of the Indian offshoring companies are talking about the opportunities presented by a more cost-conscious business environment. So how come TCS is taking the opposite view?

July 2008

Friday, 04 July 2008

Posted at 17:55

Write 100 lines: "I must not outsource my homework to India"

When I was a kid, I once did my school homework on my Commodore 64. I typed it all up using a simple word processing system (that I had coded myself) and then printed to a dot matrix printer.

I handed in my work thinking I was leap years ahead of my class in using the best technology I could lay my hands on. My teacher failed the project and asked me to re-write everything by hand.

I remembered this episode when I read recent news about Australian kids getting into trouble for outsourcing their homework to India. For a while now, most universities have had systems in place to prevent plagiarism in essays. So, if I was writing an essay on the history of Australia and I just lifted most of the text straight from Wikipedia, the automated systems would detect a pattern match and flag up my essay to the markers.

However, with software development it's much harder to detect plagiarism. If you are a first-year computer science student and asked to write a basic alpha-numeric sort algorithm, you can sweat all night over the keyboard or just post the job on a site such as Rent-A-Coder. A software developer somewhere out there will be willing to write the code and email it to you almost instantly.

Clearly there is almost nothing that can be done to detect this type of cheating. The only option for the university is to include some practical supervised tests in the course, to ensure the students really can perform on their own.

But this brought me to think of another personal example. When a friend of mine was working on his MBA a few years back, he outsourced some of his accounting module to his own accountant (my friend was managing director of a software firm). He was open with his professor about what he had done personally and what he had delegated to his accountant. The professor insisted that he complete the outsourced parts of the module himself, or he would have to fail the project.

My friend protested. Pointing out that in the real world he would never do any complex accountancy, which is why he employs an accountant. It would seem that his MBA was not preparing him for the real world in any way – which given his own business success was not really a problem, more of an observation.

I don't think we can prevent kids hiring others to do their homework. It's happened since the first homework project was assigned. We just need to be aware that with project-based sites springing up all over the internet, it's getting easier to get small tasks done. Courses need to be rethought so the right skills are taught and the testing methods are valid.

Tuesday, 08 July 2008

Posted at 10:06

In the little black book

I'm getting bombarded with press releases from companies that feature in the Black Book of Outsourcing, a book that is now being updated annually with new information on suppliers in the outsourcing business.

I have every respect for Douglas Brown and Scott Wilson, authors of the book. I haven't got the new edition yet, but I have read earlier ones and it's an interesting and well put together piece of work.

However, I still find it a little odd when I read some of the marketing hyperbole that comes through on emails about the book. Companies almost screaming with joy that they were featured in the book. If they explained what they had achieved so that they were featured in the book then it might be more interesting, rather than sending me a series of executive quotes describing what an honour it is to be in the Black Book.

As the bard of Staines, Ali G, might say, *is it cos I is English?*

Thursday, 10 July 2008
Posted at 12:41
Government loves outsourcing

A new review commissioned by the government and written by business economist DeAnne Julius positions the UK as a world leader in the outsourcing of public services. The new report, published today, goes on to suggest that the UK public sector should go even further down the outsourcing road, with many more services ripe for "significant expansion".

Listening to the news on the radio this morning, they seemed unsure about whether Britain should crow about being an international leader in the outsourcing of public services, but it can't be denied that governments across the world are beating a path to the UK to examine best practice in various areas.

Julius, a former member of the monetary policy committee of the Bank of England and chair of think tank Chatham House, writes in the report that the UK outsourcing industry has grown by 130 per cent since 1997 (notably since the Labour party came to power), and now employs around 1.2 million people. That's huge. Let's not underestimate the size of this part of the industry. It's something like £80bn a year we are talking about here.

The Julius report calls for more openness and transparency in government departments, which would promote the use of outsourcing, as it generally demands open measures. The historic use of outsourcing by government has been to reduce costs – much like the private sector – but Julius indicates that outsourcing can now be a key driver for achieving social and environmental targets that would be difficult or impossible to achieve in-house.

It's interesting to hear that this is an area in which the UK is a world leader. What do you think of your local bin collection, parking wardens, and prison logistics then?

Friday, 11 July 2008
Posted at 11:39
Outsourcing vs offshoring

A viva has finally sold off its offshore operations in India to WNS for £115m in cash. When the firm set up in India, using the Norwich Union brand, it became a poster child for offshoring. A BBC documentary even explored call centre offshoring by swapping staff between Bangalore and Norwich. Naturally, the educated young Indian call centre agent who came over to the UK was a bit disturbed to find that agents here might show up for work dressed as Elvis.

Now that's all over, but what does it mean. Certainly it's a shot in the arm for outsourcing – as opposed to offshoring. Aviva has contracted with WNS for over eight years, so there will be a smooth transition – probably the same people doing the same jobs in reality.

Aviva claims that by outsourcing to a third party they can lay off the risks of exchange rates, inflation, and all the other headaches associated with running a back office a long way from home.

This offshoring (do it yourself and save the margin you pay to a supplier) versus outsourcing (let someone else manage all the local issues) debate has raged for years. Given the uncertainties of the world economy at present, the extreme changes in exchange rates over the past 18 months, inflation in countries like India rising sharply (staples like rice and lentils have doubled in price in a year), it's almost certain that the outsourcing model is going to be more favourable for a long time to come.

Friday, 11 July 2008
Posted at 16:00
Debunking the media myths

A cademics at the Leverhulme Centre for Research on Globalisation and Economic Policy (GEP), an institute of the University of

Nottingham, have just published a new study titled The Economic Impact of Offshoring.

The report claims to be the largest ever study of how offshoring affects British companies – and jobs. The Nottingham researchers analysed over 66,000 UK companies during this research.

The first point to note is that the researchers believe that the media in general overplays the direct impact of offshoring on jobs. So they are critical of the way that offshoring and offshore outsourcing have been seen as little more than a process of firing 500 people here and hiring 500 people in India.

The real situation is far more complex. Globalisation of supply chains, automation, and greater connectivity, has all conjoined to create a far more complex reality for production of good and services.

The report summary, written by GEP director David Greenaway, says: "It is clear from our research that offshoring does contribute to changes in what is known as the 'skill mix', but our findings also show that it results in increased turnover, improved productivity, more exports and higher employment. Plainly, from an economy-wide perspective, activities that produce such results should be embraced rather than discouraged. This study shows that offshoring is not to be feared. It is something that should be welcomed and whose benefits are there to be exploited."

This is an admirable effort in analysing how work supply chains are changing, but I guess it would help if the popular media also takes a look.

Wednesday, 16 July 2008
Posted at 15:53
India vs China vs Web 2.0

Yesterday I chaired the annual sourcing and offshoring day hosted by the National Outsourcing Association. It's an annual all-day focus on all things related to offshoring. We were at the plush offices of law firm Lovells in the City – they have the most amazing auditorium at the top of their office.

The day focused on exploring some of the key themes and issues today in offshoring, so as you might expect there was a lot of debate on India vs China vs Philippines and so on, but I was particularly interested by something one of the participants said to me in the afternoon.

I was asking Stephen Page, chief executive of Sapphire Group, if he thought anything had been missed or not discussed, and he answered: "Yes, Web 2.0".

Now, that's not just because his company does a lot of Web 2.0 work. In fact, when I introduced the day I mentioned that I thought Web 2.0 and changing business models, and corporate structures would come up. After all, if you started a business tomorrow would you really invest in dozens of licences for email client software when you could just format Google Mail for free. But does it mean you just outsourced your email provision to the US?

So it was interesting that we spent most of the day focusing on the geographic regions, rather than the changing nature of business itself – that's what is likely to drive offshoring far more.

Monday, 28 July 2008

Posted at 09:38

Bye bye BPO

The Business Standard newspaper in India reported last week that a lot of the terminology used within the IT industry for outsourcing will soon change. Expressions such as offshoring, or business process outsourcing (BPO) will all be consigned to the wastepaper basket of history as business models change and we no longer use these terms.

This is obvious to say the least. I might even remind the editor of the Business Standard that Pope Benedict is, indeed, a Catholic. In fact, it is the business media and industry analysts that propagate many of these terms. If the business press stops using the acronym BPO then it's likely that the term would soon decline in use.

The more important point though is that industry in general is changing – particularly services at present as manufacturing went through globalisation rather earlier. The way a company is constructed is very different today to how a company looked 20 years ago. I'm in the process of forming a new company myself right now and I'm asking myself the question, "do I actually need to hire anyone at all, or can I just contract all this out to experts?"

Outsourcing, offshoring, BPO and so on, all these terms will be consumed within the general supply chain of future organisations – maybe all these terms will just be replaced by partnership?

Monday, 28 July 2008

Posted at 15:00

And you're in which country...?

There has been a lot in the press recently about the demise of offshore customer services. Anyone reading this blog will be aware that customer service centres went through an offshore boom in the post-millennium period as every customer services director explored offshoring – often because it was what everyone else was doing rather than for any more strategic reason.

There was an initial trend of offshore agents acting as if they were local, adopting western names and taking accent classes, well parodied in John Jeffcoat's movie Outsourced – out now on DVD if any of you want a good laugh about cows wandering into the call centre.

But, the wind of change arrived with an immense consumer backlash. Initially this could be (and was) dismissed as a fear of change, a wariness of people in far-off lands handling consumer problems. However, a scan through the press these days shows that the depth of feeling has persisted with the argument focusing far more on quality of service.

I was talking to a call centre boss recently who has agents in Hungary and the Philippines. The company used to have agents in India, but found that the Philippines worked better with British consumers. When I asked exactly why, I was interested that, for this company, it had nothing at all to do with accent or consumer perceptions of offshoring. It was the ability of the Filipino's to understand when the caller was joking, when the caller was being serious, when the caller needs help – in fact it was all about an ability to connect to the person at the other end of the line, rather than sticking to a service level agreement.

There is a lot that can be achieved working with global partners through offshore outsourcing, but will that interface with consumers always need to be handled locally? I'd really like to hear more opinions on this.

August 2008

Monday, 04 August 2008

Posted at 15:10

Preparing for a new era of employment

So the weekend has gone once again, though I am off to Kolkata in India (I still usually say Calcutta) tomorrow for the rest of the week. I always like returning to India, even for just a few days, because the people are friendly and the food is amazing – especially for a vegetarian like me.

I was relaxing and looking at the papers yesterday and I saw something really interesting in the Wall Street Journal – it has to happen now and then I guess. The story explored how the US is trying to consider meeting the challenges of offshoring and globalisation. The Financial Services Forum, a body funded by the financial services industry, has produced a new research paper suggesting that the US system of unemployment insurance is outdated and needs a complete overhaul for the 21st century.

They aren't the first to suggest this - the famous McKinsey paper on offshoring suggested this several years back, but they are articulating some of the steps that might be required to achieve this change – including new hypothecated taxes on those in employment, to fund those who are out of a job.

The US has an extremely vibrant job market. Around 25,000 jobs are created – and destroyed – every business hour, which puts the issues of offshoring into some perspective. However, foreign competition is increasing and the present legislation was designed for a USA in the midst of the depression.

Once they get the unemployment support sorted out for a new era of employment they need to get started on how to tax consumption rather than income, and how to promote lifelong education. It's going to be a rocky ride to the middle of this century for a superpower that needs to accept that the times they are a-changin'.

Wednesday, 06 August 2008

Posted at 11:28

Get smart

I was recently reading a new book by Jim Champy, the head of consulting at Perot Systems. In Outsmart, Champy gives examples of how to buck trends and outsmart your competition. It's an interesting and engaging read, written in a very easy-to-read, friendly style. I'm sure Jim would make a good companion in the pub for an evening chatting about why some companies get it so wrong.

One of the points he makes in the book is about getting caught up in industry trends, to the point that certain business strategies are followed just because investors or analysts expect it – even if it might not be the best route for the company to take. Outsourcing is a good example of this. We all know that it might not always be the best way for a company to deliver services, even though it is often a better strategy than the status quo.

Champy demonstrates this with some examples in his book of companies that benefited from looking at outsourcing and then not doing it. I was reminded of this when I saw an Information Week story yesterday about Deutsche Post not going through with a planned outsourcing deal to HP. Just because outsourcing usually makes sense, doesn't mean it is always the right decision.

Thursday, 07 August 2008

Posted at 14:59

If it's Friday, it must be India

I'm sitting in the beautiful surroundings of the ITC Sonar hotel in Kolkata (formerly Calcutta) in northeast India. I flew out from London yesterday on BA and I was interested to see that the trend of young people vanishing to exotic locations with T-shirts brandishing the legend "girls on tour" or similar slogans, along with their name on the back, has now been extended to India. I've never noticed that before.

There were two distinct groups on my plane - a whole bunch of Spanish girls all with "India 2008" t-shirts and another group of British girls on a world tour. They had all their planned locations printed on their shirts – and I counted at least a dozen, with the next stop being Tokyo.

It was quite fun listening to them in the immigration line. I guess I've become used to India, so it was interesting to hear their banter and first impressions of arriving in Kolkata. One asked if there were 16 rupees to the pound. Another corrected her and said it is more like 900. I had to give them a better idea of the real value.

Another was asking the immigration officer what their hotel looks like. I gave them a good estimate of what it would look like, given that they were planning to pay less than £20 a night for a room. They had been joking that there might be cockroaches in the room – I told them that it's probably not a joke.

Although it was just a bit of fun chatting to them about their world tour, it did remind me that there is a huge section of the British population that know nothing of India beyond the good food at the Star of India on a Friday night. Given the importance of both India and China in the world economy, it would be prudent for universities to consider how they can give students more practical knowledge of what's going on in Asia today.

Thursday, 07 August 2008

Posted at 17:05

India - moving on up

I'm at the ICT East 2008 conference in Kolkata, India. It's a major annual event hosted by the Confederation of Indian Industry (CII) - the Indian equivalent of the CBI - and WEBEL, the agency that promotes the electronics and hi-tech industry in West Bengal.

The focus of the event today was how eastern India, in particular the region around West Bengal can "move up the value chain" and offer higher value services.

Mr Siddharth, the IT secretary of the government of West Bengal, explained that only three per cent of IT service exports come from this region of India, yet there is plenty of local human resource, with over a million students graduating in this part of India alone every year. His target is to get that percentage up to 15 within a few years.

Siddharth explained how the government believes that the stimulation of demand for IT by consumers is a key way of supporting the industry.

"The government is actively involved in reaching out to regional citizens with e-service programmes, including IT education and familiarisation of IT tools," he said.

"We are going first to schools where more than 50 per cent of children are from disadvantaged backgrounds. These students then become familiar with using computers in the same way they might also learn to swim."

Ajay Chowdhry, the chairman of the CII national council, was adamant that India can no longer compete on a cost advantage alone.

"Brand India has been created by the ICT industry. ICT companies in India are already taking the next steps to moving up the value chain. We have to face up to the fact that the cost advantage is now wearing out - Indian companies have to now seek out new innovations," he said.

Kiran Karnik, the well-respected immediate past president of Nasscom, the Indian hi-tech trade association, gave a passionate lecture about how the industry should not panic, given the international challenges.

"Yes, we are seeing a credit crunch in USA, but you know we have seen it all before. It will be a temporary issue. Can you remember the downturn we experienced after the dot com downturn and then 9/11?" he said.

Karnik went on to explain that the Indian IT services industry is exceeding all expectations from even just a few years back.

"Revenue in this industry is now almost $60bn a year. Let's not talk about the industry being in trouble – we are preparing for the next stage of growth," he said.

Many of the lectures talked about the human resource issue India is suffering – the problem of creating large numbers of graduates, but with few of them ready to take on jobs in international companies.

Sanjay Jha, executive director of Dale Carnegie in India, believes that the key to the problem is that soft skills have been disregarded for too long.

"You need to create a bridge between the students coming out of college and being employable," he said.

"Soft skills are a hard business. As a country if we don't work on developing this soft skills infrastructure then we will miss the boat – and the bus as well."

Tuesday, 12 August 2008

Posted at 09:37

Blogging for India

The other day I was giving a talk in Kolkata, India, to a group of people assembled at the CII ICT East conference. I was speaking on the second day of the conference. On the first, a few of the founders of Indian business process outsourcing – such as Raman Roy – were speaking.

When I started talking to the audience the next day, I was aware that a lot of them were owners of small or medium sized companies, and eager to try doing business with Europe. I asked the entire audience: "Who wrote a blog entry about the interesting day we had yesterday with industry leaders such as Raman?"

Not a single person in the room had blogged about the conference – or about anything else for that matter.

As I went on to talk about the virtues of podcasting and social networks, I think I ended up overstepping what the audience wanted to hear. However, I still think that for smaller organisations, these are great - and virtually free - tools for getting yourself noticed above the noise of every IT company jumping up and calling out "me, me, me..."

I also challenged the companies in the room, by reminding them that they are the cream of the IT talent in India - an industry now known for IT excellence - yet where is the innovative online marketing for their efforts? Companies known for hi-tech innovation should be able to do a better job than a chewing gum company has been doing with the YouTube star Matt Harding. Take a look at the recent update to his famous 2006 'Dancing' video – this new version is just awesome!

It was therefore nice for me to land back in London, switch on the laptop, and to find an email from Moitrayee Basu, who works for MSR in Kolkata – the first thing she had done after the conference was to go and create a blog.

It's early days for blogging by smaller companies in India, but it's going to be exciting as more and more comment comes online. I'm looking forward to hearing that my CII talk may have actually influenced a second or third company soon.

Friday, 15 August 2008

Posted at 09:30

Who moved my job?

I was at a pub in Soho the other day saying farewell to Computing features editor Mark Samuels. Many of you will have seen Mark's blog on these very pages so you will realise it's a shame to see him go. I can't understand why he would want to leave the stress of weekly deadlines to edit a magazine that comes out four times and year and probably pays him more money...

As I went into the leaving party, I just received the art for my new book Who Moved My Job? I showed the images to a few people and they all universally loved the cover and the concept for the book.

In short, it's a story of globalisation – three English sheepdogs find themselves redundant after they train their own replacements. Sounds familiar? Anyway, if you like the idea then take a look at the book web site and feel free to comment – I want to hear what you think.

Wednesday, 20 August 2008

Posted at 13:11

A tragic story

I first met Mohan K Babu of Infosys when he was writing his book Offshoring IT Services. He works for Infosys and is another regular blogger – he has often helped me when I need information about Infosys quickly.

So, I was shocked to read his latest blog post – and right now I am on holiday in the US - but I still want to react to it. His baby son, just four months old, died on a flight from Brussels to Delhi. Mohan details the sequence of events on a personal blog, but basically everything was OK until the plane was descending to land in India and the baby choked.

Mohan has written a detailed critique of the procedures used by Jet Airways during the flight, the lack of emergency procedures at the airport, and the lack of empathy shown by airport staff. It's a tragic story and I hope there is some kind of investigation into how this could happen on a major international airline.

As Mohan points out, this is an extremely sad example of how procedures used by multinational companies can sometimes be the difference between life and death. In our daily life at work, we often ignore things that should be challenged. When a "perfect storm" sequence of events is triggered all we can do is rely on the people who sold us a service. When they don't know what to do, all is lost.

September 2008

Tuesday, 16 September 2008

Posted at 16:42

Will the financial services turmoil affect outsourcing?

I was in Soho today chairing a webinar with Samad Masood, a principal analyst at Ovum. At the end of the webinar I took a moment to ask him a couple of quick questions about the problems we are witnessing in the financial services industry.

In a week where Lehman Brothers has filed for Chapter 11 bankruptcy protection and Merrill Lynch has been swallowed by Bank of America, I wanted to see what his views were on how this turbulence affects outsourcing suppliers.

Samad agreed there is a problem for most suppliers.

"Financial services is a significant proportion of all the large vendors' business so the challenges we are having in financial services right now are going to affect the vendors' business, and their approach to market," he said.

"But we need to make it clear that not all financial services are suffering. Some sub-segments of the sector, such as insurance or regulatory and compliance – which will probably increase now – have been largely immune to these issues.

"Companies like Capgemini and Accenture are reporting growth in financial services projects, particularly where their consultants can advise on reducing cost."

So is outsourcing a good idea now anyway? Some people in the market are telling me that companies are holding back on purchasing or strategic decisions, such as outsourcing programmes. Some suppliers are telling me they are busier than ever, with more and more enquiries about cost reduction measures. Is an economic slowdown a good or a bad thing for outsourcing suppliers?

Samad said: "It's like any of these situations - there is never one answer for everybody. It really depends on the specific client. I don't think all projects are going to be halted, but then I also don't think that clients are going to suddenly invest in outsourcing either. It's horses for courses whether the market is rising or falling."

Samad added an interesting point about the way suppliers need to behave in a difficult business environment.

"The important thing to understand is that there is going to be more of a focus on partnership, relationships between clients and suppliers, and trust," he said.

"That means a focus on understanding the issues of each particular client. Vendors should stop generalising across their clients and really invest in getting to know each client in more depth."

Wednesday, 17 September 2008

Posted at 09:59

Is BT about to split from Tech Mahindra?

Rumours continue to swirl in the Indian press that BT Group is about to sell its 31 per cent stake in Tech Mahindra to Tata Consultancy Services. Neither company has confirmed anything yet, but it has been circulating on the blogs for a month or so and the national papers are now all reporting it as a likely deal.

There are a couple of interesting questions here. Tech Mahindra gets about two-thirds of its revenue from BT. So how might that change once they are cast adrift from each other? Second, is this one more step towards BT Global Services really taking on more of a role itself as a systems integrator/consulting firm, rather than being seen as a telecom-focused operator?

Thursday, 18 September 2008

Posted at 10:45

TCS in the news again

I find myself commenting again on Tata Consultancy Services (TCS). It's strange because I mentioned them in my own blog yesterday, and I noticed that the editor of Computing, Bryan Glick, also mentioned them. Yet I was shooting the breeze with someone who knows TCS well yesterday who confessed that things are "a bit quiet" over there.

It's certainly true that most of the major suppliers seem to have reined in some of their more extravagant promotional techniques this summer – I never got a single invitation to any test cricket this summer for example!

Nevertheless, news just broke that TCS has signed a five-year deal with telecoms giant Ericsson, to supply applications development and maintenance (ADM) on a global basis.

Not only does this demonstrate that Ericsson is still thinking beyond the business meltdown engulfing us in London today, but also it shows a strong confidence in TCS and its ability to deliver solid, steady, and reliable internal IT. A lot of IT suppliers talk up their ability to innovate, but let's face it, a lot of companies paying for ADM services just want it to work well – first time.

Friday, 19 September 2008

Posted at 09:58

Watching the fallout

Here we go with the immediate fallout of the financial crisis in the US and Europe. The 2,500 people employed at the Lehman Brothers back office in Mumbai are now expecting to be cast adrift as the centre closes by February.

Nasscom, the association representing the hi-tech sector in India, claims the fallout from this financial crisis will be very company specific and only damaging in the short term. However, one look at the interviews being given by senior executives of IT firms in India shows they are all extremely worried.

It seems a little premature of one major Indian firm to assume they are not impacted because Lehman Brothers and Merrill Lynch are not on the client list – this has not ended yet. One thing I was thinking about though is that if the Chinese sovereign funds do make some large-scale financial service purchases in the US, then where does that put the Indian outsourcers?

Monday, 22 September 2008

Posted at 11:20

South African upheaval threatens emerging IT market

Over the past few years South Africa has steadily built up a reputation in the contact centre market. South African suppliers have been working extensively with European clients either through outsourcing or captive centres, and enjoying the benefits of a similar time zone and a good cultural connection to Brits – one of the classic issues that the Indians have worked hard to rectify as this industry has grown.

But am I the only person worried about what's happening in politics there right now? Political commentators are focused on the implications of the resignation of President Thabo Mbeki, but who is exploring the ramifications for the fledging services industry that has been taking off? The growth of democracy in South Africa, since apartheid was abolished and President Mandela took over the country, has been astounding. In international services, it now shines like a beacon, offering hope to other African nations with ideas about using technology for development. I'm going to Nigeria next month as part of a UN project to help develop the IT services market in Africa through the creation of a multilateral representative trade body – so this is a very real and present issue.

With Mbeki pushed aside for his meddling and autocracy (and frankly ridiculous views on AIDS), the ANC appears unstable. If the ANC is unstable and splits, then the political future of the nation is uncertain.

The country is facing basic infrastructural problems such as power cuts, unaddressed poverty and inequality, and unemployment standing at over 25 per cent. It's going to take some tough decisions and excellent long-term vision to keep South Africa on track, but the potential replacements for Mbeki seem focused on short-term populist measures.

At least the South African satirist Pieter-Dirk Uys won't be out of a job any time soon...

Tuesday, 23 September 2008

Posted at 11:19

The changing nature of work

JP Rangaswami is chief information officer of BT Global Services and well known in the blogosphere for his eclectic Confused of Calcutta blog. I was talking to him the other day about where jobs might lead to in future, what with all the changes going on today in the way companies are restructuring and globalising.

He said something that I find very interesting and I thought I would share with you: "My father had one job. By the time I retire, I will have had seven. My son will also have seven - at the same time."

Tuesday, 23 September 2008

Posted at 12:09

IT is saving lives in India

How many IT projects do you hear about that are really life-changing? How many IT projects have the potential to really improve the life of more than a billion people? And, how many projects like this were started by one individual putting his hand in his pocket to inject some personal cash into an idea he had while walking down Piccadilly and observing British ambulances tearing up the road to the next RTC (road traffic collision – I knew all those episodes of Casualty on the BBC iPlayer would come in useful eventually)?

Ramalinga Raju, the founder and chairman of Satyam, was the man walking along the street near to the Ritz hotel in London a couple of years ago when those ambulances went by. He wondered out loud to some of his colleagues why there was no centrally coordinated emergency service in India that could get an ambulance to a person in need within minutes.

Instead of just wondering, he put £1.5m of his own cash into a personal side project, creating a call response unit and equipping ambulances with the kit they might need for 50 or so common emergencies, including pregnancy and snake bites. From this initial programme came what is now the EMRI - Emergency Management and Research Institute.

Today, this is a free service delivered through hi-tech emergency call response centres with over 785 ambulances across the Andhra Pradesh, Gujarat and Uttarakhand states in India. With the projected expansion of fleet and services set to spread across more states, EMRI will have more than 10,000 ambulances by 2010. That's a national ambulance service covering a population of more than a billion and all created within just a few years. Satyam proved what can be done with technology and now the government is coming on board to fund the expansion.

I just had a conversation this morning with Som Sarma, the European vice president of Satyam about how this project started, why it is important for Satyam and India, and how they might use this expertise in future. You can hear an audio podcast of that conversation by going to the iTunes podcast directory and searching for 'Talking Outsourcing' or by clicking here to play it back from the web.

Friday, 26 September 2008

Posted at 13:13

BA thinking ahead despite troubled times

It's interesting to see that British Airways has just signed a three-year deal for the support and testing of business critical applications with

NIIT Technologies. They have had a relationship for some time, but it's clearly a vote of confidence for NIIT.

Though it is by no means the largest IT supplier out there, NIIT has been carving out a niche in the travel and transport area. The well-known Black Book of Outsourcing ranks the firm number one in the world for technical services to travel companies.

It's good to see that BA is still making big purchasing decisions too. All the airlines are suffering right now, yet it does appear that BA is thinking very much into a future beyond the present pain.

Monday, 29 September 2008

Posted at 13:25

Too many Chiefs

Unions in the UK have become pretty wise to outsourcing. They know it's a strategy used by most major companies and so now they don't talk of strikes and pickets, they generally work with management on the best way to improve pay and conditions with an acceptance of outsourcing as a part of the mix. You can't turn back the tide, and usually it is not the process of outsourcing itself that causes a decline in working conditions anyway.

But what about where offshoring is involved and there are workers in a far-flung region all involved in the supply chain? Just a couple of months ago the BBC TV programme Panorama exposed clothes retailer Primark for using child labour in Asian countries. It's the kind of exposure most of us thought had been left behind since Naomi Klein wrote No Logo, where she detailed the abuse of Asian manufacturing workers stitching trainers together for pennies.

For a long time now, detractors of offshoring have criticised hi-tech services offshoring using the same comments – IT is creating a culture of offshore cyber-coolies, and so on. But local unions in places like India have not become beds of seething frustrated IT workers waving red flags and singing The Internationale, because the market has naturally rewarded them. How can you go to a union to complain when the company you work for pays well and gives you a whole range of fringe benefits that most workers could only dream of? The fact that good IT and business process outsourcing (BPO) staff are in strong demand also means that the companies desperately need to look after their people, as offers are always flooding in for those who can do their job well.

So it has not appeared to be the right environment or industry for mass organisation by the workers, yet I've noticed a blog recently called BPO Union with the motto: "One for all and all for one". It's a nice initiative to try using the blog environment to create a way for workers to get together and comment online about their life at work and any issues that are under the radar of the industry associations. Clearly in a modern hi-tech industry, the creation of a virtual union has to be the way to go and it also affords anonymity – important if grieved workers are going to be able to feel free to discuss issues openly.

However, I'm not sure that the founder of the blog itself needs to remain anonymous – the main contributor goes by the name "Chief" and refuses to be named even for media interviews. I'm sure there is a good reason for it, but it does strike an unnecessarily sinister tone when Chief delivers a judgement on the blog. Is it really that unsafe to openly criticise the IT industry in a place like India?

And, though the idea is good and needed, Chief should aim at targets worth shooting down. A recent blog entry claims that employees are doing unpaid overtime beyond eight hours per shift and if quantified this would be worth hundreds of millions of dollars. Read a bit closer and you see that the company in question (Evalueserve) has hired people to work 10-hour shifts with an hour to rest during the shift, and the workers are fully aware of this shift pattern when interviewed. The problem is just that the Chie' thinks it is unfair to be working more than eight-hours in a shift, so the extra is "overtime".

Frankly that's pathetic. I can't imagine my fraternal friends in the British unions getting upset about this, and let's face it anyway, who in a salaried job has not had to put in some extra time now and then? If the BPO Union in its current form is going to thrive then let's see some real issues under fire, rather than picking on companies that are actually offering their employees a pretty good deal.

Tuesday, 30 September 2008

Posted at 12:29

Which side am I on?

Zubair Ahmed of the BBC bureau in Mumbai wrote a lengthy piece on the BBC news web site today analysing the health issues of Indian contact centre workers. He quoted me in the piece, thanks to an exchange we had on Facebook, and he even managed to mention my new book – always nice to see a plug on the BBC.

I knew Zubair was working on the piece recently, but it's interesting to see it come out today as I had blogged here yesterday about some of the issues discussed by the BPO Union on its blog. When I opened my email this morning, the "Chief" had been in touch – so I know it's not only my mother reading this stuff. Actually, my mother wouldn't know a blog from an iPod. I must have the only parents in the UK who have never used an ATM or credit card.

The bottom line of what the Chief sent me today is that I can't possibly understand what it's like to be at work anymore because of the lofty position I occupy up here in an Ivory Tower commenting on the industry. Really? It sounds like the Chief has been listening to Working Class Hero a bit too often.

Well let's get a couple of things straight. I started out as a programmer. I spent a lot of long nights coding Cobol, Basic, and C++. I worked hard and gradually rose up the ranks to find myself managing technology projects across multiple countries and cultures. I switched career because I enjoyed writing more than banking technology, but it meant that I earned almost nothing for a long time.

For most of the time I worked in a bank, I was actually a member of the banking union BIFU, which is now called Unite due to a series of union mergers. I'm a member of the Labour party and my favourite singer is Billy Bragg. I'd hardly describe that as the behaviour of someone who has forgotten what it's like to be at work.

However, the debate of work and working conditions has to include pragmatism as well as idealism. I don't think it is right for employees in Europe or India, or anywhere for that matter, to be working long hours they are not compensated for. If that's a trend developing now in the contact centres then let's get the media, blogs, and unions to battle it. However, the fact is that everyone, everywhere does a bit extra now and then just because it makes life easier in the long run – for the employee and the employer. I'm not talking about repeated and regular unpaid overtime, just that bit of extra effort to make sure something is finished on time, or a project release goes smoothly. The reality of work is that some flexibility is required – not a work to rule.

October 2008

Thursday, 02 October 2008
Posted at 11:59
Safe journey?

It's now a couple of days since journalist Soumya Vishwanathan was murdered in Delhi. Most comments seem to be focused on the fact that she was a woman, out alone late at night - it was something like 3am. Delhi's chief minister Sheila Dixit - another working woman - said that for a woman to be out in the city at 3am is "adventurous".

People are calling out for rules and regulations to protect women in big cities at unsocial hours - not just when returning from parties, but those forced by their employer to work unsocial hours and return home late at night. In the southern state Karnataka, home to hi-tech Bangalore, there are rules in place that determine when a company is under an obligation to get women home safely. Clearly this is a major issue in the business process outsourcing sector, where armies of workers are forced to work nights to service clients in Europe and the US.

I have a couple of observations on this. First, the rules designed to protect women don't necessarily work. A company might pay for a taxi, but who screens the background of the driver? Second, if it is dangerous for women to be travelling home late at night then surely it is also dangerous for men?

I would also add that things are no better here in the UK. I have a friend who works in a London nightclub and she regularly finishes work at 4am. I asked her recently if the club gets her home safely, assuming they provide a taxi. She laughed and told me that none of the London clubs she has worked in provide transport for staff. Waitresses and bar staff are turfed out into the street at 4am and expected to get home – more than an hour before the London Underground starts running.

I'm sure that companies used to look after their staff better than this. If I was personally running a business that required staff to cross a major city to get home at an hour when public transport is very limited then I'd think it's immoral to just hope for the best.

Tuesday, 07 October 2008

Posted at 09:56

Where to offshore (and why not here?)

Tholons, the research firm founded by well-known offshoring guru Avinash Vashistha, has just published some new research in Global Services magazine about the most attractive cities around the world for supporting the offshoring business.

These reports are published all the time, so the average reader can get a bit jaded. How many times do we need to read another report that says India is still the number one offshoring destination? However, the Tholons research is different in that they started focusing on cities rather than countries, and in quite a lot of detail, some time ago.

If you look at the popularity of countries as measured by how many of their cities make it into the Tholons list then – not surprisingly - India is the leader. India manages to get six cities into the top eight of the list, with Bangalore, Chennai, Delhi, Hyderabad, Mumbai, and Pune all cutting the mustard.

Interestingly, there are no Chinese cities in the list of leaders, however China does dominate the "up and coming" list with Shanghai, Beijing, Shenzen, Dalian, Guangzhou, and Chengdu all being recognised as places to watch. Don't write off the Chinese dragon just yet as this up and coming list is probably where the future lies.

Makati city in the Philippines is singled out as one of the top global locations not in India. The Philippines is aiming for a 10 per cent share of the global market, which would be a substantial proportion of the entire national GDP if they can manage it. I remember attending a breakfast briefing in Manila last February and the President herself came and sat next to me. She asked me: "What do you do?" and I thought I was talking to Queen Elizabeth II, but at least I heard all these growth statistics straight from the head of state – over croissants.

Unfortunately, two British cities have dropped out of the Tholons top 50 list; Birmingham and Leeds. Both of these locations are actually hotbeds of regional talent in the UK and I recently heard that the Birmingham stock exchange – Investbx – has been doing a roaring trade helping to raise funds for local small entrepreneurs.

Perhaps the global downturn may actually encourage more regional talent and entrepreneurialism in countries like the UK, where the conventional wisdom has been that most services are going to go offshore? How about the UK being offshore for others?

Thursday, 09 October 2008

Posted at 13:46

The Filipino roadmap

I attended an event in London earlier this week hosted by the Philippines embassy. No, it was nothing to do with Harry Enfield, this was a series of lectures themed around the title "Philippines as an outsourcing destination" and featuring private sector industry leaders and government representatives.

The Philippines Ambassador, Edgardo Espiritu, started the event by declaring: "Logica is transferring operations from Bangalore to Manila. The business process outsourcing (BPO) sector is the fastest growing sector of our economy and we are now starting to focus even more on the higher-value services sector."

After this opening summary, undersecretary Edsel Custodio from the department of foreign affairs in Manila described why he felt the relationship with the UK is of utmost importance. "We are very interested in London and business in the UK. You are one of our top trade partners globally as the third largest investor into the Philippines," he said.

Everyone from the government referred to Custodio as the "usec" – a nice abbreviation for a title with a lot of syllables.

The usec went on to directly address the elephant in the room – the news that outside our office walls, the financial sector was continuing it's freefall into oblivion.

"In the Philippines, our banking sector is very strong. Our banks have not been affected by the present financial crisis. This is because we have seen some very difficult situations in the past 20 years or so and we have gone through restructuring of our foreign debt before. We really had to back in the 1980s so we could avoid becoming the laughing stock of the developing world," he said.

He went on to further emphasise this point when he added: "Our position as far as the financial sector is concerned is very strong and solvent. We are ready for long-term growth in a time of crisis – so if you have a long-term investment horizon then the Philippines can offer you a source of confidence."

The bottom line for this industry in the Philippines is that they need to move beyond the call centres that have become so established there. The government estimates that the hi-tech services sector will be worth around $13bn in foreign exports by the end of this decade, so it is critically important for them to get this right.

Step forward the man who is most likely to make it happen, Oscar Sañez, chief executive of the Business Processing Association of the Philippines (BPA/P). Oscar initially outlined the advantage the Philippines has in terms of human resources.

"In a country of 90 million people, we have 36 million in the labour force and last year there were 454,000 new graduates, nearly half of whom are from IT, engineering, or business courses," he said.

"We have been able to sustain the supply of workers, so we have not seen the uncontrollable wage inflation in some neighbouring countries. We have heard a lot of these stories from places such as India and Malaysia."

In fact, when I was studying the numbers Oscar was displaying on screen I did feel a sense of sadness for the romantic lover of English literature in me. Out of all those half a million young people heading off to university, only 7,000 studied arts or humanity subjects. I know that in this industry we are obsessed with people who get engineering or technical degrees, but I personally find that people with a more rounded knowledge of the world make better employees and managers.

Anyway, personal observations aside, Oscar described how his organisation is approaching the task ahead.

"We are focused on four broad themes for our 2010 roadmap. These are talent, next-wave cities, business environment, and the BPA/P team itself. We are supporting a deeper bench of supply through training programmes and focusing on curriculum changes," he said.

He went on to describe further more specific measures as he went into more detail: "We want to change business perceptions of risk and to encourage efficient government support, with input into things such as the new data protection bill. We are working hard to bring up the next wave of major cities all around the Philippines, because the next 15 major cities after Manila can easily supply a further 300,000 FTEs."

The Philippines has a real roadmap for the future and they have a chance to seize a great opportunity due to the uncertainties in India before the next election. I had lunch yesterday with a friend who is a senior think tank analyst with years of experience in India and all we talked about was what on earth is going to happen there in the next six or seven months – it's too hard to predict at present. It looks like the time has come for some genuine challengers to the dominance of India in this market.

Friday, 10 October 2008

Posted at 16:26

Cost becomes king again for outsourcing

I was at the office of the analyst Datamonitor in London yesterday. The plan was to go and meet Peter Ryan, the lead analyst for call centres and business process outsourcing (BPO), and to go for some dinner. Peter is based in Canada, so he is not on this side of the Atlantic very often.

I took advantage of him being around to get some opinion on the present threat of recession. I have heard conflicting views in the outsourcing community – some suppliers are looking forward to a wave of new business as cost cutting becomes more important, and some fear the worst.

Peter dragged his colleagues Pat O'Brien and Ed Thomas into the room to talk as well – both London-based analysts focused on the BPO sector. We talked about the potential recession and how it might impact the BPO and general outsourcing marketplace. The entire conversation can be played back on the Talking Outsourcing podcast, but I've captured a few key messages in this blog post.

Pat opened the conversation by declaring: "Outsourcing suppliers seem to be suffering as much as the wider market in terms of share price. The idea of outsourcing getting more popular in a downturn has not been reflected by investors. The suppliers that have been hit hardest so far are the ones with the most exposure to financial services."

Clearly Pat does not agree with those vendors who think the recession will be a boon. Following on from this, Peter said: "A lot of people seem to feel that contact centre outsourcing is about to see a lot of new business, happy days for all. But if there is a downturn in the economy then there are fewer consumers purchasing fewer products leading to fewer opportunities for queries about products and so fewer contact centre interactions. Of course, that means there is also less scope for outbound sales as well."

Oh dear, it looks glum based on the chat so far, but Ed injected some enthusiasm for the future by reminding us that the world has yet to end.

"Contract signing might be falling off, but acquisition activity is not. Look at the recent news of HCL trumping Infosys for Axon and TCS just picking up the Citigroup BPO activities. Companies clearly still have cash available and are investing it with an eye on the future," he said.

Based on this chat with the Datamonitor analysts, a few points became very clear. There is no automatic boom time ahead for outsourcing suppliers just because of a potential recession. However, there is much more focus on the price of the services – forget about the past few years of strategic outsourcing and flexible resourcing. Now, cost is king again.

Wednesday, 15 October 2008

Posted at 15:16

Testing the waters across the pond

I just jetted into New York City. I'm staying at the legendary Hotel Chelsea, famed as a literary haunt and for the downfall of such diverse characters as Dylan Thomas and Sid Vicious.

The organisers of the conference want me to chair a couple of debates here, one focused on the development of Eastern Europe, and the other on currency and attrition risk in outsourcing. I've been planning these sessions with some of the speakers over the past week, but I'm keen to see what the audience thinks about the present financial meltdown. In my view, it's the only topic worth focusing minds on this week.

The markets appear to be reacting positively to some of the government-led rescue plans and our very own Prime Minister is being presented in some quarters as a global saviour, as it is the British rescue package that is being replicated the world over. Perhaps the war on credit will be Gordon's equivalent of Maggie's Falklands war? He certainly needed it.

But just because of some initial market acceptance that the major banks won't go under, there is no assurance that a recession is not around the corner. I heard informally yesterday from another major Indian supplier that they are weathering the storm quite well so far, but at the same time I hear these platitudes from the delivery teams, the investors are beating down share prices.

I'm going to take some notes and get back to the blog, hopefully with some views on what people are saying Stateside about the potential for an ill wind in outsourcing.

Wednesday, 15 October 2008

Posted at 17:17

Going down Mexico way

Congratulations to the team at MexicoIT for winning the Outsourcing Marketing Excellence award at the Midsize Enterprise Summit this week in Dallas.

MexicoIT is the trade body dedicated to promoting and developing the hi-tech services industry in Mexico. It should be a no brainer for organisations in the USA to consider working in Mexico due to its close location, lower costs, highly skilled people, and great food. But I'm becoming more interested in the region now as a more general source of talent.

As India falters, is it now time for Mexico and other locations in Latin America to come out from under the shadow of the US and start talking to the rest of the world?

Thursday, 16 October 2008

Posted at 13:20

Getting social about business networking

I was chairing a panel discussion at Outsource World in New York yesterday. The focus was on whether offshoring was still viable in an environment where we are seeing rising costs, rising attrition, and rising currency risk. Joining me on the panel were Bill Bierce, a partner in law firm Bierce and Kenerson, and Amrita Joshi, president of consulting firm Ahilia.

It was a good discussion and well received by the audience. Strangely enough for these events, the audience was getting bigger as the talk went on – rather than the opposite, so it must have been of interest. It was just a shame that as Bill was entering into a great monologue about pricing issues, the conference organiser came and tugged my arm, asking me to wrap up. I was confused about how long we had to talk and it seems like we were running over time.

There was a guy from HCL who came up to ask questions. He made sure everyone knew he was from HCL - so don't forget about what HCL is doing in remote infrastructure management. That's the HCL from India, in case you don't know them...

It was a good session. You know it has been a good discussion when time is running out and there is still more to discuss, but a few people came up to me after and said it was great how much we had managed to cover in a short period of time. That's nice to hear. And we also managed to plug HCL during the talk thanks to our friend asking questions.

Something interesting happened at lunchtime that's worth mentioning. I was sitting at a table chatting to Uldis Salenieks, the economic counsellor from the Latvian embassy in Washington DC, about my dog Matilda. Every business card I have is unique – they feature photos from my Flickr account so no two cards are the same. I'd just given a card to Uldis and it had a photo of my dog on it, so we were talking about her. Then, a guy who was on the other side of the table said: 'Hey, you're Mark aren't you?' It was David Kinnear, board member of the Global Sourcing Council – someone I have chatted to on Facebook, but have never met in real life.

What was really interesting was that we picked up straight away on some Facebook chats. When I explained to Uldis that I had never met David before he couldn't believe it!

I also managed to connect with Chocko Valliappa from Vee Technologies thanks to me noticing that he would be at this conference in his Facebook status.

Who says social networking is all about wasting time and killing vampires?

Monday, 27 October 2008

Posted at 09:59

Every one a winner. Except the losers.

A few days ago, the annual awards ceremony hosted by the National Outsourcing Association (NOA) took place in central London. I was there, as one of the judges, and enjoyed a front seat view as the finest outsourcing minds in the country all celebrated their nominations and awards.

The NOA chairman Martyn Hart made a big mistake in his opening speech by suggesting that a forthcoming recession might be good for some companies in the outsourcing sector. Comedian Dominic Holland was MC for the evening, and once he heard Martyn's comments he never let it go. Though, a heckler from Alsbridge did start giving Dominic himself a hard time too, so the crowd turned on some of the negative comments from the MC!

My own role at the NOA is focused on cross-border outsourcing and offshoring, so I would just like to send a large message of congratulations to the team from Egypt – who won the offshoring destination of the year award. The competition was tough and Egypt has made enormous strides in the past year telling the story of what it has to offer.

It can be really tough judging these awards. I was button-holed during the evening by a consultant from a big advisory firm who was very upset that her project was shortlisted and had not won the award. I apologised and said that I'm sure there was a good reason for it, but she was very insistent and wanted an immediate explanation and justification. In my view, the problem by that point was the free Champagne, so I thought it was better to walk away quickly rather than start trying to justify why any particular company should have come second. Sometimes these things happen.

Monday, 27 October 2008

Posted at 14:02

Helping small businesses go global

A few days ago, I went to give a talk to a group of customers from QuickStart Global. It's a company that is only about a year-and-a-half old, but has been growing rapidly by making the offshoring path easier – especially for small to medium-sized enterprises (SMEs).

QuickStart basically allows smaller companies to go global and create their own captive offshoring unit, because Quickstart already has offices and facilities all over the world – so if you want to get 10 people set up in India, you no longer need to fly over there, find an office, hire an HR person, fire a lawyer - Quickstart can cut through all of this and gives you desks and other infrastructure in its offices.

It's a model that works really well for the SME sector as the resource use can be aggregated with the offshore facilities. None of the small clients could justify getting their own office facilities, but together they can make it work.

I've seen similar business models to this come and go over the years, but one look at the growth being enjoyed by QuickStart Global makes me suspect they have got it right. Clearly it's not an answer for big established companies that have the volume of work to justify their own offshore facility, and the outsourcing vendors are appealing to ever smaller customers these days, but it's a great way of helping SMEs to go global.

Wednesday, 29 October 2008

Posted at 09:59

Outsourcing of Africa

I have been working over the past few weeks with Mfanu Mfayela, chief executive of Business Process enabling South Africa (BPeSA), the national co-ordinating body that represents the outsourcing industry in South Africa.

Mfanu and I were presented a challenge by the International Trade Centre (ITC) - create the framework for a new outsourcing association to represent the African continent; an African Outsourcing Association (AOA). The ITC is a joint organisation, created by the United Nations and the World Trade Organisation, so to get a request like that was exciting – and a real challenge.

Part of the challenge was to come over to Abuja in Nigeria and to present our conceptual ideas to a wide range of technology professionals and government representatives. The idea being that we should try creating some momentum for the idea across several African countries.

So, here I am in Abuja. Yesterday I got up and presented some ideas on the private sector and the need for Africa to reinvent itself for a modern technology-enabled era. My presentation went down very well (my various YouTube interludes were popular!) and it led into a discussion session hosted by me and Mfanu, to gather thoughts on the AOA concept.

The discussion went extremely well. The ideas we presented were accepted by the conference and there was a unanimous vote of support to take the proposals further. We decided to organise a focus group, with a single representative of half a dozen African countries, to look at the scope of the proposed AOA and to refine the proposal before we go further.

I should have feedback from that focus group in the next few days and I will then be working with Mfanu to see how we can implement an AOA that helps to reposition Africa as somewhere that can benefit from the global IT and IT-enabled service industry. It's an exciting time here in Abuja today, so you can bet that if we manage to get further progress on the AOA then there might be a group of us celebrating over Star beers in the Elephant bar tonight...

November 2008

Tuesday, 04 November 2008
Posted at 09:39
Literary insights into India

It's not often that I talk about books in this blog. Now and again there are some decent business books that cross my desk, but by and large I personally tend to read more fiction than management books. I'm a firm believer in the art of learning about business mistakes from Richard III.

So here is a tip for those of you who want to combine a love of literature with outsourcing. This no longer has to be an oxymoron. Just take a look at the winner of the 2008 Man Booker prize, The White Tiger by Aravind Adiga.

The White Tiger tells the story of Balram Halwai, a man with a dark secret who recounts his life in a series of letters to the Chinese Premier Wen Jiabao. Balram lives life as a servant in India, rising from the darkness of servitude to the relative freedom of chauffeuring rich businessmen. He eventually winds up in the outsourcing centre of India – Bangalore.

Adiga's beautiful story documents a side of India that most foreign business people never see and yet the darkness is always connected to the light. It documents the outcome of moral or amoral actions and the mental torture of the poor in India.

If you have not read this book then I strongly recommend you do so. I would not say the same of last year's Booker winner, but then that's my personal taste. This year the judges have chosen a very deep and complex novel that exposes the true India – and it's full of references to outsourcing too!

Wednesday, 05 November 2008

Posted at 13:04

The audacity of offshoring

A ll is well. President Barack Obama is now going to reward his kids with a new puppy for their support. I want to know if that means we are going to be treated to a new series of dog cams, in the same spirit as the "Barney cam" videos produced by President Bush. Perhaps the instigation of this video series was his finest moment in the White House? I don't need to be impartial here. The sooner Bush is on the conference circuit earning big bucks for speeches about fireside chats with Tony, the better.

But what everyone around the world wants to know is how far President Obama will go towards fulfilling his campaign pledge to restrict offshore outsourcing. He promised a restriction on outsourcing, but was it just electioneering or a serious threat to all those suppliers in India, the Philippines, China and other fast-developing regions?

It's obviously difficult to rein in international business. What can President Obama do to prevent Microsoft developing software all over the world, including in hi-tech Indian delivery centres? And, when Microsoft argues that this global development actually results in the healthy operation of a US company, can he seriously tell the corporation to retrench and retreat to behind the US border? Then, once Steve Ballmer is dealt with, how about the thousands of other American companies that operate globally?

Nasscom, the software and services trade association in India, is playing down the threat. They believe that Obama will focus more on the domestic economy and the creation of jobs at home, rather than shutting off links to overseas locations. Of course, Nasscom might be expected to play down the danger, but its member companies are continuing to see healthy double-digit revenue growth in a business environment where many company executives are only considering which ledge to leap off.

I don't think Obama will threaten the offshore outsourcing industry, but not because he is not going to fulfil his pledge. I think he will examine the legal and tax framework around service transfers, but I think it is a long way down the agenda and not something that will even be reviewed for a couple of years.

Don't forget, he made an even bigger pledge to pull US troops out of Iraq. These big-ticket foreign policy pledges and the crashing economy are far more pressing than the effect of offshoring on US jobs – which is actual terms is tiny compared to the effect of economic uncertainty on jobs.

But who knows what he will pull out of the hat in the New Year? Let's enjoy the festive season and hope that the new US president ushers in a new confidence for 2009. Or in Star Wars parlance, a New Hope.

Monday, 10 November 2008

Posted at 17:29

Smile Jamaica

A few years back, the offshoring community was engaged in a constant firefight over the negative headlines associated with work being sent to remote offshore regions. Now, most reporters are more careful in their analysis. It's never a black and white case of good and bad where offshoring is concerned and this is reflected in the journalism of the past few years. The reporting has matured.

However, when I was in New York speaking at the Outsource World conference recently I met some government representatives promoting Jamaica. I was interested in what they had to say because I had heard of some banks setting up facilities in Jamaica back in the 90s, but eventually moving on to places such as India. I was wondering if there was now a good case for investment in the region, a boom in the local service industry perhaps?

I met a charming man who runs a contact centre in Jamaica; he then introduced me to the government people. I explained who I was and told them about my recent book Who Moved My Job? Suddenly I got a reaction that was colder than the London rain outside my window today. They said they don't want to talk to me as I am only going to write negative things about Jamaica. So I explained that I write about the industry for magazines such as Computing and for my own books, and that I was hardly likely to write up a hatchet-job if there is something positive to say. I felt about as welcome as President Bush at a Democratic convention.

If this is the way Jamaica goes about promoting the benefits of working there then heaven knows why anyone would want to invest in the region or do business there. The government representatives travelling the world to promote Jamaica need to learn about destination branding. They need to learn about who is out there writing about their own industry. They need to learn about what is going on outside the USA. And most of all, they need to learn some manners. What gives some stuck-up diplomat the right to treat me like something she just trod in on 11th Avenue?

Thursday, 13 November 2008

Posted at 14:47

Christmas come early

On Oxford Street in central London the joke is that Christmas comes earlier and earlier each year to the point at which we might one day expect to be returning our summer holidays only to see the decorations going up. I know I snapped a picture in department store John Lewis last month because I was astounded to see the place resembling a winter grotto more than two months before Christmas.

The same applies to the business projections from analyst firms. Expect every company to be sending out their views on what is in store for 2009, and every magazine printing those same views ad infinitum. But credit where it is due to Equaterra who appear to have sent me the first list of outsourcing projections for next year. That's not to say that they are going to be the most correct, but they are the first to approach me with their predictions, so let's have a look at what they are saying will happen.

• Globalisation is set to continue, but at a slower pace – so sourcing decisions will take longer, but the business benefits of sourcing will ensure it is a strategy more often used in hard times.

- Locations will be reassessed more thoroughly and more often – so lower-cost higher-risk regions now have a greater chance of winning new contracts.

- Learning curves will be steeper for buyers using outsourcing as a cost mitigation strategy and also for suppliers who may well be going through a lot of M&A activity now.

- Volatility in the foreign exchange markets means both buyers and sellers need to pay more attention to hedging risk if they are trading services across borders.

- Wage inflation pressures will decline for a time due to the pressures on buyers.

- Buyers will shift towards longer term partnerships rather than project based solutions

- Greater flexibility and blended delivery models

So that's a good start for 2009. I'm quite interested to notice that in the face of economic hard times, all the Al Gore green measures seem to have dropped off the list. Does anyone care for the environment when they are struggling to keep their business afloat? Let me know what you think about this and if you have your own outsourcing predictions for 2009 then please send them to me. I can't promise to reprint all of them, but I will try collecting the best ones together – closer to the end of the year... 2008 is not over just yet!

Wednesday, 19 November 2008

Posted at 13:03

It's the economy, stupid

The big theme this year at the National Outsourcing Association annual summit in Westminster is the economy, stupid. As might be expected, all the conference small talk is about what will happen in 2009. I even went to a very nice dinner at Gordon Ramsay's Maze restaurant last night – thank you to Cognizant - and found that in our sumptuous surroundings, we were still all focused on the doom and gloom of where the country is headed.

Professor Mari Sako of Oxford University gave the keynote speech this morning focused entirely on the economy and several other speakers have approached the subject, but in my opinion the issue is far more that there seems to be little consensus on how the international trade in services will be affected. Everyone has a different opinion and some are biased. Suppliers talk up the market and the cost savings that can be achieved and buyers are holding back on spending decisions. With the market in flux, fear, uncertainty, and doubt reign supreme.

Outsourcing can play a key role in giving companies some certainty over their outgoings and service levels. It's not a panacea and it's not always going to be cheaper, but with a reputable supplier it is certain that you will get what you contracted for. That certainty has to be the big sales proposition for outsourcing in the hard times to come.

And, a final point... how come at a conference about hi-tech services there is no wifi supplied to the delegates? The only wifi on offer at the QEII conference centre costs £10 per hour. That's daylight robbery – hence my decision to blog this from Starbucks...

Friday, 21 November 2008

Posted at 12:47

How far can outsourcing go?

I notice I mentioned Cognizant in my last blog. Without meaning to start mentioning them every day, I just want to recount a few comments made when I had a chat to Martin Kochman today. Martin is the head of Business Process Outsourcing (BPO) operations for Cognizant in Europe and we had a chat on the phone earlier about some of the changes in the BPO sector.

What was particularly interesting were some of his views on the hard times faced by many companies as we head into recession. Martin remains very positive about the business outlook for the BPO sector as a whole. He said: "I still think that the total size of the market is growing, but we may see a slowing in the rate at which earlier growth targets are met. The fundamentals are still in place for this to be a significant market."

He added: "Cost reduction will always drive some activity, but the boundaries between what organisations have considered 'outsourcable' will continue to be pushed and more is going to come into the realms of outsourced contracts."

Martin clearly believes that the retained organisation is going to shrink. This implies that as times get harder, companies may even be exploring the outsourcing option even more than usual. In summary, Martin thinks it's going to be a busy time for companies in IT and BPO services: "The market will grow. On the demand side there is more global recognition of the skills and standards required and so things like Knowledge Process Outsourcing (KPO) are becoming easier to package up and deliver remotely."

Wednesday, 26 November 2008

Posted at 15:59

Setting the standards for outsourcing

The National Outsourcing Association (NOA) here in the UK has just launched a new series of qualifications in outsourcing. It's an attempt to ensure there is a best practice benchmark for outsourcing knowledge in the industry. So companies should be able to use the courses as a part of their own training programmes, and individuals can use the courses to boost their own CV when trying to get a job in the industry.

The NOA has created a new arm called NOA Pathway to administrate the courses and they are all accredited by Middlesex University. There are a number of qualifications, beginning with the most basic foundation knowledge of outsourcing, called the NOA Gateway. The NOA Professional Certificate is equivalent to the first year of a degree course, and the NOA Advanced Professional Certificate is equivalent to the third year of a degree. The NOA Diploma is the gold standard, being classed as equivalent to a master's degree.

There have been some other attempts creating outsourcing certification, but this is the first time a comprehensive suite of university-accredited qualifications ranging from a foundation course to a master's degree has been offered all as a single package. I am on the inside as a director of the NOA, so I know how much work has gone into bringing this to the market. Yvonne Williams, the NOA Professional Training Director, has worked for the past couple of years to get this programme looking so good.

Take a look at the NOA website for more information on the NOA Pathway and enjoy your studies!

Thursday, 27 November 2008

Posted at 09:46

Perspective on Mumbai bombings

The Times, the Guardian, and the Independent all lead with front-page stories about the terrorist attacks in India yesterday, where at least 80 people were killed and hundreds injured. The Times is particularly striking, with a cover featuring blood on the floor of a railway station and the headline 'Carnage in Bombay'.

Gunmen targeted major hotels, such as the Oberoi and the Taj Mahal. As I write this blog, the Indian army has surrounded both hotels because more than 200 people are being be held hostage inside. The BBC radio news this morning has predicted that the England cricket team will abandon their one-day tour of India. Not that England can win now anyway.

This attack is being linked to al-Qaeda, but it's the latest event in a string of violence that is scarring India and making the world's largest democracy appear unstable and unsafe.

Regardless of why this particular attack took place, I've been predicting civil unrest in India for a long time now. In very simple terms think about it like this. The BJP government that lost the general election in 2004 were widely seen as out of touch with the millions of poor Indians that have yet to benefit from the outsourcing riches. The farmers and poor elected the Congress party on a wave of hope and with a mandate to focus less on hi-tech 'India shining' campaigns and more on lifting hundreds of millions of people out of poverty.

Now, with a general election looming, what has happened? Not a great deal that is discernable for the poor Indians with such high expectations. So can they switch support back to the BJP again? Well, that's not quite so easy. The BJP was always a Hindu nationalist party, but during the last few years they have become more vocally nationalist in their agenda. So the choice for voters is a Congress party that seems to be going nowhere or the BJP alternative seeking division along religious lines.

With this level of political tension, and now al-Qaeda stirring the situation, I'm afraid to say that we can expect more violence in India within the next few months.

Friday, 28 November 2008

Posted at 10:14

India will remain open for business - but that's not the real story

One of the duties I have to fulfil as a director of the National Outsourcing Association is to talk to the media and to give some views and opinion when they call – to give a human voice to the association. Usually the chairman will do the media stuff, but as my focus is offshoring I often get called on to comment on international sourcing issues.

But as a part of the media machine myself, I can sometimes feel disappointed when I see my own words incorrectly quoted back at me. Yesterday, a rival publication to Computing called me for a comment on the Mumbai terror attacks. I rambled on about how business people might be thinking twice about visiting India right now, and possibly even in the next few months up to the general election, but I categorically stated that as I intend to go to India soon myself, I could not recommend a policy of not going. What was the headline that appeared on the story? "Mark says don't go to India…" How did that happen?

So just for the record, in case my friends in India are reading this blog, I don't think that everyone should stop travelling to India - far from it. I think we should all exercise caution when planning international travel, but India has not suddenly become a no-go zone. Some business people stopped visiting London after the 7/7 terror attacks in 2005, but the Australian cricket team played on. I remember seeing Shane Warne in Kensington three days after the bombing – close to a beer and a girl, so business as usual there - and the real business visitors returned soon after.

The terrorist attacks on India this week were tragic and it's my fear that it could happen again unless prime minister Manmohan Singh clamps down on the perpetrators. But nobody really seems to have an idea of who is responsible at present – so the situation really is uncertain. However, in this present climate we all have to adopt a heightened sense of security. It's not unique to India and the next mindless and brutal attack could be in London, or Washington DC.

Let's remind ourselves that the real story here is not about whether this atrocity is good or bad for business in India. At least 119 people were going about their business in a place I know and love, and now they are dead.

December 2008

Wednesday, 10 December 2008

Posted at 11:38

An Indian bailout plan

Among the charges often levelled against trade unions is they are combative, antagonistic, and their existence creates a "them and us" culture that shouldn't exist in an era of flat management structures.

So, I was interested to see an email from the BPO Union about their proposals in India. The organisation seems to be pre-empting measures the Indian government might offer to help the local outsourcing industry and IT service companies ride out this uncertain recessionary period. The suggestion is that staff across the industry would take a pay cut of 10-15 per cent if the reduction were directly subsidised by the government. Instead of government coffers being emptied directly into private companies, the union is suggesting that employees should be protected just as much as the companies – and this idea of a hypothecated subsidy sounds, on the surface, like a reasonable suggestion.

My only uncertainty about this kind of bailout plan among the Indian service firms is that some of them stand to gain from economic slowdown elsewhere, so it's not a universal problem. Tata Consultancy Services was recently quoted in the FT saying it is now actively reducing its dependence on the US as a source of business – can you imagine that statement from an Indian IT supplier just a few years back? Companies in the same sector, such as Cognizant, have been posting increasing revenue and many are quite bullish about the year ahead because of the amount of hunkering down that needs to be done if companies are really going to cut costs and survive.

Services are still required by companies in all sectors, but areas of business that have strongly supported outsourcing – such as banking and financial services – remain in a state of flux.

Wednesday, 10 December 2008

Posted at 11:42

Creative destruction or more bailouts?

I received an email this week from a friend of mine that gives some eye-watering figures.

Just over a year ago Royal Bank of Scotland (RBS) paid $100bn for ABN Amro – 80 per cent in cash. For this amount, RBS could today buy:

* Citibank for $22.5bn;

* Morgan Stanley $10.5bn;

* Goldman Sachs $21.0bn;

* Merrill Lynch $12.3bn;

* Deutsche Bank $13.0bn;

* Barclays $12.7bn;

* And still have $8bn change

I haven't checked these numbers, but the fact is that in the current climate it is entirely believable. It also reminds me of a recent message on the blog of US documentary-maker Michael Moore, hardly known as a friend to big business, but certainly an astute commentator.

The US auto-giants GM, Ford, and Chrysler are all haemorrhaging cash and now going cap-in-hand to the US government for a $34bn bailout. Moore pointed out that all common stock in GM could be purchased for around $3bn. So, we could save the government a load of money by just supporting earlier intervention and then supporting a massive wave of innovation in transport – a Marshall plan for the auto industry. Why bail them out with more cash when the current bosses will just deliver more of the same?

Joseph Schumpeter popularised the term "creative destruction" in which companies or industries would naturally die, to be replaced by the newer and stronger. It seems we are now witnessing Schumpeter's vision on a daily basis.

Monday, 15 December 2008

Posted at 13:21

Not so captivated any more

Fidelity has put the IT support part of its back-office in India up for sale. The centres in Chennai and Bangalore employ more than 2000 people, though this sale is not affecting some of the actual knowledge-based processes performed there – such as business analytics.

It's one more nail in the coffin of the big offshore captive centre. Now GE, Citigroup, Aviva, and Fidelity have all endorsed outsourcing above offshoring their own resources to another country, is the argument won?

Tuesday, 16 December 2008

Posted at 10:32

The uneasy global supply chain

A lot of people and companies still consider social networking tools such as Facebook to be a frivolous waste of time. Yet, work consists of more networking and communication than ever before. The tools are merely reflecting the way we work today, and are becoming an essential part of the working day.

I mention this because there was an interesting post on the discussion board of the Outsourcing Experts Group in Facebook yesterday. Preet Chandhoke, a director of software development firm 01Synergy, posted up his views on the five regions to watch for offshoring in 2009:

* Argentina

* Bulgaria
* China
* Egypt
* Philippines

Preet highlighted his thoughts on the pros and cons of each location and I tend to agree with his views. But one factor I expect to become more important in the coming year is political stability – something Preet mentions with regard to both Egypt and the Philippines.

International terrorism and civil disputes are going to be considered a greater risk than before in the present climate, leading to a greater willingness to explore different options, where before it might have been a straightforward decision to go offshore. Those options might even include getting the work done in your home country by using a smaller company, or just going for a nearshore option. There is a definite increase in unease at having critical components of the supply chain halfway across the world right now.

Wednesday, 17 December 2008

Posted at 12:22

Keeping it in the family

H ere is a challenge from the moral maze of business life. You are the chairman of a major international - and publicly-traded - IT services company. You are concerned about the effect of the credit crunch on the IT services industry, so what do you do? Perhaps try using spare cash to diversify the company offerings by buying into companies in other industries, such as construction?

It sounds like a classic diversification strategy, but what if the $1.6bn investment is spent on companies that your family already owns? Ask Satyam chairman Ramalinga Raju, because it's exactly what he just tried to do. And he expressed surprise when shareholders and institutional investors slapped down his proposed investments as scandalous.

With his best poker face Raju claimed it was a genuine move to develop the future of Satyam in new business areas. So that's OK then. Nothing at all about sticking a few billion somewhere safe, like the family business...

Wednesday, 24 December 2008

Posted at 11:22

Seasonal bargains

Is there now a bargain to be had from every member of the banking sector trying to divest service units to free up cash? Wipro has certainly found one this week by purchasing Citi Technology Services from Citigroup for $127m.

The deal also includes a six-year contract to continue providing services to Citigroup, and this is a business unit expected to turn over $80m this year. That six-year deal could be worth about $500m, so the purchase price looks like a tremendous bargain. Entire chunks of the banking sector are being sold off like the pick 'n' mix at Woolworths... expect more in the New Year.

January 2009

Friday, 09 January 2009

Posted at 16:04

Satyam latest: See for yourself

Yesterday, the interim chief executive of scandal-bound Indian IT services firm Satyam, Ram Mynampati, took questions from the media about the fraud engineered by founder Ramalinga Raju. You can watch the first half of the press conference here and the final half here.

Friday, 09 January 2009

Posted at 16:09

Satyam scandal is a one-off - hopefully

As expected, there has been a lot of talk about the massive fraud perpetrated at Satyam, and the business press has already started using "India's Enron" as shorthand for the scale of the disaster.

Salil Tripathi, writing in the Wall Street Journal, seems to have detailed the impact of the scandal more eloquently that most other commentators. In particular, Tripathi draws attention to the question most industry watchers are thinking about, but are too scared to ask: Is the "outsourcing to India" bubble about to burst?

As I looked around the internet for more information on the scandal, I stumbled across an article on the Gerson Lehrman Group Expert Network site. Author Paul Massie says: "The revelation of such massive fraud in a company that has been public since 1991 and was considered one of the three or four top Indian outsourcing companies is inevitably going to raise questions about all the other Indian outsourcing companies. Clients and potential clients are going to be asking the question: 'If this could happen at Satyam, why not at Wipro/Infosys/TCS/Cognizant?'"

Why not indeed? It's what Tripathi is concerned about. And after all, PricewaterhouseCoopers audited the books at Satyam – a name known and trusted across the world, in the same way Arthur Andersen was known and respected prior to the Enron collapse.

But the dust has yet to settle on the Satyam scandal. We are commenting on a moving target, as the forensic accountants will need to examine what has been a systematic fraud of accounting overstatement over several years. I tend to feel that this issue is confined to Satyam. I can't imagine that every other hi-tech Indian company has been mis-stating its margin and revenue in the same way as this one company.

So I don't feel the Gerson Lehrman comment is really valid or fair. The entire industry won't collapse because of this fraud. Satyam will collapse for sure, but other players within the industry will absorb their clients – possibly delivering the service from India. But just imagine the nightmare for the service industry in India if another Satyam is found in 2009.

Tuesday, 13 January 2009

Posted at 11:24

Learning the lessons of Satyam

What does the recent scandal at Indian technology giant Satyam teach us about the nature of 21st century business?

First, that old-fashioned trust is still at the heart of any business-to-business relationship. Buying a service from a supplier is not just a procurement exercise in beating a company down to its lowest possible price. Does anyone remember the old Japanese theories of looking after and nurturing your suppliers from back in business school?

Second, the increased use of outsourcing has blurred the edge of the traditional organisation. Academics have talked about virtual organisations for a long time, but here they are in the news every day. There are companies that would be in real trouble if a supplier such as Satyam goes to the wall – because the supplier is such a critical part of the supply chain that they are effectively a part of the client organisation.

And third, the old-school Indian habit of management cronyism has to be addressed if Indian firms are to integrate themselves further into foreign customers. However, this is not just an Indian problem. Boards are stuffed full of friends in many places, including cultures closer to home, such as France. However, we are involved in the hi-tech future of industry so the hi-tech leaders need to work hardest.

Let's behave like it's the 21st century and reintroduce some transparency and trust into some of these corporate relationships.

Tuesday, 13 January 2009

Posted at 12:43

Outsourcing seminar next month...

I tend to mix my time between the business and academic world. There is much to be learned from both the detailed academic approach to business, and the day-to-day practical reality of working in business.

So I'm pleased to just note here on my blog that if any of you are interested in an entire day focused on outsourcing at Loughborough University, then put 6 March in your diary.

The fourth seminar on Careers & The Migration of Business Processes (Outsourcing & Offshoring) will be held at the business school at Loughborough - and I'm speaking. Other speakers include Phil Taylor from Strathclyde University, Virginia Doellgast from the London School of Economics; Angelika Zimmerman from Loughborough, and M.N. Ravishankar from RMIT in Melbourne, Australia.

More outsourcing and business school experts will be added to the agenda over the next month or so. If you are interested in more information then contact Champa Patel at Loughborough.

Tuesday, 13 January 2009

Posted at 15:25

Offshore providers need to prove themselves even more

The National Outsourcing Association has issued some predictions for 2009. There is an entire bullet point list that you can find here, but I wanted to quote from one section of the press release:

"The UK economy is weakening and with the value of the pound continuing to fall, companies will not be able to see the same level of cost savings from offshoring that they have experienced in the past. Also 'patriotic' sentiments and rising unemployment will encourage UK organisations to seek out areas in the UK to site new outsourcing business or bring back poorly performing operations. This may feel good, but whether this is economically right entirely depends upon each situation. Once users start to bring work back to the UK, offshore suppliers will see a loss of the economies of scale that made them initially attractive and therefore a rise in their own costs. "

It may seem counter-intuitive to the conventional wisdom that as we enter a recession, more companies will be looking to slash costs by offshoring. However - think about it like this: The appetite for risk and major change programmes is reduced in this environment, the weak pound is making it harder to achieve major savings, and the perennial nationalistic spirit will only grow stronger in a downturn. It's actually quite a hard market for the offshore players because they have to prove themselves even more in this kind of operating environment.

Wednesday, 14 January 2009

Posted at 10:47

Slumdog Millionaire - as inspired by Indian outsourcing

Last night I went to see the brilliant new film Slumdog Millionaire. Directed by Danny Boyle and based on a novel by Vikas Swarup, the movie tells the story of a young man from a Mumbai slum who achieves success on the TV game show Who wants to be a millionaire. His horrific experience of life in the slum gives him the exact knowledge required for each of the quiz answers. The movie has just won four Golden Globes this week and is being tipped for Oscar success, so it comes strongly recommended by most critics.

My Facebook status indicated that I was out watching the movie and this morning I noticed that Anil Tikoo, from the Indian technology firm NIIT, had posted a message on my wall suggesting that his firm was the inspiration for the movie! I dug around on the internet and - sure enough - he was right.

In 1999, Dr Sugata Mitra carved a hole in the wall of the NIIT offices in Delhi, a wall that divided NIIT from a neighbouring slum. Mitra left a computer there, available for the slum kids to use, but without any training or instruction. Within a month the kids were familiar with the operating system and could use the computer to access the web. The 'hole-in-the-wall' experiment became a well-known example of innate ability and Mitra and NIIT have developed a strong corporate social responsibility programme thanks to the success of this experiment.

When the experiment was publicised, Vikas Swarup heard of it and was fascinated by the idea that anybody from any background could do something extraordinary, provided they get an opportunity. He wrote his novel based on this idea, and the rest is history.

Thursday, 22 January 2009

Posted at 18:05

No offshore fears with Obama

Wasn't the inauguration of US President Obama just stunning? I just love this Techcrunch photo of Washington DC from taken from a satellite. Ever felt you were about as insignificant as an ant? Well, here is the proof.

A number of countries with a lot to gain from offshore outsourcing are concerned that some of the anti-offshoring rhetoric employed by Obama during his election campaign might now come into force. I don't think so.

Note that Obama's first move in office was to end the terror suspect trials at Guantanamo Bay. He has more on his plate with the ongoing Middle East military campaigns and the crashing economy than possibly any other incoming president.

There might be some pro-US job measures that are designed to shore up the economy, but I can't foresee any major anti-offshoring legislation with all these other issues on his plate. Offshoring is an emotive topic, but there are far greater factors affecting the US economy right now and Obama will be targeting them one by one.

Monday, 26 January 2009

Posted at 10:11

Customers to desert Satyam?

The dust is starting to settle on the financial scandal at Indian outsourcing giant Satyam. While the founder and chairman Ramalinga Raju languishes in jail, confidence in his company is collapsing.

In the Financial Times last week, Ashutosh Gupta of research firm Evalueserve recommended that customers should be hiring private investigators to poke around and ask difficult questions.

The Wall Street Journal claimed that at least half a dozen major clients of Satyam are preparing to leave if they don't see some stability and certainty restored within weeks.

We are now only a fortnight away from the biggest Indian technology conference – the annual Nasscom Leadership Forum. Who wants to bet what is going to dominate the agenda this year?

Thursday, 29 January 2009

Posted at 10:16

Hiring the skills for outsourcing

I was recently scanning through the Offshore Futures report by consultancy Alsbridge. It was published about a month ago, and I saw I had been quoted in there, but given that I have lunch with the author on Friday I thought I should give it a closer inspection.

One thing that jumped out at me relates to human resources. Many in the industry have argued for a long time that partnering with companies demands a different skill set to procurement and purchasing. For long-term outsourcing to work, suppliers need to be included within the supply chain – and therefore to share in the success when the operation is working well.

The author of the report, Paul Morrison, states: "Outsourcing specialists would be a career evolution for procurement professionals, technical specialists and industry experts. A successful function is multi-disciplinary. A big core will come from IT and procurement because they are natural starting points."

I agree with Paul, but I have not seen a lot of firms really specify this kind of multi-discipline approach in their hiring – it's just the same old "have you got some experience of outsourcing?" I'd be interested to see just how this develops over the next few years. Perhaps those of us with a good combination of technical, industry, and communication skills might have a bright future after all?

Friday, 30 January 2009

Posted at 13:11

Helping small businesses

I often type 'outsourcing' into Google to see what comes up. Obviously Google News is a useful tool, but it's interesting to also see the organic search results too.

Usually the Wikipedia entry for outsourcing and the National Outsourcing Association come top of the list, but I was surprised today to see that the second entry (after Wikipedia) is the UK government's Business Link service.

Business Link is a national advisory service that offers practical information and help to UK companies, typically smaller or medium-sized enterprises, and I've never noticed much in the way of outsourcing advice from them in the past. However, there is now a useful introduction to the subject developed by Cranfield School of Management published on its web site.

Smaller firms are going to need to understand strategic sourcing strategies even more than ever in the present market conditions so anything Business Link can do to get that message across is welcome.

February 2009

Wednesday, 11 February 2009

Posted at 15:01

News from NASSCOM

So the first day of the NASSCOM India Leadership Forum is over. I'm passing up the opportunity to sit in the bar so I can make sure you get a blog update from me today.

John Chambers, CEO of Cisco, gave a great keynote speech to open the conference. He drifted between two parallel themes – how Cisco has pulled through bad times before, and how collaboration is going to define the company of the future.

Chambers foresees a world in which content, rather than software or networks, is what we are concerned about. He has a great vision, but let's face it – most companies are still stuck in the Stone Age with their bans on any form of social networking. Chambers was quite blunt about companies who bar interaction via the Internet – he asked if we really expected a younger generation, who consider Internet-driven social interaction to be a way of socialising and doing business, to want to work for our companies?

The media, all seeking information on Satyam, mobbed Kiran Karnik - former President of NASSCOM. He was there to introduce Chambers and was not really planning to talk about the Satyam recovery plan, but it's what the press pack wanted to hear.

There was a useful debate at lunchtime focused on the questions raised by offshore outsourcing in continental Europe. Chaired by Mukesh Aghi, Indian head of Steria, the debate ranged far and wide, but gave some interesting insights into the realities of offshoring from several European locations.

In my opinion though, the most disappointing session of the day was a panel featuring board-level execs from TCS, TPI, HCL, and Infosys. The panel was supposed to focus on the realities of the recession and potential impacts to the service industry in India. Unfortunately the only speaker with any real sense of passion was Infosys's Nandan Nilekani, and even he was giving some high-level platitudes without really dealing with the nuts and bolts of the argument. But as I said to someone just after the talk, Nilekani was flying overhead giving a helicopter view of the issues, but the others were 11km up in a 747...

It's been a good start to the event. Now this is with my editor I might just get that drink.

Monday, 16 February 2009

Posted at 10:20

Indian providers gloss over downturn

I'm feeling a bit cheated. One of the things I really wanted to see at the NASSCOM India Leadership Forum was some intelligent debate on how the hi-tech service business in India can cope with the economic downturn in the West.

Yes, it's a topic we were all talking about in the corridors and bars, but the official discussions seemed to either skirt the issue or treat it less seriously than it deserves. I don't want to sound like a harbinger of bad tidings, but the majority of hi-tech services delivered from India are for US firms, and a large majority of those are in financial services. That worries me, and it worries several other people I met in Mumbai last week. So how come it wasn't really discussed in detail?

But the reason I really feel cheated is because a friend of mine sent me a text message on Friday to say she has been laid off. She works (sorry, worked) for Tata Consultancy Services (TCS) in London. A big chunk of their UK marketing team was just culled along with part of their consulting group.

As I mentioned in my last blog, I've just recently listened to the CEO of TCS talk about specific strategies for steering his company through the downturn. He never mentioned any redundancies. Everyone in India has been careful to not mention redundancy. Natural attrition and a hiring freeze was the rule of thumb, yet here we are with permanent staff being booted out – casualties of the credit crunch.

It's a bit like that line in the Scorsese movie Goodfellas, "murderers come with smiles", only in this case the Indian tech firms are telling the Indian press one thing in India as they simultaneously discard their staff in Europe – and no doubt the US too.

Wednesday, 18 February 2009

Posted at 15:18

The world has changed

N ASSCOM tends to always get a big hitter in to speak in the final, Friday afternoon slot before the annual India Leadership Forum closes and we all head off for a Bollywood party. This has ranged from big name corporate leaders to the President of India, but last Friday they mixed it up a little by getting the well-known academic CK Prahalad to talk about management in turbulent times.

And what a talk it was!

Throughout the entire three-day event I had wanted someone to give me some insight into the changing nature of business in this economic slowdown. I'm really fed up of hearing doom-mongers explained how it's the end of the world or optimists telling me that consumers will start spending again by the middle of this year. All these comments are just random opinions shot from the hip and are quite often self-serving because corporate chiefs need to play up their own particular market segment.

Prahalad was different. He said the world has changed, and we have yet to move on to a new way of dealing with business in this environment.

Instead of just talking of a vague 'recession', this is how he summarised the issues of the present situation affecting businesses involved in global services:

1. Markets do not extinguish risk, they distribute it

2. There is a complexity of denial, pressure for growth, profit, and compensation

3. Regulatory design, unfettered innovation, poor oversight

4. There is ongoing systemic risk

5. We are underestimating complexity; individual deals vs. interdependency [supply chain]

I was pleased to see this analysis because it goes so much further than most in global services have been prepared to admit. Prahalad summarised that the problems managers in the current environment are going to face is:

• Managing trends – the future used to be like the past. Now growth, seasonality, competitor behaviour, consumer preference... none of it can be easily predicted.

• If you are dealing with volatility then you cannot deal with trends – you need to deal with discontinuity... the past is not a predictor of the future

• There will be wild swings in input cost, revenue, and product mix because of sudden shifts in consumer preference, technologies, and consumer crises

• You will need the ability to scale up and down, but also the capacity to hold on to operations,

What does Prahalad advise leaders to do? Well, he admits that he does not have all the answers for the long term. If extreme volatility is going to be a new factor in business life then we may well need new business models to handle that. However, he had some specific pointers for the short term than should help companies survive:

1. Conserve your cash

2. Declare a war on waste

3. Do not build your business to carry any stock

4. Create a lower breakeven point

5. Shift to newer businesses where possible

6. Business portfolio choices may need to be adjusted

7. Focus on your core competencies

These basic actions will allow you time to:

1. Increase your capacity to support operations

2. Reduce the impact of market swings

3. Mitigate risk in your service portfolio

I found his lecture quite thought provoking and useful, and extremely relevant to the outsourcing market today. If the supplier community thinks that we are looking at a temporary downturn that will all shake out in a few months then they won't be in business next year. It's time to fundamentally reconsider which game you are playing, because the game has changed.

Thursday, 19 February 2009

Posted at 10:00

Warm welcome for government offshoring plans

As my Computing colleague Angelica Mari has reported this week, a new UK parliamentary group has just been created with the objective of stimulating UK-India trade and investment opportunities. The expectation is that this would benefit both national economies, with technology being a leading part of the relationship – given the strength of the Indian hi-tech service sector.

I thought I'd ask a few people with an interest in this parliamentary group to comment. First, I approached Sangeeta Gupta, vice president of NASSCOM - the Indian hi-tech trade association.

Sangeeta said: "We are very happy with the announcement of the UK government, and our research shows clearly that government spends a great deal on IT services. It's really about competitive advantage. It's not about moving jobs offshore. It's more about Indian companies going there and creating jobs, which will benefit the UK economy. It is about the advantages of using the Indian companies experience and Indian companies have already become partners to many European companies anyway."

One man with real experience of running an Indian technology firm and working for the UK public sector is Ashank Desai. He founded Mastek in the early 1980s and the company has recently been involved in work on the London congestion charge and NHS spine projects. This is one Indian tech player with plenty of experience in the UK, much to the dismay of those of us who forget to pay the congestion charge. Ashank explained to me: "I think that it is not about cost, that's not the main reason for the UK government to come to India. Just look at the great knowledge Indian companies have in the IT domain. It will benefit of the public sector in the UK to leverage that knowledge and to use it to the advantage of UK citizens. You need to look very holistically, at the benefit of the project as well as the local jobs."

Clearly, both commentators from India are keen to stress that the new emphasis on sourcing public sector services from their country can only be a good thing – for both the UK and India. I wanted to ask some Brits their view – of course one would expect the Indians to support this new parliamentary committee anyway, so what did John Willmott, chief executive of BPO analyst group NelsonHall, think?

"The cliché is that it's good for government efficiency. India is a key part of our future and so it may seem like one-way traffic right now, but trade flows both ways and encouraging the two-way flow of trade has to be a good thing," he told me.

So, John is broadly supportive, believing that any short-term pain will be offset by better long-term relationship with India. I asked the same question to Alex Blues, a member of the management group at PA Consulting. Alex is one of the most experienced consultants in the field and he told me emphatically: "The UK government can no longer tinker around the edges. For the first time they are going to really have to start on being citizen-centric and focused on outcomes, much like the Canadian government is doing. With the current financial crisis underway, to achieve their financial objectives they can't just trim here and there. They need to embrace globalisation and do something different. And if they are embracing globalisation then that means embracing India. I do agree that in the long term that has to be good for the UK."

So the commentators I approached, both from the UK and India, all feel that increased public sector trade can only benefit the UK and India. I agree with their sentiments, but I would also exercise caution. The UK is experiencing a wave of public nationalism that has not been seen for decades. The Daily Mail today ran a front-page story screaming about the fact that FOREIGNERS perform 13 per cent of jobs in the UK! Sentiment is against long term economic initiatives, so it will take strong leadership by the British government if they are going to make this new idea work.

Thursday, 19 February 2009

Posted at 14:42

A NIIT at the movies

Last month I wrote a story in this blog about Dr Sugata Mitra and his experiments with slum children in India – inspiration for the award-winning movie Slumdog Millionaire. As you might recall, Mitra performed these experiments while he was at the Indian technology firm NIIT - he is now a professor at Newcastle University here in the UK.

Last night, at the private screening room of the Mayfair Hotel in London, NIIT and Pathé Films hosted a private viewing of Slumdog Millionaire, but with a slight difference. Mitra was there in person to talk us through the experiments he performed with the slum kids around India before we got to see the movie. It was funny to hear that Mitra had been to see the movie at a cinema in Newcastle without ever realising that his work had inspired the novel the film is based on!

Mitra's research focuses on innate learning and I found two of his examples fascinating. He knew kids could teach themselves to use a computer without a manual, but he wanted to see how far this learning-without-guidance paradigm could be stretched so he loaded up a computer with information on biotechnology, all written in English, and left it with a bunch of Tamil-speaking kids for a couple of months.

The end result, these kids could talk to him about DNA, cell structures and other complex matters of biotechnology that they should not even be aware of, given their environment. Mitra has tried some similar experiments closer to home here in the UK. He has proved that eight-to-10-year-old, primary age kids, can easily handle GCSE-level exam questions designed for 16-year olds, providing the teacher guides the children using similar methods to his original slum experiments. That is, let the children find the answers using the internet and make them work in small groups that encourage peer co-operation – and some peer pressure, or a desire to do better and know more than the other kids.

It was a fascinating talk by Dr Mitra and a great opener for a great movie. Kudos has to go to the NIIT team for arranging this. I wonder if they arranged it because they saw my earlier blog?

Monday, 23 February 2009

Posted at 10:58

Harsh times for outsourcers' most valuable assets

My recent blog on redundancies at TCS has created a flurry of activity, with messages from disgruntled IT workers being sent to Computing and also to the various social networks I inhabit.

One batch of very suspicious redundancies is going to get some further investigation by the Computing team, so please keep mailing these comments. You know where to find my personal email and phone number if you don't want to leave public blog comments.

I just want to mention one interesting case that came to me via someone contacting me on Facebook. It's another Indian outsourcing firm with a lot of staff employed in the UK. The contact took maternity leave – so you can at least guess her gender – and returned to work as agreed. Once she returned to work, she wanted to avoid the peripatetic nature of consulting life because of her baby, so she asked to avoid travel where possible. She was told in no uncertain terms that she should start looking for a new job.

Fortunately she found one, but is this how all the IT outsourcing giants are treating their staff today? What are your stories of outsourced IT? Is there a difference in the way a "local" firm behaves compared to the Indian majors?

Tuesday, 24 February 2009

Posted at 14:28

A spot of pyramid selling

I'm in Egypt today, enjoying the hospitality of the Information Technology Industry Development Agency (ITIDA) at the 600-acre Smart Village on the outskirts of Cairo. ITIDA is focused on promoting and developing the information and communication industry in Egypt and for a couple of days they have arranged for some of the leading industry analysts to all be here at the Ministry for Communications and IT.

The joke being passed around the analysts here is that the ministry is actually for a lack of communication, as it's impossible to access any communication tools such as MSN Messenger, Yahoo! Messenger, or Skype – they are all banned. However, to give them the benefit of the doubt, this is a government office so one might expect them to have some tough firewall restrictions.

The Smart Village is a world away from the crowded streets of downtown Cairo on the edge of the city. Those of us without any earlier experience of Cairo had our noses pressed to the glass as the car took us along a main road with the famous Pyramids clearly visible in the distance. Smart Village is an impressive miniature town, filled with beautiful offices that seem to all have some connection to the area, like the Egypt Telcom office featuring glass pyramids.

This morning, the well-known London School of Economics academic Professor Leslie Willcocks outlined some of his thoughts on fourteen non-BRIC (Brazil, Russia, India, China) economics, with some emphasis on Egypt for this audience in Cairo.

Willcocks, and the LSE outsourcing unit, found that these are the key global sourcing trends they predict for the period 2009-2014:

1.   IT outsourcing (ITO) and business process outsourcing (BPO) will increase and become more common

2.   Multisourcing is going to remain the dominant trend – though companies using more than 5 suppliers will struggle

3.   India from low costs to... where? India needs to define a future beyond low cost.

4.   China signals promise but it is not being realised.

5.   Emerging greater country competition across South America, Eastern Europe, and East Asia.

6.   Software as a service will change the entire business model into 'netsourcing'.

7.   Outsourcing disciplines insourcing because internal departments can learn from outsourcing.

8.   Nearshoring will be a strong trend in favour of long distance offshoring.

9.   Knowledge process outsourcing is increasing and so services are getting more complex.

10.   Captives are established and then being sold.

11.   Outsourcing, success and disappointment – don't forget we have seen a lot of disaster and will see more, but we will learn from the past.

As might be expected, Willcocks and the LSE team found that these are the key issues that regions need to focus on when considering their attractiveness to the market:

1.   Costs; labour, infrastructure, corporation tax.

2.   Skills availability; skills pool, vendor expertise.

3.   Environment; government support, business environment, living environment, access and travel.

4.   Infrastructure; telecoms, IT, real estate, local transport.

5.   Risk; security, disruptive events, macroeconomic, Intellectual Property.

6.   Market potential; captive, outsourcing, ITO, BPO.

Of course Egypt is still growing into this market, but it looks like it could become a real player for international offshore outsourcing. However Willcocks did mention some negative points, specific to Egypt:

1.   High illiteracy remains – though mostly in rural areas.

2.   Low percentage of educated population.

3.   Lack of management skills.

4.   Middle managers are imported and there is a local law capping foreign workers to 10 per cent of a company.

5.   Retention of good staff is becoming an issue.

6.   It's just not yet common to outsource offshore software development to Egypt, so it remains a hard decision.

The LSE published these recommendations for ITIDA and the Egyptian government:

1.   Focus on improving the local management skills.

2.   Attract more high value development work from western clients.

3.   Change the negative risk perception, especially in the USA where it was admitted that Egypt is often confused with other Arabic-speaking nations.

4.   Improve the local public transportation system.

5.   Explicitly address the differences in the working week with western clients – and national holidays – as support is difficult when working days are different.

6.   Develop a long-term strategy for widening the education system.

It was a useful session and gave a good outline of the opportunities for Egypt, though there is more to come for us in the hours ahead – focused on what real companies are doing on the ground.

Wednesday, 25 February 2009

Posted at 15:00

Empire building in Egypt

I'm sitting in the mother of all traffic jams at 8am trying to get from central Cairo out to the Smart Village, the hi-tech campus on the outskirts of the city housing both the IT ministry and several IT and BPO firms. Perennial traffic seems to be a major problem with this city, but that's something shared with many major capital cities – including London.

Just before I went for dinner last night (very nice and on the bank of the river Nile) I managed to chat to Amin Khairaldin, strategy advisor and board member of ITIDA, the agency charged with promoting hi-tech services from Egypt.

I asked Amin about the realities of Egypt. It's a fact that many countries around the world are trying to promote their offshore outsourcing credentials, though not many seem as well organised in their communications as Egypt, but are they creating a mirage rather than a reality? He said: "We got the work first before we started talking about it. We created the vision and started to execute before we started talking to the world. What you see today in Egypt is a reality and we are executing to international standards."

Amin explained to me that the IT sector in Egypt has grown organically over time. There has been a strong local IT industry for several decades, though it's mainly with companies of SME size and with a focus on serving the Gulf region, so those of us in Europe are probably not very aware of what's happening here. What was interesting to learn though was that ITIDA has entirely bootstrapped the business process outsourcing (BPO) sector from nothing. He explained: "We have more then twenty years of history in ITO, with companies like IBM who came here in the 1970s. When we assessed the strategic capabilities for Egypt, we found there was a BPO opportunity and there is now a real starting point with companies like Xceed and the multinationals will come."

I asked Amin about the main areas of focus for Egypt moving forward and he said: "We have a great SME programme as we see a lot of opportunities in this market. Many multinationals will work with us because we are in the right place to address the world from Egypt, the US, Europe, and the Gulf region."

This has been a useful and educational trip to Egypt for me. ITIDA kindly arranged for the visiting analysts to dine at the pyramids this evening, but unfortunately my diary is full this week and I need to be back in London tonight. Egypt has a story to tell though, so I'm sure I'll be back.

Friday, 27 February 2009

Posted at 14:33

Job cuts biting harder

Over the last few weeks I've been getting messages about layoffs and cutbacks at various outsourcing suppliers – to the extent now that the national press in India has been chasing me to comment on sentiment over here in London. In the last three weeks though I've visited Bahrain, the Philippines, India, and Egypt – and the message from these places is much the same. They see opportunity in a crisis.

Here in the UK though, the news is depressingly bad as each day goes by.

One of the most noticeable effects of this economic doom and gloom is the rise of the nationalist agenda. The press is currently full of stories of how many "foreigners" work here – implying that those same foreigners are stealing jobs that Brits could be doing.

The first comment I would make is to be extremely wary of this nationalistic agenda. London has long been the most culturally diverse city on earth, in terms of the number of languages used within the boundary of the M25 ring road. Pointing to this now as a negative when it has always been seen as positive is not going to change the way the economy operates. Nothing has changed; it's just that the commentators are shining a light on the facts in a different way.

But, let's get back to the outsourcing companies and their tales of woe. HP has angered their workforce by asking them to take a pay cut. TCS has increased working hours and frozen variable pay. HCL just laid off 450 people in India. Though in a somewhat ironic headline, the Economic Times (India's equivalent of the Financial Times) reported: "Tough times ahead for Infosys employees" – the story being that pay rises this year might only be around the 10% mark. Ask the people at HP what they think of that.

These are companies that have only ever known hyper-growth for a decade. The Economic Times is not kidding. There probably will be Infosys employees upset to only get a 10% hike, because they expected to keep on seeing future progression the way the past operated. Get real.

Friday, 27 February 2009

Posted at 14:48

Will temporary workers haunt Indian outsourcers?

I'm getting worried about the UK system of companies granting their own work permits. Computing has been commenting recently on the responsibility of the India IT sector to behave in a mature way, comparable to the companies they compete with in Europe.

I've commented many times in the past that Indian IT companies should hire people in the country where they operate, rather than flying in cheap workers for extended periods of time. Non-UK companies such as Capgemini, IBM, or EDS, just don't have this tendency to resource projects by bringing waves of staff into the UK from India.

When specialist project expertise is required, or where a knowledge transfer has to be managed then it's obvious that people need to come from HQ and work here temporarily, but how long is a temporary transfer to the UK supposed to last? Can a project transition really require a couple of years? I've known people that were brought in "temporarily" and given a per diem by the company to compensate their transfer to the more expensive UK environment – then 12 or 24 months later they are still around working on the same project on the same terms and conditions.

I've been a champion of the Indian technology sector for many years, but it feels like a disaster waiting to happen in this economic climate if they can't start driving up the perception that they really do make a valuable contribution to job creation in the UK.

March 2009

Wednesday, 11 March 2009

Posted at 10:54

Local jobs not for local people?

Take a look at this headline from the Essex Echo last week: "Essex County Council outsourcing scheme could take work abroad".

The story is about a county council plan to outsource clerical work. It explains: "Council leader Lord Hanningfield held talks with Mumbai-based Tata Group when he visited India last year on a trade mission. At the time, the firm was on a shortlist of companies bidding for the council contracts."

Though Tata is no longer on the shortlist, the newspaper keeps reminding the reader that "New York-based" IBM is on the list, though it seems that having "Milton Keynes-based T-Systems" on the list is OK. I always thought T-Systems was German? But then again, do you worry about Coca Cola being American when you pick up a drink on hot day?

Anyway, this story highlights several of the major issues about outsourcing from the public sector. The council clearly wants to make its back office more efficient. It probably has decades of entrenched processes to sort out, so a change is long overdue. However, the moment some private sector experts are brought in to have a look at improving things, the balloon goes up. Quite often, outsourcing is going to be the only solution because it is politically impossible to improve service within the existing organisation structure.

Other councillors are going to gain political capital by opposing the scheme and saying it will cost council workers their jobs. Then, the spectre of offshoring is introduced not only by suggesting that public servants might need to "answer to a boss thousands of miles away", but in the context of the recession and a need to invest locally in Essex.

It feels hard to criticise the local newspaper. They are just reporting the row at the council, but surely the reasons for the outsourcing idea could have been explored further? There must surely have been a study or audit that looks at council performance and suggests that outsourcing would be a solution. And if not, then why not?

Monday, 16 March 2009

Posted at 15:57

The power of publicity

O h dear. ANZ Bank in Australia is caught somewhere between a rock and a hard place.

The bank has issued a stern press release distancing itself from press assumptions that by focusing on creating value in their Indian technology centres, ANZ will cut local jobs in Australia. The Australian press has been reporting that around 500 jobs are set to be lost, but the bank has stated: "ANZ did not announce job losses in Australia related to offshoring. Employment in ANZ's Australian operations increased by over 500 full time roles in 2008."

Isn't it strange when a company has to release a shotgun press release like this? Reading it creates a sense of panic and fire fighting in backrooms. Just look at some of the themes covered in the first few lines of the release: we are growin; we have been using technology services in India for 10 years; no call centres or customer-facing work is performed in India; anyone affected by the use of offshore technology services is being redeployed in the bank...

It's all good stuff, every message in the press release is positive. However, it's interesting that the media in Australia seems sceptical, because that would tend to indicate that the man on the street also disbelieves these corporate statements.

ANZ is probably doing a great job, and being a responsible employer, but the public are extremely jittery at present. The company will be more effectively judged by actions, rather than words.

Tuesday, 17 March 2009

Posted at 15:20

Don't shoot the baggage handler

Aconsumer pressure group just announced that airlines around the world mishandle around 42 million bags each year, and over a million are irretrievably lost.

I was eating my breakfast and listening to this story being debated on the BBC Radio 5 Live breakfast show.

A representative of the Air Transport Users Council was recounting her own experience on losing her baggage and then reporting it to the airline. The airline said 'we outsourced baggage handling, so it's not our fault the bags are lost'.

This is a typical complaint on outsourcing and it's a shame that the airline involved feels that by blaming the supplier they can make the situation better. The poor passenger without any clothes to wear doesn't care how you structure your baggage handling. It could done internally, it could be outsourced, it could be Coco the Clown and his mates, the passenger doesn't care so long as the bag arrives in the same place that they just arrived.

The fact is that when a service is outsourced, the responsibility for making sure the service works is not transferred to the supplier. It's the client who is selling their own product or service to their own customers. That they may have outsourced a part of the supply chain is of no interest at all to their customers. Outsourcing can't be used as a poor excuse for poor service.

In my first example, if a bag is lost then it's still the airline to blame even if their employees were not handling the bag. They retain responsibility for the service and accountability when it goes wrong.

Wednesday, 18 March 2009

Posted at 11:40

Protectionism and publicly-owned banks

Here we go, more nationalistic reporting from the US, this time in the Columbus Business First newspaper.

The paper is upset because JP Morgan Chase & Co employs nearly 15,000 people in the central Ohio region and yet they have an IT outsourcing programme that's about to be implemented and is costing around $400m.

42 members of Congress have signed a letter to the company asking why this outsourcing plan needs to go ahead when the company has just accepted $25bn in government funds – as a part of the financial services bailout better known as the Troubled Asset Relief Program.

We are witnessing a very dangerous mixture of the public and private sector. Look back a couple of years and can you remember what the economists would have said about Chase outsourcing IT work to India? It strengthens ties with India, it raises income levels in India, it becomes more likely that Indian companies will buy from US companies... the bottom line was that international trade actually enriches the nation because more money flows back to the US from the regions where the US does business.

So what is different now, apart from the sentiment that a major employer in Ohio should be creating more local jobs? But if that suddenly seems like the right thing to do now, then doesn't that mean that it was always the right thing to do – in good times or bad?

Were the economists wrong?

Thursday, 19 March 2009

Posted at 11:54

Recessions fuels offshoring fears

D on't try doing any business with France today. The entire country has gone on strike in protest at President Sarkozy's economic policies.

More than two million people are expected to down tools or leave their desk, paralysing the nation for a day, because unemployment in France has now soared past two million people (sounds like the UK). Government figures suggest that 10% of workers will be unemployed within a year, with 350,000 layoffs expected in the coming months.

I love the fact that people in Europe, France especially, remember who put the politicians in power. In too many countries, the political classes exert such power over the population that we seem to forget it was the people who elected them as representatives - not kings.

But national strikes like this are scary and unsettling. There has already been sporadic violence and industrial action in Europe over the past few months. If French workers are now arranging their second national strike in two months then how much further are the protests going to go?

The relevance for those working in international sourcing is clear. People on the streets are calling for tax cuts to be reversed, for public sector jobs to be preserved, and for jobs to remain local. There is a tidal wave of nationalism sweeping Europe and the US and I have not seen anyone in the industry getting prepared for this.

The last economic downturn hit Europe after the dot com crash and the 9/11 disaster in America, but the last time there was a real recession that actually hurt people away from the trading floors was right back in the early 90s. That's before the explosion in global sourcing took place. None of the suppliers know what is about to happen.

We are entering uncharted waters now. In times of growth, it's easier to explain global sourcing. The economists used to point to the hundreds of thousands of job vacancies in the UK, the continued growth in the UK economy, and all kinds of indicators that showed how trading internationally brought long term gains. How do companies explain and justify this strategy though when the general public, in places such as the UK and France, are facing massive unemployment, jobs are hard to come by, and the economy is in decline?

I predict there is going to be a lot more unrest ahead. Companies on the buy and sell side of the outsourcing equation need to think long and hard about how they present their strategy, because in this climate its going to be very easy for the consumer - and their employers - to misunderstand what's going on.

Friday, 20 March 2009

Posted at 17:13

Outsourcing is not a security weak link

The BBC called yesterday and asked me to comment on a sting operation they set up involving a reporter travelling to India and buying personal data on British consumers from a crooked contact centre employee.

A lot of the data they were sold was invalid and incorrect, but they did manage to purchase some valid credit card information that would allow a smart fraudster to create cloned cards.

When this type of story is featured in the media, the automatic reaction is to point the finger at the contact centre, or the fact that the details are being processed thousands of miles from the customer.

Stop and think a moment. If the consumer (that's you and me) wants access to their bank account, their credit card balance, or to an insurance quote on a 24/7 basis then it means some personal information is going to be flowing around the world on computer systems.

Outsourcing does not create this issue of fraud. It's a consequence of us as consumers insisting on the 'always on' society. Our personal information is now on computer systems and in contact centres like never before. Of course, security has to be stepped up in the contact centres, but the behaviour of consumers has to change if we are really going to prevent this kind of fraud. Blaming the contact centre is like shooting the messenger.

Tuesday, 24 March 2009

Posted at 13:48

Pricing outsourcing deals will remain complex

Closing down sale. Prices slashed. Inflation morphing into deflation. That's the reality on the high street. And the hard times out there are having interesting consequences.

Gartner just published some new research indicating that IT outsourcing prices will drop between 5-20 per cent in the next year. The weak economy and constraints on budgets are going to hit the outsourcing suppliers hard in the coming months.

It's a complex market at present though and I think that there are really several factors changing the nature of IT outsourcing prices:

* New vendors entering the market are changing the nature of competition. This means both niche players who do the job much better than the big 'generalist' boys, as well as the offshore vendors developing more credibility and becoming real players.

* Offshoring is becoming extremely politically sensitive and so the perceived risk is greatly increasing – meaning prices will need to factor in those new fears.

* IT is really industrialising, at last. Prices for commoditised services like storage or infrastructure are bound to fall anyway as these standard, but essential, services increase in scale and vendors compete for bigger and longer-term deals.

* The market is uncertain. Big spending customers are taking longer to make decisions, so vendors are having to promise a lot on price to get their signature on a contract.

It's true that times are hard, but there is still plenty of opportunity out there for those who are offering high quality at a good price. What we are witnessing is the death of the mega-margins and hyper-growth. Some of the offshore outsourcing margins used to be obscene anyway. I don't like this uncertainty in the market any more than the vendors, but I feel that they had it so good for so long that it's about time we saw who is really offering genuine value to their customers.

Thursday, 26 March 2009

Posted at 11:33

Some sound advice

I don't normally react to many surveys or awards to 'best companies'. There are some really worthwhile industry awards and surveys out there (Computing included), but a lot of them are just lists of companies that have paid to be featured. It's often just a PR exercise.

So, even though it's unusual, I want to draw your attention to the fact that KPMG has just been awarded the top outsourcing advisor award by the International Association of Outsourcing Professionals.

The full list of the top twenty advisory firms will be published in the 4 May edition of Fortune magazine, but it's an interesting choice to name KPMG as the number one. I was chatting to Edge Zarrella from KPMG just the other day. He is the global partner in charge of IT advisory and is one of the leading outsourcing advisors at KPMG.

As you might expect, KPMG is known throughout the world for audit, tax, and advice, but it's not so well known for advice in the sourcing environment. However, with awards like this that is likely to change. And one of the things Edge said to me the other day did stick in my mind. We didn't discuss any absolute numbers, so he was guesstimating, but he said that they are probably doing more advisory work in outsourcing right now than several of their competitors combined.

That's a big operation, and clearly the fact that they don't offer their own ITO/BPO services means they can offer impartial advice – unlike some consultants in the marketplace right now who also have their own offshore delivery centre...

So, as I started, I don't normally promote these surveys, but I do think KPMG has an important position in the advisory market that's not being reported. People like Edge are leading this area and deserve an audience.

Thursday, 26 March 2009

Posted at 14:26

Don't pull up the drawbridge just yet

Just recently, a column I read online featured a stinging attack on offshoring. Not from the perspective of any strategic failing, but because it encourages the use of labour in a foreign country. It's the protect-local-jobs debate all over again.

Now I'm all for protecting local jobs as well. I wouldn't want to see the UK become nothing other than a destination for tourists who want to photograph Windsor castle, but the problem is a lot more complex than the pull-up-the-drawbridge approach being advocated by some.

Two years ago I wrote a book with Dr Richard Sykes of Intellect and we highlighted that changing nature of the IT industry itself was going to affect jobs far more than offshoring ever will. And even though the book is a couple of years old, the arguments still stand up.

Let's face it, 'the cloud' is going to affect jobs far more than offshoring – yet it's constantly presented as innovative, wonderful, and the way forward. Or what about software as a service? What's going to happen to all those IT application support teams, desktop maintenance teams, or database administrators if most organisations are using browser-based tools?

I could go on and on, but this is a blog so I recommend you either give me a royalty by going and buying the book, or if you have less time, read this article. It's an interesting insight into the real nature of how the IT business is changing.

Tuesday, 31 March 2009

Posted at 15:21

A risky business

I can't confess to being a regular reader of Financier Worldwide, but a story in the latest edition of the magazine caught my attention because of some comments by Peter Brudenall, a partner at law firm Hunton & Williams.

Peter is one of the leading legal advisors on outsourcing based in London, so I always tune in to his comments in the press or at conferences.

In the Financier Worldwide article he warns: "Few companies truly appreciate the value of their IT systems to ensuring the efficient and stable functioning of the company."

He goes on to say: "Many companies only appreciate the level of dependence when something goes wrong – whether it be a major systems failure, a problem with a key service provider if, for example, the operation and support of IT systems has been outsourced, or when data is lost."

The bottom line is that risk is back on the agenda – if it ever went away. This is particularly important when applied to the issues around offshoring, especially the negative public perception of offshoring. The world is about to come together in London for the G20 summit to explore a coordinated economic effort to escape the recession, and offshoring is on the agenda of more than just a single political leader.

You can expect risk (operational, country, regulatory, reputational) to rise up the agenda of outsourcing decision makers after the events that will take place this week, because as Peter mentioned, many companies underestimate the importance of their IT systems and so the client/supplier relationship is going to be explored in detail once again.

April 2009

Wednesday, 01 April 2009

Posted at 12:05

A destination too far?

I was asked yesterday about my opinion on offshoring to Myanmar. I was a bit taken aback, not least because I still refer to the country as Burma. After all, a military junta enforced the name change in 1989 soon after killing thousands of innocent civilians who wanted nothing more than their democratic rights.

It seems the government there is now eyeing up the international services and outsourcing market as a way of generating some foreign revenue and potentially increasing their own legitimacy.

When we work around the world it's a fact that standards of governance and democracy are different, but isn't Burma a fairly clear-cut case of a place that should be avoided? The Prime Minister-elect, Aung San Suu Kyi, has languished in jail or under house arrest for years – and the election she won was back in 1990. That's almost twenty years since she really should have been Prime Minister, yet it has been impossible for her to adopt the position and form a government.

This all strikes me as distasteful – how could companies consider working with a place with such well-known prisoners of conscience? I'm interested in the wider opinion of Computing readers though – perhaps I'm judging this through British eyes and others have a different view on Burma?

Monday, 06 April 2009

Posted at 13:26

Destination Dubai

I was interested to see that the BBC current affairs programme 'Panorama' is focused today on the story of economic growth in Dubai, and some of the harsh realities being faced there as the economy starts to falter.

It's interesting because I had been invited to speak at the Arab outsourcing conference in Dubai later this month. In fact I can't make it due to some other commitments, but it looks like I am still listed as a speaker on their website - I can assure you I'll be here at home in London.

I don't think the BBC investigation will have much of an impact on outsourcing in the Middle East, Dubai in particular. This 'hidden' aspect of Dubai has not really been all that hidden over the years – it's just that most visitors tend to put it to the back of their mind as they stare in awe at the 7-star hotels.

What is potentially interesting though is how commodity-rich economies in the Middle East will lend themselves to international technology-enabled services. In the long term, the oil wealth will naturally diminish so these nations are seeking a future income beyond oil and tourism.

But Dubai doesn't have the attribute that most places sell when they talk of their attractiveness to the offshoring marketplace – an abundance of people. What they do have is a government that is very keen to create an environment where the legal and physical infrastructure is extremely supportive, and attracts investors and entrepreneurs to the region. In short, they want to make it the best place to locate a hi-tech services company with the people coming from wherever they are needed to support that company.

I know several of the speakers at the conference, so I'll give them a call in a couple of weeks to update some of these thoughts with views directly from Dubai on what is happening in the region.

Tuesday, 07 April 2009

Posted at 16:21

Is bringing the jobs back home a serious strategy?

US student loan firm Sallie Mae has decided to cancel its Indian offshore operations, a back office that employs around 2,000 people.

Why? The recession.

The troubled economic climate means that jobs are being lost in the US and Sallie Mae has decided to hire locally back in the States as a response. Is this just a marketing gimmick or is there really something in it? Don't forget that the US is a big place and back office staff in Boise, Idaho will not cost the same as those working on the Avenue of the Americas in Manhattan.

I believe that this story has the whiff of a firm having some trouble with their offshoring plans and deciding to create some positive spin by shutting down the Indian operation, but if we see it developing into a trend then it could become a serious worry for some of the Indian BPO firms.

Thursday, 09 April 2009

Posted at 11:32

Microsoft's Indian deal clouded by uncertainty

It's no surprise to read that HCL has signed a five-year deal with Microsoft worth around $170m. After all, Microsoft has long been operating with global resources and HCL is one of the Indian giants.

But, take a look at the comments on the Techflash blog in Seattle. Techies in the Pacific northwest of the US are particularly upset that this deal could involve around 600 people in India – 600 people they assume could be working in the USA.

One of the comments on the blog claims that Microsoft has recently given around half their staff a 10-15% pay cut. This is because a large proportion of Microsoft staff work on contracts, rather than as permanent staff, and the agency rates have been renegotiated. This is on top of an ongoing programme to reduce overall headcount by around 5,000.

What would really help us all when new outsourcing deals are announced against a backdrop of redundancies is to announce what the deal is actually for. Reputable news sources such as the Economic Times in India, and even Reuters, don't really have any information about the HCL deal other than the contract size.

Come on HCL and Microsoft. We have to assume it's an important deal for you both so please issue some more information to let us know what it's all about...

Thursday, 09 April 2009

Posted at 11:35

Sainsbury's renews its faith in outsourcing

Who can remember the heady days of 2004 when Sainsbury's dumped the IT systems being built by Accenture at a reputed cost of around £3bn? The supermarket chain hired over 3,000 shelf-stackers to handle stock control systems manually and beefed up their internal IT team instead of relying on the fine words of the external consultants.

Now, zip forward to today. Sainsbury's has just announced that IBM will roll out the Wesupply system for them, aimed at improving stock levels across the chain.

In fact, with an average of 30,000 product lines in each store and the recent addition of a home delivery service that relies on picking items in-store, it's no surprise that Sainsbury's have finally decided that the pencil and paper approach has had its day. Goodbye, shelf-stackers. Hello, IBM IT implementation experts.

Let's hope this is going to be a better marriage of client and supplier than the earlier attempt at stock control. I can remember an Accenture executive speaking at a conference about the Sainsbury's issue as a positive example of how Accenture can exit a deal gracefully.

Now, that's the mark of a truly great consultant. Getting a good case study together from every kind of client experience!

Tuesday, 21 April 2009

Posted at 13:18

Beware the outsourcing rumour mill

I was quite amused to read this statement in the Economic Times this morning: "In a press statement PA's Executive team and Board has clarified that Cognizant Technology Solutions are not, nor have ever been, in talks with PA about anything whatsoever."

I do like the flourish of that final "whatsoever". It just sounds as if PA Consulting has had its nose completely put out of joint by a false news story in the ET.

And yet, news on mergers and acquisitions in the outsourcing market is notoriously unreliable. Everyone wants to be the first to report on a merger or takeover and so some papers will run the story before there is anything other than smoke and mirrors. Who can remember all the rumours about Infosys and Capgemini from about a year back?

That these stories still hit the press in such a way shows that analysts and journalists still feel such a deal is likely – not necessarily this one, but a similar pairing of companies. If one of the offshore major Indian technology companies wants to really grow and acquire new clients in the middle of these difficult times then they certainly need to offer some deep business consulting abilities, but is this really the right time for the offshore firms to be expanding their footprint? Some firms, such as TCS, seem to be scaling back their consulting ambitions to focus on what they do best – lower cost, reliable, safe, offshore delivery. Time will tell.

Tuesday, 21 April 2009

Posted at 13:22

No more surprises from Satyam?

Last week it was announced that Tech Mahindra would purchase the troubled Satyam. Yesterday, they published details of the new board and all the initial welcome messages to the new management team.

The press release from yesterday details the financial offer that has been confirmed for Satyam: "Following the Company Law Board's approval on 16 April, 2009 of Tech Mahindra as the successful bidder to acquire a controlling stake in Satyam, Tech Mahindra has deposited the initial subscription amount of approximately Rs. 1,756 Crores (approx $351m) and the total funds necessary to consummate the mandatory public offer being approx Rs. 1,154 Crores ($231m), in separate escrow accounts today. Tech Mahindra is expected to announce plans for the Public Offer, shortly."

Forgive me if I sound surprised, but nearly $600m in cash is changing hands? They must have supreme confidence that Satyam is not going to lose more clients because of this scandal - and that more accounting trickery is not going to materialise once the forensic accountants really get going.

Friday, 24 April 2009

Posted at 15:47

The visa debate is heating up

A couple of weeks ago, the New York Times featured an extensive series of debates on foreign workers using the H-1B visa system to work in the US. The debate centred on whether these are skilled workers urgently needed by the economy at large, or just workers that depress the value and viability of the local jobs market.

I'm quite fascinated by this debate. The UK finally reorganised it's own visa system for skilled workers quite recently, introducing a points-based system to simplify eligibility and also allowing companies to self-issue visas to their own staff. The design of the new system, and the lobbying that led to it, was all in the context of the good old days – when the economy was growing and skilled people were needed as fast as they could arrive at Heathrow. I know because I attended several debates and meetings where companies in the IT industry pressed their case upon government ministers.

Yet, what happens now we are suddenly looking at the worst economic climate since the Second World War? it took several years of lobbying and planning to create a more flexible work visa system, yet it seems as if the economy has just fallen off a cliff and collapsed in under two years.

IT firms working in the UK with global resource are just getting used to their newly found freedom, where the government trusts them to follow the guidelines and supervision is minimal. Will the weight of the 'British jobs for British workers' debate mean the work visa system is overhauled again before the ink is dry on the last revision?

Friday, 24 April 2009

Posted at 15:50

British public sector outsourcing agreements can excel

The Treasury here in the UK has released its final report on operational efficiency, the programme of work aimed at improving the way the government operates. I did see it mentioned in Computing, but given the British annual budget was announced this week the efficiency review appears to have been largely overlooked.

The UK government is obviously going to be a big fish for suppliers selling outsourced services. It's interesting then to note some of the case studies within the efficiency review that are held up as best practice within the government at present:

• HM Prison Service (HMPS): HMPS has implemented a shared services centre that delivers finance, procurement and HR functions for all 128 Prison Service establishments. It is expected to deliver a 32 per cent saving in staff costs and just over 30 per cent savings against the gross costs of corporate services;

• National Health Service (NHS): A joint venture, shared business service between the Department of Health and Steria now serves over 100 health trusts. This shared service delivers 20 to 30 per cent savings on like-for-like services; and

• Department for Work and Pensions (DWP): DWP has set up a shared services organisation providing some HR and finance functions to the department, its executive agencies and to other parts of government. Savings from shared services of 15 per cent have been achieved already, with further savings of 13 per cent expected for 2008-09.

I've written in the past about the NHS deal with Steria, back when Xansa announced it in India (Xansa was subsequently purchased by Steria in October 2007). It's interesting to see that it has grown so large now, with over 100 health trusts within the NHS now using this joint venture company to process their finance and accounting work.

The spirit of this joint venture was originally that both the NHS and Steria should be able to benefit by creating the deal as a joint venture with a profit share arrangement. It was an innovative arrangement back when it was formulated and clearly it's getting recognised now as an example of best practice. Perhaps the private sector should take notice and learn from the government?

Thursday, 30 April 2009

Posted at 16:50

Doubts creep in over the wisdom of multisourcing

Computing published a story yesterday about some new research from PA Consulting, with the emphasis on issues being found with multisourcing.

It's not a surprise to me that there is a groundswell of opinion now shifting against the multisourcing miracle. Although many other industries (just look at big construction projects) have used similar procurement models for years, it just doesn't seem to have become all that accepted in the technology and services sector.

Why? Just as PA Consulting is pointing out, there are many more risks associated when working with a basket of suppliers - that was always known. But the real reason is that it's just too complex!

I wrote a white paper on this about three years ago, back when books like 'Multisourcing' were spouting off about how this is the future of outsourcing – even though they had precious little in the way of case studies to back up the predictions.

If a client wants to multisource, they don't just need to create a vendor management department, they need an entire range of new resources and skills, a whole new ability to programme manage several external suppliers who may all be dependent on each other for your project.

So, it's interesting to see research like this. Is the era of multisourcing over? Did it ever really start?

May 2009

Friday, 01 May 2009

Posted at 9:00

The value of networks

Straight after I had listened to PA Consulting telling me all about their new research – as featured in my last blog post – I caught a bus to Shoreditch. I wanted to go and have a chat to Charles Armstrong, the CEO of Trampoline Systems.

This was an interesting and quite random connection. I met a girl in a bar last year in Idaho in the US – we chatted and shared a few glasses of local Idaho beer. She worked in music promotion and introduced me to a venture capital guru, who introduced me to Charles – all through social networks and without any motive other than sharing contacts where it looked like we might add value or get along together.

Shoreditch remains a kind of forgotten wilderness within London. It's just minutes away from the financial centre of the city and is not quite a part of the trendy art scene around Hoxton – though I noticed a few studios as I walked to Trampoline so perhaps that's changing. Charles was also making more of an effort to fit into the local art scene than the world of corporate IT, with purple trousers and space invader graphics stencilled across the office.

Charles showed me some of the things he has been working on and for those of you still wondering how the concepts of social networks apply within a corporate context – here is your answer.

The tools created by Trampoline can plug into any standard corporate email system and monitor traffic, relationships, and context... A visual map can be displayed showing who is talking to who, when, how often, about what, and which companies link to your company – and where.

If this all sounds a bit 'Big Brother' then just consider some of the upsides. Rather than this being a tool for snooping, the idea is to shine a light on networks that exist, but are not usually visible.

329

Suppose you need to find someone in your own company with investment banking knowledge as well as a good understanding of some particular tool, let's say SAP. The visual maps Trampoline offers let you easily find who might be the right person, and not just by skills alone, it becomes obvious who sits at the hub of several critical relationships when you can see expertise and influence being displayed graphically.

I mentioned that I had been talking about networks recently to someone at Capgemini. Charles plugged his name into the system and we could immediately see who, from his company, has the best relationship with that Capgemini person.

I loved it. But the reason I'm blogging about it here is not to plug what Charles is doing - he already has some very well known clients. It's because of the serendipity in having a lunch at Gordon Ramsay's restaurant and listening to PA Consulting talk about how multisourcing has become impossible because multi-company networks are too difficult to manage. Then, later in the afternoon, I see the solution staring me in the face.

Friday, 01 May 2009

Posted at 17:47

Going for green

This week I chaired the first meeting of a new 'Going for Green' steering committee, organised by the National Outsourcing Association.

It was a useful meeting because we had an excellent mix of contributors on both the buy, sell, and advisory side of the outsourcing mix, including HMRC, Gartner, Adec, Capgemini, IBM, and Fujitsu.

This was only the initial meeting of the steering committee, but the group already highlighted a number of areas where the NOA could really get their teeth into the green supply chain. These are going to be written up by the NOA team into a white paper that should be published within just a few weeks.

The aim is to create some momentum within the industry on the real green issues – measurements, standards. These are the changes that matter, rather than the usual 'greenwash'. The group should be meeting again in late June. If you would like to participate then contact the NOA team here.

Tuesday, 05 May 2009

Posted at 11:20

Local job plan doesn't spell the end for offshoring

M uch of the press has been talking today of how disastrous the new proposals of President Barack Obama might be for regions around the world where outsourcing flourishes. It was an ongoing fear during his election campaign – that he would actively discriminate against companies that send work offshore, but what's the reality here?

Obama is planning to emphasise tax breaks on companies that create jobs within the American economy, so companies creating new overseas jobs would forego the tax incentives they are now used to.

In my opinion there are a couple of things to remember here. First, there is a global market in services anyway, despite what trickery governments perform with the tax system. Obama is sending a patriotic message to those who elected him, but he won't suddenly shut down international investment overnight.

Second, we are in a recession anyway so it's sensible for any company that has a lot of consumer interaction – any B2C firm – to be looking at ways to create local jobs. It helps the company to look good in marketing terms, it can encourage staff loyalty, and it does help to stimulate the economy, however minor the local investment.

It's entirely understandable what Obama is doing. He can't roll back the economy to a time before the Internet, or before companies could split their departments and structure and locate staff across the world. However, he can at least show to the American taxpayer that incentives from the government only go to companies creating local jobs. And he is doing this in a way that is not punitive to the thousands of American companies that already work across many borders.

These measures won't have much of an effect on the international market in offshore services, but they will make Obama look like an astute leader. If the technology and service companies in places like the Philippines and India are really worried about losing business because of this tax incentive change then I can't imagine their business proposition was really all that attractive anyway.

Wednesday, 06 May 2009

Posted at 11:22

It's looking tough down Mexico way

As we might have expected, swine flu is finally affecting outsourcing. With business in Mexico almost paralysed by the flu, contact centres and other services there are suffering from the uncertain business situation.

In a recent statement, Peter Ryan, head of contact centre outsourcing analysis at Datamonitor, said: "To date, medical research has shown that swine flu is most commonly transmitted in areas of limited air circulation and close human proximity. For a location like Mexico, in which contact centre agents frequently use public transportation to travel to and from work, it is very possible that many could choose to stay at home rather than risk contracting the virus during regular commutes. This is also the case in regard to the contact centre facilities themselves, in which large numbers of individuals share common space."

That's especially an issue for the contact centre industry, where agents are critical. But those agents need to be there on time and usually on a 24/7 basis, so the uncertainty over people coming to work or not could have a major effect on the viability of some centres in Mexico at present.

Ryan goes on to say: "The current outbreak of swine flu, furthermore, is only one of a number of challenges facing the Mexican contact centre outsourcing space, the most notable of these being that of ongoing border violence. Earlier this year, Datamonitor commented on the negative impact that drug cartel wars with authorities could have on the investment climate in Mexico, in regard to attracting foreign clients. Concerns over swine flu will only exacerbate worries associated with this location, and make other offshore markets potentially more attractive to investors."

It's looking tough down Mexico way at present. Hopefully the swine flu will be a temporary disturbance, but it could be enough combined with these other factors to convince investors that there is an easier ride somewhere else...

Wednesday, 06 May 2009

Posted at 15:23

The song remains the same

Two years ago I wrote a book for the British Computer Society with Dr Richard Sykes, who some of you may know as a board member of Intellect – the British hi-tech trade association.

Richard is a friend of mine who has had a long history in the IT business, including time as the technology head of ICI and chairman of advisory firm Morgan Chambers.

The book, Global Services: Moving to a Level Playing Field, has finally been distributed to the USA so readers over there can buy it from local stores, such as Amazon.com.

I was always disappointed that it never got much distribution in the USA, as it's the natural home for a book like this, so it's pleasing to see that the publisher has finally got their act together.

Although I wrote this book with Richard and I'd be inclined to talk it up, I hope American readers of this blog do go and take a look. The interesting thing is that when I look at the book now, it hasn't really dated and the arguments are still very strong.

This book explores outsourcing in the context of how a global market in services is being created and so we were more concerned with that way technology and the robust infrastructure of 'the cloud' is changing the very nature of companies and how they are structured.

We made the book short and direct with strong arguments and a lot of examples, including case studies such as the Samuel L Jackson movie, Snakes on a Plane. It's even more relevant today now the recession is forcing companies to change faster than they might like so if you have never heard of this book because you are in the USA, then take a look and feel free to get in touch with me if you have questions about it.

Monday, 11 May 2009

Posted at 12:56

A little knowledge goes a long way

The thing about the offshore outsourcing market is that trust is a genuine currency, hence the importance of brands in that marketplace.

Major IT firms, like IBM and HP, have strived for years to create a sense of trust in their brand and so when they offer a service that is delivered from offshore you can be pretty sure it's going to work well – at least within the boundaries of the agreed service levels.

And it should be quite obvious to any of the smaller service providers that this is the case. Think about the client who might be considering an offshore project. Whatever part of the supply chain they are thinking about outsourcing, it's going to be a vital part of what they do – no matter how simple or standard it is.

Yet I keep on reading of suppliers who talk of how advanced they are and how far 'up the value chain' of services they have ascended – to the heady heights of knowledge process outsourcing (KPO). They tend to treat basic services with some disdain, preferring to focus on high-margin and sexy services that involve a lot of mathematics and analysis.

Well, the truth is that I'd be surprised if any outsourcing contract went to a supplier that was not trusted by the client – at least initially. So, it must be getting harder and harder for these KPO firms to win any business if they are not cutting their teeth with the basics first, right?

Monday, 11 May 2009
Posted at 16:00
A matter of trust

O n the subject of trust in outsourcing, how many more times do I need to receive emails from suppliers in far-flung corners of the world promising me a percentage of any projects I can find for them in the UK?

If a supplier wants to work with me then I'd be only to happy to advise them on how to improve their presentation for the European market, how to talk to the media and analyst community, how to create a great online presence. I can do all this stuff, because that's what I do, when I'm not writing.

One thing I certainly don't do is take percentage cuts on 'deals' because here I am commenting about companies in the media. I couldn't claim much integrity if I was earning bonuses from companies that I talk up in the press. When I mentioned this 'problem' to one supplier from India in the past they offered to make payments to my parents. I don't think they quite understood my concern. Or maybe that's how others behave and I'm missing out on the goods in the trough?

But are any of these suppliers that are offering shady salespeople a percentage cut really doing any business worth talking about? And who would outsource a project to a salesperson that has only a vague connection to the company that might actually end up delivering the service?

Wednesday, 13 May 2009
Posted at 11:08
Cutting through the greenwash

I can remember a couple of years ago feeling certain that environmental concerns were going to become the critical issue in outsourcing. The belief was that companies in high energy-consuming industry sectors would demand better green credentials from their suppliers – to improve the carbon neutrality (or in an attempt to reach that status) of their own supply chain.

It started off that way and some companies made very public pledges of carbon neutrality. However, this area of the outsourcing marketplace has been flooded with greenwash – the false promises hyped up to appear like your IT supplier does anything and everything for the environment.

I was interested to see the 2009 Green Outsourcing Survey from the Brown Wilson group – the guys who publish the Black Book of Outsourcing. I was browsing through this 38-page study yesterday and I was impressed by their ability to filter out some of the less credible environmental claims.

I'm sure you can obtain a copy of the report from Brown Wilson, so I'm not going to detail all the findings on a blog entry, but I would like to say that it's interesting to see Patni on top of the 'innovative green' rankings. Patni occupies the top spot, surrounded by the 'big boys' such as IBM, HP, and CSC as other Indian suppliers languish much further behind.

Even though clients are presently concerned with short-term survival, rather than the rain forests, these green credentials must surely give Patni some advantage in the market? Any opinions?

Thursday, 14 May 2009

Posted at 14:21

Can BT become a credible services player?

I remember having a chat with Andrew Kemp, Director, Group Planning and Analysis, for BT, at the NASSCOM conference in Mumbai last February. During his conference presentation, Andrew had talked of how BT was positioning itself well to weather the recession – all except for BT Global Services where the poor results at the end of 2008 led to CEO François Barrault falling on his sword (albeit with £1.5m in the bank as a farewell gift).

Last year, BT Global was all set to reinvent their involvement in the IT service sector. Traditionally just focused on corporate telecoms, they openly set a course towards becoming a full service IT company, including systems integration and development.

Those ambitions have been cast to the wind now the group has announced a £134m loss.

But how does that change of heart affect the wider industry? BT Group owns nearly a third of Tech Mahindra, the company that just bought the beleaguered Indian tech firm Satyam.

BT may well wish to sell those share, but they need to see if the Tech Mahindra share price will increase over the next year or so. It's highly unlikely BT would just bail out immediately, unless they felt any uncertainty over the Satyam acquisition.

But what was their strategy really anyway? Why would they be developing BT Global into a full services IT player when they hold a significant share in a rival firm, and use that firm for their own IT services (amongst others)?

BT has a global footprint and a tremendous brand so it's a shame to see that the troubles with BT Global have contributed to the calamitous losses announced today – and those losses are going to lead to thousands of jobs vanishing across the group.

If they could refocus what BT Global does well and remove the Tech Mahindra connection then they could slowly build themselves into being a credible IT services player. The question is, do they have the appetite to grow that business in the present cash crisis?

Monday, 18 May 2009

Posted at 11:56

A new era of management consulting?

Could the recession be good news for management consultants cast adrift by the lack of advisory work? It could be. After all, another effect of this economic slowdown is a reaction against 'foreign' service companies, so many companies – like the Indian tech majors – are keen to be seen hiring locally in places such as the UK and US.

We have seen this before. Many of those same firms started hiring locals a few years back in an effort to create a strong cultural fit with the markets where they were winning business, but as business started thinning out, a lot of those six-figure-salary consultants were shown the exit door.

Now the consultants are cheaper, because they can't find the work, so companies like Wipro are back in the market and looking for good, local domain experts again. Wipro has seen their workforce contract this year, rather than growing as they have always been used to.

It's an unusual work market for both the employer and employed, but many of these non-European firms are poised to start winning more juicy public sector contracts, so this could be the dawn of a new management consulting era

Thursday, 21 May 2009

Posted at 14:00

MTV turns to India to reach out to viewers

Indian tech giant HCL has just announced a new IT outsourcing contract with MTV. It's reasonably interesting because MTV is a pretty cool brand for any IT company to associate itself with, but what was more interesting to me was the list of different work to be included in the deal.

According to the media in India, the contract includes the development of a new media player, and a new social network – in addition to other software development, such as bespoke games.

In an environment where the internet has a surfeit of free social networks and media players, it's interesting to see the music giant commissioning an IT firm to develop these. Clearly they must have an ambition to capture the immense potential of a youth network connected by music, something the British magazine NME has been working hard to achieve – with some success.

MTV has been interacting with the web very closely, from right back in the early days when their VJ Adam Curry personally registered the domain mtv.com. He went on to become known as the 'podfather' for his work in pioneering the adoption of podcasting, and the website is packed full of information in a multimedia format, but clearly there is a greater long-term ambition.

Watch this space. Next time I visit the guys in HCL, I'll ask if I can join them at the virtual Headbangers' Ball.

Thursday, 28 May 2009

Posted at 15:56

Some harsh truths about technology

The Evening Times newspaper in Scotland features a front page story today about the 850 jobs Hewlett Packard is planning to axe in Erskine. The manufacturing plant is being reduced in size, with more focus on increasing production in the Czech republic.

This is a blow for the local economy in Renfrewshire, and the newspaper has pointed out that in the last quarter alone HP made profits of £1.1bn.

This is an emotional decision for anyone who cares about job creation in the UK, but who is right and wrong in a case like this? Companies such as HP do have to think of all stakeholders when they make these decisions, and clearly they believe that continuing to offer a better deal to their millions of customers is more important than the livelihood of a few hundred people in Scotland.

Someone in Glasgow using the name 'openmind' posted a comment on the Evening Times website saying: "We're masters of our own destiny. We want everything cheap - computer printers for £30, laptops for £200. The cost saving has to come from somewhere so that companies can maintain margins to stay in business. We've got no right to complain therefore when manufacturers seek to cut labour costs so we can still buy stuff cheap in the shops. Learn to live with it."

And that's the hard truth. Most of the staff losing their jobs never even had a contract with HP – they were almost all agency staff employed on short-term contracts.

If the people of Britain want to buy hi-tech products at almost giveaway prices, then how can those same people expect the manufacturers to offer stable long-term jobs in Scotland?

Friday, 29 May 2009

Posted at 14:37

IT services providers feel the pressure to specialise

I had a meeting this morning with a group of consultants who are trying their best to come up with a way of selling advice on services, without it sounding like outsourcing. Their dilemma is real, because if you break up the value chain within a company, only a small section of it is related to outsourcing at present, but we were having a discussion about how they might create a grand unified theory of services.

One of them even declared that the IT outsourcing supplier community, as we currently know them, will eventually die off – they are too general and try to be all things to all men.

I'd have to say I certainly agree with that. I'm about to enjoy a beer in the English sun with Dr Richard Sykes, co-author of my book 'Global Services: Moving to a Level Playing Field'. When we wrote that book two years ago, we predicted that suppliers would have to specialise, they would have to know as much about a business area as their clients do. If they can't offer that expertise, then what else are they going to offer? IT skills.

Hmmm, how hard is it for me to source commoditised IT skills? The supplier community had better wake up because the contents of that book are becoming even truer today, as companies are demanding better ideas from their suppliers – just to survive.

June 2009

Thursday, 04 June 2009
Posted at 14:56
Offshoring in decline?

The Financial Times published a very interesting piece of analysis based on their own research on offshoring from the UK yesterday.

The analysis suggests that offshoring has rapidly declined because of the recession. That's not a surprise if you are regularly reading this blog. There is a tendency to assume companies will use offshoring more in a recession – as they need to cut costs fast – but it's not always true, and the FT research indicates that offshoring from the UK is presently at miniscule levels.

The report said: "An FT analysis of job losses announced since the recession began last July suggests little more than 4,000 job cuts at 17 locations can be wholly or partly attributed to work being moved abroad. This figure is minuscule compared with the nationwide total of 700,000 redundancies over the past three quarters, according to data from the Office for National Statistics. Most of those were caused by lack of demand or failure to access credit."

That's a robust defence for those who have to defend offshoring decisions. The actual number of redundancies caused by offshoring is tiny, compared to companies going under and firing staff because they just can't find finance – or they are just not goo at what they do.

The FT research indicates that it is the fear of investing a large chunk of operating capital up front in a change programme that is preventing most offshoring. The report also points out that the cost advantage is dwindling – it has become more expensive to hire offshore resource in locations such as India, and in many cases it has become cheaper in some parts of the UK.

I'd also add that the consumer backlash risk is also being taken far more seriously today. Even though a consumer-oriented company may logically feel they can offshore some functions, they might choose to not do it just because they want to be seen actively creating jobs in the local market. We live in an era where single-issue campaigns can be distributed very fast over social networks, so it is easier to target companies who ignore consumer concerns.

So, if offshoring is declining then what of the outsourcing market in general? I've been talking to people involved in public sector outsourcing – and that includes several of the Indian suppliers – about government sourcing. I'm going to posting several blogs over the next few days focused on those conversations...

Friday, 05 June 2009

Posted at 14:18

Delving in to the detail of the OEP

The recent British government budget emphasised that public services need to be delivered for less – because debt levels are so high right now. In the same week, the Operational Efficiency Review (OER) led by Dr Martin Read came to a similar conclusion, that more must be delivered for less. More recently still, the Child Maintenance and Enforcement Commission (replacement for the Child Support Agency) commissioned India IT firm TCS to redesign their IT. Connected? Possibly.

Perhaps there is a new wind of change in the public sector that means an emphasis on efficiency is going to force public bodies into more outsourcing? I spoke to some industry experts to gauge the opinion of those in the market.

Almost everyone I spoke to feels that outsourcing will increase, yet some feel that any outsourcing will not even approach the levels of savings required by the government.

Brian Woodford, Public Sector Director at Tata Consultancy Services said: "It comes through the OEP, government cannot continue to fund the level of public sector that it does at present. Savings are needed in the back office and from procurement. The Read report looks at back office operations IT and there is a huge case for shared services. It might not mean outsourcing – it could be shared internal services. They have looked at internal shared services as a good example of best practice, so it's not just outsourcing that could answer the questions."

Richard Marchant, Local Government Strategic Partnerships Director at Capita goes into more detail on the level of planned efficiencies: "The targets set for savings over the next three year for the public sector are very tough. Government departments cannot keep top-slicing budgets as they have been doing without looking towards a broader range of solutions to best meet the efficiency agenda."

Marchant goes on to say: "In the recent budget, the Government announced that it is seeking £15bn of efficiency savings across public services. £6bn of savings is the focus in the current spending review period and an additional £9bn of savings will be sought between 2011 and 2013/14. Outsourcing or strategic partnering could well present government departments with a viable option as they seek to implement change, re-engineer services and achieve efficiency savings. A strategic partnership is not just about achieving short-term savings but is also about making the most of an experienced private sector partner to deliver in the medium and long term. An example of this is our joint venture with Birmingham City Council, Service Birmingham, which aims to deliver cost savings of £1bn back to the council over 10 years."

Gary Bettis, Director of IT Advisory Services for Serco Consulting, believes that the story is not so much about new outsourcing – it's improving what is already being done. He said: "We did in fact advise a great deal on the Read OEP report. The reality is that in government right now there is a lot more scope for outsourcing, but the real story is in the existing outsourced services. If they could introduce better standards across some of the existing contracts then they could save a huge amount."

Bob Scott, Vice President, Public Sector Outsourcing UK at Capgemini said: "I think that this efficiency drive will manifest itself in the short term by extending and expanding outsourcing that is similar to what we have seen in the past. The operational efficiency programme has to be put alongside other forward-thinking programmes, because it's aligned with cost reduction and yet we should also be looking at this in parallel with things like Lord Carter's Digital Britain programme. We can't just continually look to cut costs for evermore. Intellect commented on this recently saying, if all we do is cutting ICT budgets then we will have failed the public."

Stuart Ford, Head of Public Sector, Europe, at HCL Technologies said: "Yes I do think there will be more outsourcing – I've spoken a lot with Martin Read and depending on where you look in the government there are different feelings. In general though, there is a view that transformational outsourcing will greatly increase. The feeling is that outsourcing can get public sector staff back on the frontline, doing what they should be doing."

Andrew Warren, Head of Public Sector Practice at Vertex, said: "Yes of course this is going to happen. There are some subtleties though. We will see fewer green field outsourcing opportunities and the government will itself explore new ways to deliver their own services. That might be smaller agencies outsourcing to bigger ones, as well as more traditional outsourcing to suppliers. Local government will go much faster than central government, with considerable new contracts in the next two years."

Geoff Llewellyn , Head of Public Sector Business Europe at Wipro said: "We expect a lot more government outsourcing. There is the cost driver, but also the transformational government programme. Given the prominence of shared services in that, we expect outsourcing to complement a move to more shared services. The most important review is the transformational government push from the Cabinet office, trying to get departments to think more radically about how they deliver public services, and what facilities they use to underpin their own service."

Mark Brett, Member of the Management Group (Partner, Public Sector Advisory) at PA Consulting, said: "It's a story of two halves. Given the way government operates, there will be pressure in departments to employ more outsourcing. But it's going to be pressure from within each department because of the pressure they feel, rather than a cross-government strategy. It is easy to forget how much the government has already outsourced. They have a lot of experience already just that most of it is in fairly low-end mundane processes."

Brett adds: "Some departments are really trying to work hard at increasing the levels of shared services, but some are still only flirting with the idea. I can't see there being a common drive across government at all. If you look back through the 90s then many departments had some form of efficiency review forced on them, but that was usually quite tactical – outsource your IT support or something like that."

It's clear from these comments that most industry players expect far more outsourcing to be commissioned across all forms of government. Improving the use of shared service centres and creating models where departments can outsource to each other will be a critical part of making this work though – rather than just a bonanza for the supplier community.

I'm going to dig deeper into some of these issues in my next few blog posts. They are going to be a bit longer than my usual blogs, but I've been talking to a lot of people recently and I want to get these conversations online.

Tuesday, 09 June 2009

Posted at 15:32

Sales calls can find you anywhere

Here is something interested that happened to me today. Someone added me to their phone book on Skype. I wasn't sure who the person was – other than the name meant it was obviously a tech firm – so I said hello on chat. It turned out to be a firm called GKS Technologies in India.

First, it's a big surprise to me that anyone would just randomly trawl Skype looking for potential customers to call in locations that just might have some business – will they call everyone in London looking for some IT work? Then, wouldn't the process of using unsolicited Skype calls like this alienate anyone who might even potentially give them some business? By switching to chat, it also highlighted some pretty dreadful presentation skills on their part.

You can guess what I think of GKS Technologies, but just so you can see what happened, here is the conversation:

Mark Kobayashi-Hillary

hello

hello?

you just added me

GKS Technologies

hi

Mark Kobayashi-Hillary

hello

GKS Technologies

hi mark

This Is Neha from Mumbai/India

Mark Kobayashi-Hillary

hello

GKS Technologies

This is Neha

Mark Kobayashi-Hillary

Hello Neha, what can I do?

GKS Technologies

Mark, we offer cost effective web site and software solutions from India, and was wondering if you may be interested in outsourcing your web /software development services to us are you interested?

Mark Kobayashi-Hillary

I'm not sure where you got my details or who you think I am - have you looked at my web site?

GKS Technologies

It's just an random search performed on Skype

Mark Kobayashi-Hillary

Based on what criteria - being in London? I'm just wondering how you found me - you added me to your Skype address book earlier. Was that because I am in the UK?

So, at this point Neha stopped talking to me. Then another Skype user picks up where she left off:

Software & Web Developing Company Based In India

Hi Mark

Mark Kobayashi-Hillary

Hello

Software & Web Developing Company Based In India

This is Gulab Nihalani here

Mark Kobayashi-Hillary

Hello Gulab

Software & Web Developing Company Based In India

Earlier Neha have had a chat with you on Skype

Mark Kobayashi-Hillary

I saw that yes

Software & Web Developing Company Based In India

Mark just to clarify it was purely a random search performed on Skype

Mark Kobayashi-Hillary

That's fine. I am just interested in how you found me though if it was random - you mean based on my location then?

Software & Web Developing Company Based In India

Yes, am sorry if you have been disturbed

Wednesday, 10 June 2009

Posted at 11:09

Taxing time for Indian IT industry

Way back when the Indian technology industry was taking off, the companies managed to negotiate a raft of tax breaks that allowed the hi-tech sector to operate without the usual burdens placed on Indian business. All those benefits are due to end next year.

All the commentators in the sector knew that this was going to happen, but in the past couple of years whenever I have asked people in India about their fear of having to start paying considerably more tax, they have all said that the Indian tech sector is maturing and doesn't need these special benefits anymore. Almost everyone in the industry, including the trade body NASSCOM, imagined that once the sector has matured enough then these additional benefits from the government would not be required.

Roll forward and what's in the Times of India today? NASSCOM is calling for the tax breaks to be extended by around five years, because the tech companies are struggling due to the global economic slowdown.

So when will Indian tech grow up and pay the same taxes every other firm in India has to pay?

Thursday, 11 June 2009

Posted at 12:07

Government and outsourcing - a mixed bag of issues

Following on from my recent blog about the public sector in the UK, I'm going to expand on the theme and explore some more public sector questions in more depth.

This time, I'm interested in how the government views the suppliers that fulfil their IT contracts. Is there a group of suppliers more 'favoured' than others or just more experienced at playing the public sector bidding game? And when will we start seeing more contracts going to the Indian firms that are charging into the public sector marketplace?

When I started this discussion with Wipro, they almost took offence at me suggesting they were up-and-coming, rather than seasoned. Geoff Llewellyn , Head of Public Sector Business Europe at Wipro said: "Companies like Wipro are global. It's just a logical move to leverage what we have done elsewhere in the world and to bring those skills into the UK public sector. We think that we can bring some new thinking. There are some well-established players, but we have a lot to bring to the party."

He added: "We have a lot of public sector experience in other markets than can be brought to the table in the UK, even if we have not had a lot of experience here. Wipro is a grizzled and experienced campaigner and has worked with many private sector companies like gas and water – where those companies were public sector until recently, so we are not on completely unfamiliar ground at all."

Llewellyn has a point. And what's worth noting is that most of the big Indian suppliers have plenty of staff on the UK payroll too – using an Indian company doesn't have to mean the deal involves offshoring.

When asked if the Indian suppliers stand a fighting chance, Stuart Ford, Head of Public Sector, Europe, at HCL Technologies said: "I must think so, or I wouldn't be with HCL. I think things have slipped the other way now. The really big suppliers are out of favour. Senior civil servants are actively looking for some new players to enter the market. If you pick all the top five players, you can find a major screw-up at every one of them. "

Tata Consultancy Services has been a high profile winner of a major government contract, the technology required to deliver the Child Maintenance and Enforcement Commission – a replacement for the disastrous Child Support Agency. Brian Woodford, Public Sector Director at Tata Consultancy Services said: "There is a difference between what people think about the market emotionally, versus how procurement processes create winners of different suppliers... clearly the government wants to see a wider set of suppliers and engagement is really happening – we are proof."

The view from inside government is that most managers are tired of the small pool of suppliers who keep popping up when contracts are tendered. Mo Ali, Former Head of Procurement for e-Government Services in the Cabinet Office, said: "There is no group of favoured suppliers. It just so happens that when we go out to bid, it tends to be the same suppliers who always apply. It's not that they are favoured, and in fact there is usually some frustration and desire to get fresh blood, but many of the other companies have a lack of understanding of the bidding process."

But there is a tendency to avoid risk, as observed by Dr Colin Ashurst of the University of Durham: "No one ever got fired for buying IBM. That's a part of the problem here. The system itself is complex because of the scale and so smaller suppliers cannot afford the overheads of large bids."

Addressing the initial point about the same old faces cropping up, Alan Downey, Head of Public Sector UK at KPMG said: "It's not favouritism. It's more related to experience of those companies. When you are talking about offshoring then it's a much bigger risk. Theoretically it's not a bad thing for a company to be headquartered in India, but politically it's very sensitive. No department wants to be on the front page of The Sun for offshoring." Downey stressed that the reality of security in India is good, but it's still a sensitive subject in government.

He said: "I went to India recently and looked at some of the delivery on the ground there. I found that in most cases the security was better than the UK. The people were good. The private sector has already bought into this model because they see the benefits, but the government has this additional consideration of how it looks politically. They will always be more risk averse than a bank."

Mark Brett, Member of the Management Group (Partner, Public Sector Advisory) at PA Consulting added: "I don't agree that there is a favoured group of suppliers. There is a small group that were very successful at winning government business, but many of them are on the wane now. It's never been seen as a favoured body from within the government. There is a view from the inside that feels that many of these companies are better at bidding than at delivery. Some are improving delivery and some are really struggling to deliver at present. "

Andrew Warren, Head of Public Sector Practice at Vertex, mentioned the NHS and Steria joint venture – where the finance and accounts for many primary care trusts have been offshored to Steria teams in India using a joint venture scheme to return value to the NHS: "I don't believe that there is a favoured list. I do believe that there are some companies in this country that have had a lot more experience in the public sector than others. In the big transactional departments there is a strong desire to increase the quantity and quality of private sector supply. The government departments have targets for contestability that drive them to actually widen the group of suppliers they use, so I can't believe they really exclude anyone."

Warren adds: "If your premise is that you are going to offshore work, then that is a totally different conversation with the state. There is the NHS joint venture with Steria, but can you name another big offshoring example? I can't speak for IT services, but the conversations I have had with people make me believe that there is no appetite at all to commission offshoring in BPO. There is some interest in working with suppliers that use offshore services in some way, so the offshoring is indirect. So there is an interest, but no appetite to be seen offshoring to far off locations – where people are really interested in is deploying people across the UK and taking advantage of services delivered from the Highlands of Scotland for example."

Two clear issues emerge from these comments. There is no intentional favouritism, but it is certainly confirmed that more experienced suppliers know how to bid for contracts far better than new entrants. There is an attitude within government to help and encourage new suppliers though and I personally recall a conversation I had with government CIO John Suffolk in 2008 where he suggested that he is trying to make all government contract bids entirely open – even to the extent of all document submissions – so smaller suppliers could easily learn from the submissions of the big players.

Secondly, there is no political will at all for any form of offshoring of services. It is just too sensitive to be seen offshoring government services overseas. New entrants may be coming into the market, from countries such as India, but they will compete on a level playing field using local staff – not as low-cost offshore businesses.

Friday, 12 June 2009

Posted at 13:28

Satyam casts a shadow over World Cup 2010

I was sitting in the Dolce hotel close to Brussels last night listening to BBC Radio 5 on the iPlayer. They were broadcasting a special programme focused on South Africa because it is exactly a year until the FIFA World Cup tournament – that's football, not cricket. The Twenty20 World Cup final is next week in London.

But one of the commentators was reducing expectations on the technology that will be possible, claiming they can't hope to meet the exceptionally well-organised World Cup in Germany in 2006. However, I thought that FIFA had outsourced the entire technology programme to Satyam.

Ah, Satyam - again. So has the World Cup technology been affected by the collapse of this Indian giant? Maybe someone from Tech Mahindra can give me a call to let me know because there were some serious doubts on the BBC last night...

Monday, 15 June 2009

Posted at 11:12

Did outsourcing lead to MPs' expenses scandal?

D id outsourcing cause the expenses scandal that has rocked the foundations of the Palace of Westminster in London? It's highly likely as The Daily Telegraph managed to get hold of more than a million pieces of information related to expense claims by British parliamentarians – all in a single place and stored digitally.

According to a report in The Times last Friday it looks as if the information that was leaked was a comprehensive collection of paper documents that were scanned and were to be edited and filed – not used in their raw form.

So, could it have been a leak from the printing firm TSO, formerly Her Majesty's Stationery Office?

If so, it makes all the other outsourced data leaks we have heard about in the past pale into insignificance. This one could end up changing the very nature of government in the UK regardless of who wins the next election.

Hat tip: Thanks to Alan Lee at London South Bank University for pointing me to this article.

Tuesday, 16 June 2009

Posted at 14:12

Breaking the helpdesk bottleneck

I was wandering around the Gartner outsourcing summit in London today and I bumped into Christoph Neut, the European head of Techteam.

Techteam was founded in the US in 1980, so it has been around for a long time, but I'm not really familiar with the company. Christoph explained to me that they have been working in Europe since 1996 – which is when he joined the company.

Techteam focused on helpdesks – the poor guys and girls who get the brunt of users' anger when their IT falls apart. But they have an interesting angle on the old helpdesk model.

Christoph explained to me: "We all know the egg timer. Microsoft uses it extensively and we all love the symbol because we need to look at it so often when waiting for applications to open. I want to use it as an analogy for business and IT though. The top of the egg timer can be considered to be the business, and the bottom is the IT organisation. The bottleneck in the middle is the relationship between then two and that is usually through a help desk."

Christoph's analogy is certainly true, and IT staff are forever being asked to try behaving like the business – especially in anything that advises them on their career. What Techteam seem to be offering though is a re-organisation of the way the helpdesk is structured, so the technical team is completely aligned with the business.

Christoph went on to explain: "Helpdesks are rarely staffed with the A-team. However this needs to change. You need to reposition the role of the helpdesk and to change so it moves away from just being a part of the IT organisation. Helpdesk agents often report to a helpdesk manager who reports to an infrastructure manager who reports to the CIO. It makes the helpdesk team feel like they are stuck at the bottom of the IT organisation!"

He added: "Business owners need to operate with the helpdesk, creating a combined business and IT function. This results in the neck of the egg timer widening. It can change the whole way of dealing with IT and it becomes more of a service desk approach."

Their approach seems very interesting. I even heard a couple of the IT suppliers from India talking about the Techteam approach with some grudging respect.

When Christoph was explaining his analogy he added: "You know that TV show The IT Crowd? That's a lesson in how NOT to run a help desk!" I tweeted that comment after the interview only to find that minutes later the writer and creator of The IT Crowd, Graham Linehan, had tweeted a message back saying: "They're right!"

Techteam has a new fan thanks to the wonders of Twitter.

Tuesday, 16 June 2009

Posted at 15:09

The benefits of Brazilians

I came late to the Gartner outsourcing summit yesterday. I knew I had to be at the conference all day on Tuesday because I was presenting, but Monday was going to be more of a networking day.

When I did arrive, I talked to a few people and then went to a session highlighting the outsourcing opportunities in Brazil.

Robert Janssen of Brasil IT gave an interesting presentation, of course full of all the usual information one would expect, but used an interesting analogy I'd like to repeat.

Robert said: "I was at my favourite pizza place in San Francisco the other day. The owner was smiling so I asked him what was so good today. He told me that he had just had his best day ever for pizza deliveries – even delivering more than the local pizza chains like Domino's. I asked him, what 's his secret? How can he deliver more pizza from one store than Domino's can across the Bay region? The pizza restaurant owner replied: 'I only hire Brazilians to deliver my pizza.'"

Robert then went on to explain the reasons the pizza restaurant owner gave for his choice of delivery riders: "There are three reasons.

Firstly, if they can ride bikes like they do in São Paulo then they can deliver fast anywhere. Second, they just get things done, whatever happens, and third, they are completely flexible. Whatever unforeseen event occurs can be dealt with – my riders come to me with solutions, not problems."

It's a nice little outline of some of the cultural advantages of Brazil. The usual presentations listing the number of college graduates and internet connections can get a little boring so kudos to Robert for livening it up.

What made the session even better though was that the global technology head of HSBC in Brazil, Jacques Depocas, was there and he talked at length about the experience HSBC has had in the country. This was supposed to be a closed session – no bloggers allowed – but I got special permission directly from Jacques to reproduce some of his comments.

He said: "So why did we set up our centre in Brazil? There were many reasons, but it started off because, when the decision was taken in 2005, the global head of the GLTs had previously worked in Brazil for three years and he knew that due to the maturity of the Brazilian IT industry he could find skill sets that were very hard to find in other regions. The time zone is favourable. There is a strong cultural similarity with Americans and Europeans. People think of their career in the long-term and there are good union relations in the industry, plus it's a very mature industry - about two million people work in IT in Brazil. There are other factors, such as political stability and good infrastructure, but the real difference is in the experience of the people. Brazilians often work through university, so they are getting valuable work experience much earlier than in most regions. If you look at my team, almost 25 per cent of my people have more than 10 years' experience - that's very hard to find in some other areas."

That final point was supported in some of the other Gartner sessions today as a key differentiator. There are a lot of people out there more worried about the quality of their team than the cost reductions. And for those organisations it looks like Brazil has something to offer.

Wednesday, 17 June 2009

Posted at 15:44

Touchy subject?

When I do talks about outsourcing, I often try to illustrate different points by using video or images. Let's face it, someone talking to PowerPoint slides for an hour is about as interesting as a rail timetable, so I try to find ways to liven it up a bit.

I like using this video when reminding people that most people out there find outsourcing to be annoying, useless, or pointless.

It's a funny little viral that has been sent all over the web in the past couple of years, but it does explain some of the issues around outsourcing in an amusing way. The useless high-priced American is replaced by an Indian, who is in turn replaced by a Chinese computer - so it not only illustrates human call centres, but the industrialisation of customer services.

I think it's funny and a useful way to remind managers that not everyone sees the point of their change programme. But I was talking to an MBA class a few months ago and I used this video and one of the students said it was racist and I shouldn't be using materials like this.

Was he just a bit touchy or do you think it's offensive?

Monday, 22 June 2009

Posted at 16:35

Trade lessons from Indian IT

I was at the Confederation of British Industry (CBI) this morning because their equivalent body in India (the CII) had brought a large delegation of Indian business leaders over to London to talk about trade between the two nations.

I was most interested to hear a speech by the new commerce and industry minister, Anand Sharma. The minister has only been in the job for three weeks and yet he spent last week in the USA talking to business groups there and here he is today in London talking to similar British groups.

The general debate, and Sharma's speech, was not specifically themed around outsourcing or the tech industry, however the tech sector was mentioned a number of times – particularly when the discussion turned to work visas. Minister Sharma sounded somewhat frustrated when he talked about the recession-led protectionism that is flaring up in the USA – particularly over the granting of H-1B work visas. He stated that there are some critics who might want to look at the 250,000 or so jobs already created inside the USA by Indian technology firms.

It felt at times like the minister wanted to yell 'I told you so' to the assembled British business leaders. Because the Indian government had never given their banks such freedom as we did in London, their banking system has not collapsed in a similar manner. In fact, the minister was talking of GDP growth rates in India creeping back up to 7%, with strong predictions that the trend can soon get back up to 8% or 9%.

That's astounding - if it happens as the politicians are predicting. What can't be disputed is that a fifth of all the children in the entire world are Indian. Think what that means for the future of doing business with the region. In our sector we are already getting quite familiar with the India story, but you can bet there are other industry sectors out there that India will excel in before long. They had better start taking a look at what we have been up to in technology.

Thursday, 25 June 2009

Posted at 12:44

Skills for a global industry

Rob Preston's blog in InformationWeek earlier this month caught my attention recently. He recounts a recent event in New York where the CEO of HCL Technologies, Vineet Nayar, said he doesn't hire greater numbers of American graduates because they are 'unemployable'.

Notice the focus on 'greater numbers' though. HCL does employ a lot of Americans, but when he was pressed on why they are not hiring more kids straight from college Nayar explained that he just felt that the American college system is not preparing them for work in the technology industry.

We have heard similar arguments about technology or computer science courses in the UK for a long time. Commentators always argue that the universities need to include more project or programme management, more relationship-led soft skills – not just the hardcore code cutting.

What's interesting though is that Nayar thought some other skills were missing from university curricula in the developed world. Global history and foreign languages were two areas he cited that would prepare tech workers for life in a more global industry.

I studied Computer Science and Software Engineering and my first job was with a big German tech firm, then Japanese, then French, then American... and this globalisation of services has only just begun. I think Nayar is on the right track, but what do you feel about his comments?

Thursday, 25 June 2009

Posted at 14:33

Infosys co-chairman makes government switch

So an Infosys executive has finally made it into the upper echelons of the Indian government, but it's not the one everyone has assumed would eventually seek an elected office. Though rumours about Narayana Murthy one day standing for a senior government position (possibly even President) have swirled around tech business circles for years, now it is actually Nandan Nilekani who has taken the leap into public service.

Nilekani has been a frequent visitor to media studios recently as he has used his celebrity in business circles to write a book about imagining a new India. The government handpicked Nilekani to run a new scheme assigning a unique identification number to every citizen.

With over a billion citizens, that's a tall order, but asking one of the founders of Infosys to run the programme seems like a shrewd move.

Monday, 29 June 2009

Posted at 10:21

Unwelcome rumours

A supplier asked me recently if I could provide them with information about which CIOs are 'thinking' about outsourcing, so they might have some advance warning and they can pitch for business earlier.

It struck me as a strange thing to ask. CIOs don't just randomly share their thoughts about what areas of the business might be outsourced, and even where they might be considering an outsourcing programme it is likely they will keep it very silent. Even their own staff won't hear about it until the strategy has been decided, because rumours and discussions about plans that are undecided could cause chaos in most companies. And I might add, that where a CIO has asked me for some opinions in confidence, I'm hardly going to repay that trust by ringing up a few suppliers with the news.

So I get tired of seeing supposedly respected news sources, like the India Times, running stories like this. If UBS wanted to go on the record and talk about their plans then there would be a story. If the newspaper can't confirm the story then why print a rumour? Unless they just want to force the UBS public relations machine into issuing a confirmation or denial? It's no better than the mish-mash of rumours and speculation that filled the Internet when Michael Jackson died.

If the boss of UBS wants to talk to someone who understands what they are doing and can comment on their plans without resorting to rumours then it's obvious how to reach me.

Tuesday, 30 June 2009

Posted at 15:27

Carving out a niche

As outsourcing destinations go, Sri Lanka is not having the best of times. Protests have been taking place non-stop in London for months, with Tamils trying to encourage the British government to do something about the civil war in Sri Lanka – generally by making a lot of noise for their cause in Westminster. The heat of these protests has barely died down, though since the death of the Tamil Tiger's leader, the Sri Lankan government has now declared the country officially 'at peace'.

So it was with some trepidation that I took a call today from the director and general secretary of SLASSCOM, Madu Ratnayake. SLASSCOM is the Sri Lankan hi-tech services chamber of commerce – and the name sounds familiar to those of us who know similar organisations, such as NASSCOM and BRASSCOM.

With Sri Lanka in the British news over the past year for all the wrong reasons, what was he going to tell me about outsourcing to Sri Lanka that would make it a compelling proposition?

He had some good - and confused - messages in my opinion. The good thing is that Sri Lanka has accepted they need to specialise. They are drilling down into some specific industries, like the legal, and leisure businesses, and trying to focus on becoming a destination of choice for companies in that space. They are also keen to target the Small to Medium sized Enterprises (SME) that often elude much larger offshore destinations, such as India.

The SME focus is essential for Sri Lanka to succeed. They have a very different service industry to some of the larger locations, with over 300 suppliers in this sector. They really do have the potential to be a hub for SME activity because it always works better for smaller companies to work with smaller partners.

But, on the downside, the outreach for SMEs is far harder. SMEs in the UK don't often go on trade missions, or attend big conferences in London, let alone Colombo – so how do you reach them? Unfortunately

SLASSCOM don't seem to have much of a plan on that yet, though to be fair Madu said it was early days and they not only need to figure out how to reach people, they need to change the war-torn perception of the country too.

The thing I found most unsettling though was the tired low cost argument. I guess it's one of those things in offshore outsourcing – everyone always returns to cost of labour and service as the primary driver. I asked Madu about why SLASSCOM tries to position Sri Lanka as a specialist, a niche operator, and then returns to the low cost of labour as a 'key differentiator'. In fact, low cost is the primary reason for outsourcing to Sri Lanka according to their website – and it's something Madu echoed when we talked. He even stressed that it's the "primary reason" for anyone to be outsourcing offshore.

But surely that defeats the purpose of SLASSCOM focusing on niche areas, focusing on having top class talent, and focusing on the quality of life in the country? I think SLASSCOM needs to work a bit more on their messaging, but they are at least away from the starting blocks.

July 2009

Wednesday, 01 July 2009
Posted at 17:34
Outsourced

I attended the UK premiere of John Jeffcoat's movie 'Outsourced' at the Soho hotel screening room in London last night. I was fortunate enough to be introducing the film as I started the ball rolling and created the possibility of arranging the screening in the first place.

It all started a couple of years ago when I saw this video on youtube. I liked the fact that someone had turned a current affairs story into a human-interest story – an actual movie that would interest people beyond the business community. I started using the video in some of the MBA classes I teach, as an example of business strategies crossing into general consciousness. One day I just thought I would contact the person who uploaded the video – out of interest. I was surprised to soon receive an email from the director (and writer) John Jeffcoat!

I then had some chats with John about the movie and how we might arrange a London screening. I started trying to put it together as an event that the National Outsourcing Association (NOA) could host. What I found though was that all the companies I approached for funds (to pay for the cinema, drinks etc) were all a bit scared of the subject matter. The film has some amusing sections, comic situations involving cultural misunderstandings and many of the companies I spoke too just shied away from associating themselves with comedy when the press is often accusing them of stealing jobs from the UK and sending them to India.

Eventually the NOA board even rejected me. Not that they didn't like it – we had a private screening on DVD and the board liked it, but they were wary of using membership funds on an event that was 'fun' rather than educational or research driven.

However, the NOA provided a sponsor in the end. Buffalo is the marketing and communications agency that works for the NOA. I had an offer of some cash from the law firm Olswang, but it was not enough to completely cover all the costs. Buffalo stepped in and said they would match Olswang and cover any additional costs so the event could happen!

So... Buffalo did a lot of work and organised a great event at the Soho hotel screening room. There were drinks, and a really nice screening in a great theatre. What was really nice was that I managed to get hold of the actress Ayesha Dharker via John Jeffcoat – i was communicating with him the day before the screening on Facebook and he sent some text messages from the USA to the actors from the movie. She was in London and managed to change her diary for the day so she could come to the screening and also do a Q&A after the movie finished. You can see some video from the Q&A session here...

If you haven't seen this film then I'd recommend trying to obtain a DVD copy. Yes, it's a love story, but a friend of mine described it as a cross between Local Hero and Slumdog Millionaire. That's not a bad description of the film – and it's about outsourcing too.

Tuesday, 07 July 2009

Posted at 14:17

Outsourcing growth being driven by cost

I read an interesting story on the continued growth of IT outsourcing today, written by Allie Young - a research vice president at Gartner.

Young puts forward the view that Gartner has observed things slowing in the marketplace, but not collapsing. She said: "Looking back at the contracts signed in 2008, many of our points of analysis - contract size, contract terms, vertical uptake, deal type and 'mega-deals' - show continuations of past trends. Yes, there was some softness in large deal signings, but no catastrophic declines. In part, this continuation of past behaviours is because external forces don't change the basic drivers of outsourcing - firms still outsource for cost, efficiency, access to skills, focus on core business, innovation, modernisation and business transformation."

I'd agree with this. Young also states that the market is going to be driven more by cost reduction as we go forward. That's a given at present, regardless of any increased market optimism there is a sense that right now we all just need to batten down the hatches.

Young also observes that a number of poor deals that collapse in the next couple of years are likely to be signed during this time when all the emphasis is on cost, rather than service. It's going to be a shame if that really does happen, after the industry has had years of maturity in the good times why should it all go to pot as companies focus more on the bottom line?

Thursday, 09 July 2009

Posted at 15:23

A novel approach to building trust

I had quite an interesting call with Derek Kemp from Patni just now. Derek heads up their Communications, Media, and Entertainment practice and so he is focused on a lot of advisory work, rather than the usual delivery of pretty basic systems integration services.

Based on my earlier experience of Patni, I had thought of them as more of a player in the embedded systems space, but Derek actually described their advisory work to me in a way that sounds quite different and exciting.

They have focused entirely on the business itself, and hired people with senior business experience – regardless of their IT knowledge. Their advisory work is positioned as quite separate to the rest of what Patni does. Derek explained: "It's the deep industry knowledge that makes us different. Some of our guys have been CIOs and CTOs in the past, so we understand the pain of being a buying organisation and we are not just focused on trying to create downstream revenue. We want to be known as a trusted advisor."

I think it's always hard for a service provider to be known as a trusted and independent adviser. Any client that hires them will always suspect they are talking up the need to sell their downstream services. For example, it has always surprised me how Accenture has managed to maintain their advisory reputation for so long, when they are also selling the kind of services they advise on.

Derek's description of how Patni is developing this area of their business impressed me though. I'll be interested in following what they get up to over the next year – and particularly in some of the newer markets that they are exploring in the Middle East and Africa.

Friday, 10 July 2009

Posted at 12:25

Infallabile opposition to outsourcing

The Holy Father, Pope Benedict, has warned of the dangers of outsourcing. Yes, you'd better believe it. The Vatican is now stepping into the world of corporate globalisation and commenting on areas of business where the Pope has concerns.

I have to 'confess' that I hadn't read the latest encyclical letter published by the Pope. I am a Catholic, but not one that spends a lot of time worried about what the Pope is publishing.

However, in today's edition of the Wall Street Journal, there is a feature analysing what the Pope's opinion's mean for international business. The specific fear of the Pope is that outsourcing will lead to the destruction of social security systems and job losses.

The WSJ is not very complimentary. In polite language they point out that the Pope is an idealist. That's not a bad thing, but perhaps it's a better qualification for a spiritual leader than a business leader.

Thursday, 16 July 2009

Posted at 13:19

Collective wisdom can helps SMEs outsource

Outsourcing is hard enough for the big guys. There are consultants out there who make a fine living helping companies answer questions like:

- Which part of my supply chain can be outsourced?
- Should I find a partner or go offshore myself?
- If I need to find a partner then who, and where?
- How do I keep it all under control so I am improving things and not just making the whole situation worse than now?

Now, imagine if you are a much smaller company, a Small to Medium-sized Enterprise (SME). If you are a company needing to buy a service from someone else on a small scale then you are not likely to think of offshoring it. You might think of outsourcing to an offshore partner, but for a small project there is no way you can go and personally check out the suppliers – the business trip might be worth as much as the project cost.

And, what about the suppliers? You might be an experienced supplier with a good track record of delivering smaller scale projects, but how does your potential future client know about you? They might be on an industrial estate near Coventry as you sit in an export-processing zone near Mumbai airport.

Outsourcing for smaller players is really difficult.

I asked Jaroslaw Czaja, the Chief Executive of Polish software development firm Future Processing, about some of these issues and he explained: "Currently a lot of our business comes from word of mouth recommendations and I think this is the most powerful tool for SMEs. Web 2.0 marketing, through its personal, groundswell-based nature, also works well and plays to SMEs strengths of being more flexible than larger companies and therefore sometimes being more willing to try something new. The online/forum grapevine of horror stories from destinations more geared up to larger scale outsourcing also works in our favour."

Jaroslaw went on to say: "I think Future Processing is like many smaller outsourcers, we are an SME ourselves and often have limited resources to put into business development while always putting existing customers first.(But we also have a lot in common with our customers which is a great plus point). Some sort of online community for outsourcers who are SMEs themselves to find other SMEs to partner with would be really useful."

I've been hearing these complaints from SMEs for years. Government agencies and trade associations often arrange trade missions for SMEs, but at the end of the day, unless the SMEs talk to each other there will be no progress towards creating more outsourcing opportunities for smaller companies.

It might seem self-serving to mention it, but I have tried putting together a new business network that aims to try addressing some of these issues – to try driving small companies together, wherever they are located. It's called Peerpex and it goes live in September, though you can register now if you are interested. Take a look and let me know what you think – especially if you are an SME!

Thursday, 16 July 2009

Posted at 15:28

Are Tier 1 outsourcers strengthening their grip on the market?

N ew research from Ovum suggests that despite the recession, the big outsourcing suppliers are bearing up well – even growing their market share.

It's good to see some observations like this backed up with empirical evidence, but it's not too surprising. After all, the pressure on budgets has forced many companies to explore outsourcing where they might have wavered before. And so, the top ten suppliers stand to do well.

I remember at the National Outsourcing Association awards ceremony last year the NOA Chairman, Martyn Hart, quipped that many of the suppliers are going to do well out of the recession. The chatter in the bar was that it was in poor taste to say something like that, but here we are with analysts saying exactly the same thing.

The real story will be in the second or third tier of suppliers, particularly the offshore suppliers. If the top suppliers are cutting amazing deals just to maintain market share then who would bother looking to the second tier anymore? Those firms are going to be working flat out just to maintain the clients they already have in this market. How they generate new business when the market leaders are just getting stronger is anyone's guess.

Thursday, 23 July 2009

Posted at 11:05

Speaking globally...

Voice-to-text firm Spinvox is under fire over claims that their technology is not quite what they had claimed. Spinvox claims to use voice recognition technology to turn voice messages into text that can be sent to your phone, however a BBC investigation has found that human agents in South Africa and the Philippines are transcribing the messages manually.

Spinvox have featured at National Outsourcing Association events in the past and their offshore operations were no secret in the industry. They always liked to talk up their technology, but never made any secret of the fact that they had people checking messages too, so it's interesting to see the 'human checking messages' aspect as 'news'...

However, it looks like the Information Commissioner will be interested in the story as Spinvox claims to not transfer data outside the EU. This does appear to be a breach on how data is handled, and what has driven the BBC investigation is the personal nature of the data – private phone messages. Spinvox claims to slice and dice the messages so that a person hears only small chunks – but the word from former offshore agents is that this is not true, they have access to complete transcriptions.

Perhaps if the firm had been a bit more open about the global nature of their operations in the first place they wouldn't have Rory 'Katherine' Jones from the BBC breathing down their neck?

Conclusion

These are turbulent times for outsourcing. The global economic downturn, initially triggered by the credit crunch in the American banking sector, is having a number of effects on corporate purchasing and partnering.

For many years, a wave of offshore outsourcing was driven by the financial services industry. Banks and insurance firms needed armies of back office staff to process accounts or claims and take calls from customers. Yet these are the organisations hardest hit by the downturn – take a look at my blog post from December 10 2008 for an observation on just how hard the financial service sector was hit by this downturn.

But, the outsourcing suppliers appear to be doing just fine; the industry is not quite flourishing, but is far from despair in a general climate of international decline. Some observers even argue that this cautious optimism is precisely because of the present economic uncertainty. As the scale of this crisis started to become clear, most company executives initiated cost-cutting measures. The road to survival in a recession depends on both reducing ongoing costs and being able to fix future costs with some predictability. Outsourcing, and particularly offshore outsourcing, facilitates this and so even though it has been taking longer to get budget approval, major projects are still being approved.

So outsourcing still helps to reduce costs, and that just became more important than ever, but do you recall the marketing efforts of the supplier community from just a couple of years ago? The service cost had dropped way down the list of strategic reasons to outsource, as it became uncouth to suggest that a company just uses a strategy like offshoring to reduce cost. Well, that shyness has all but vanished.

Outsourcing is not a panacea and experience has not helped every organisation that has tried it. Many have tried and failed to make it work, especially where offshoring across vast distances to unfamiliar territories or cultures. All too often a business case with an unrealistic expectation of savings drives the relationship, rather than a realistic acceptance of what is possible. When the main driver for the work is just a reduction in operating cost, and the transition to working with a supplier is also fraught with the potential for error, the chance of reducing service quality is very high. Though most companies want to reduce cost, they don't want to reduce the service quality to a level where they find their operation is beset by constant problems.

Offshoring has driven much of the drive to create a lower-cost international service infrastructure for companies, but offshoring needs much stronger governance than typical outsourcing deals, though there are many ways of structuring a relationship. Even where the offshoring programme only involves employees from the same company working across borders, it is likely that some of the structures of outsourcing will be introduced to help manage the interface between the onshore client and offshore delivery centre – tools such as key performance indicators or service level agreements are common standards. And if the offshore delivery is outsourced to a third party then these standard agreed measurements are essential.

But these measurements can't prevent a disaster. The accounting scandal at Indian technology giant Satyam early in 2009 was an issue that the entire industry feared might destroy trust in India, but it was surprisingly well contained by the interim management team. It never developed into a wider distrust of offshoring in general, and the beleaguered company was snapped up by Tech Mahindra just months after the story broke. This is a story that continues to evolve, as I have documented in recent blog posts. Who really knows how much Satyam should be worth before allowing the forensic accountants in to dig around and determine the true depth of the fraud? Yet, the company was acquired anyway.

So what are the real trends that are driving outsourcing today, based on the observations in my blog? If I focus first on the offshoring market then I'd suggest that there are three major areas of the business that are changing now, when compared to a couple of years ago.

The first is the trend towards nearshoring. There was a big rush to go offshore early this decade. India was the place every company executive was jetting to, but the time and expense of travelling to remote locations has been noticed. The time zone differences are not really the benefit once mooted – who really manages to extend the working day considerably because of time zones? And most developed regions have a cluster of lower-cost resource pretty close by – Mexico and South America for the US, or Eastern Europe for us here in the UK. There is a definite swing towards using offshore partners that are at least much closer and can be visited easily. The India vs. China debate used to be a staple at every conference focused on offshoring, yet this is not even discussed today – no one is interested any longer because crude country comparisons are not really very useful anyway, but mainly because both India and China seem less attractive than closer alternatives.

The predicted growth of knowledge process outsourcing (KPO) is another area where I am noticing a difference to what was predicted. KPO is the higher-value more complex service, such as research or analytics. This was predicted to explode and to become more significant than the humdrum business process outsourcing (BPO) sector – well it never happened. The reason? Because clients are scared of outsourcing these very high-end processes to companies they don't know. They will outsource these processes to partners they trust, so the real potential is for those humdrum BPO companies to expand the range and depth of their services – not for a sea of new start-ups with unpronounceable names to expect KPO contracts.

The consumer backlash against offshoring has continued and this has changed the strategy for many. Initially, it was seen as a bonus to offshore a company function such as the customer service help line to agents in India. The call centre agents are better qualified than locals, highly intelligent, and cheaper. It all seemed perfect, but consumers hate calling their bank or insurance company and hearing someone thousands of miles away dealing with their details. These consumer concerns have shifted the thinking of most companies so that offshoring of high-touch consumer services to an offshore location is becoming far less desirable, even if other services like IT remain acceptable because consumers have no idea where their bank locates IT infrastructure.

Africa is the story really waiting to break in the offshoring market. I've recently been to Nigeria and I'm planning to visit Kenya and Uganda soon. These are places where a huge number of smart young people want to work in hi-tech services and the infrastructure is now starting to catch up. Just a year ago there was not really enough broadband capacity in Kenya to make offshoring feasible, but that's all changed now. Once customers get over their initial fear of working with partners in Africa, it's going to be the next big thing in offshoring. South Africa has already established a reputation for contact centres, so expect their neighbours to join the party soon.

The BRICs (Brazil, Russia, India, China) hypothesis was also an extremely popular view on how services might develop when this blog started back in 2006 – I even wrote a book about it (Building a Future with BRICs - Springer 2007). However, with the maturing market in India, the focus on the domestic market in China, and the political uncertainties in Russia, it looks like Brazil may be the only brick in the brics with strong outsourcing growth ahead. All these regions will see some continued success in services, but it will almost certainly be different to that imagined before the global economic slowdown.

If I widen my own perspective away from offshoring alone and out to outsourcing more generally, what are the other trends that come up regularly in the blog?

The green agenda has changed considerably in the past few years. There was a period of time documented in this blog (see June 13 2007 for an example) where the strength of feeling in the market about carbon neutrality was so strong that it seemed to be imperative – go green or go bust. That strength of feeling has not survived the economic downturn, with most companies preferring to focus on survival rather than the environment. However, many of those good intentions are not going to be wasted as legislators gradually increase more requirements for environmentally conscious services, particularly when supplying services to the public sector. There will be a green revolution, only a bit slower than I had imagined a couple of years ago.

There is still no easy way for small businesses to reach out across the world and interact with each other, using the outsourcing lessons learned by larger companies. I have indicated in blog posts as far back as November 16 2006 and March 19 2007 that the small business sector has a lot to gain from being able to explore networks of partners internationally using the Internet. Some services, such as eLance or oDesk do exist, but the user experience is far from satisfactory. My own Peerpex network is aimed at improving this, though it is still in its infancy.

An ability to innovate and create added value for clients beyond the basic services documented in the contract is a perennial topic of the blog. I've mentioned this back on November 17 2006 – and it is a topic that consistently creates the same doubts and concerns. By it's nature, innovation is hard to define in a contract. Recently I have seen some more genuine examples of innovation in outsourcing, but this is years after every supplier started believing that they looked a lot better if they defined themselves as "innovative". In some cases it is also an oxymoron. Some of the supplier community make a virtue of being reliable and always delivering the same level of service. That's understandable because contracted service levels need to be observed, but it is not a creative or innovative environment, yet some suppliers appear to make claims of both innovation and safe reliability.

Public sector outsourcing is becoming more common the world over. Governments are finding that they need to improve their own service delivery to citizens and the supplier community is scrambling to demonstrate their expertise – though in many cases public sector contracts are on a scale that cannot be imagined in the private sector. Public sector offshoring remains quite unusual for obvious reasons, it is an unpopular strategy with the electorate and so the elected decision-makers tend to steer away from it as a strategy for services. Keeping jobs local still wins votes.

With new regions looking at the success of India, and the international economic slowdown causing an intense focus on operational cost, companies will use more outsourcing in the foreseeable future. The future for most suppliers in this market is bright, provided they can deliver a quality service at the right price.

Outsourcing has changed so much over the past three years, as demonstrated in this blog. Expect more change to come as companies utilise ever more innovate sourcing strategies in a bid to emerge stronger than ever once the economy recovers. The next three years will see this market change beyond recognition.

Talking Outsourcing

Mark Kobayashi-Hillary

www.talkingoutsourcing.com

Global Business-to-Business Exchange

www.peerpex.com

www.ingramcontent.com/pod-product-compliance
Lightning Source LLC
Chambersburg PA
CBHW051221050326
40689CB00007B/754

* 9 7 8 1 4 0 9 2 8 5 6 8 7 *